AF580776

BANKING ON BELONGING

BANKING ON BELONGING

WHY INVESTING IN REFUGEE ENTREPRENEURS BENEFITS EVERYONE

JOHN KLUGE JR. AND
CHRISTINE MAHONEY

Columbia University Press *New York*

Columbia University Press
Publishers Since 1893
New York   Chichester, West Sussex
cup.columbia.edu

Library of Congress Cataloging-in-Publication Data

Cataloging-in-Publication Data is available from the Library of Congress.

ISBN 9780231218122 (hardback)
ISBN 9780231562089 (EPUB)
ISBN 9780231567534 (PDF)

LCCN 2026015284

Printed in the United States of America

Cover design: Noah Arlow
Cover image: Ronny Hartmann/Getty Images

GPSR Authorized Representative: Easy Access System Europe,
Mustamäe tee 50, 10621 Tallinn, Estonia, gpsr.requests@easproject.com

For Mirren:
May you grow up in a world
where everyone knows
that each of us is loved and
we all have a place to call home.

REFUGEE BLUES

Say this city has ten million souls,
Some are living in mansions, some are living in holes:
Yet there's no place for us, my dear, yet there's no place for us.
Once we had a country and we thought it fair,
Look in the atlas and you'll find it there:
We cannot go there now, my dear, we cannot go there now.
In the village churchyard there grows an old yew,
Every spring it blossoms anew;
Old passports can't do that, my dear, old passports can't do that.
The consul banged the table and said:
"If you've got no passport, you're officially dead":
But we are still alive, my dear, but we are still alive.
Went to a committee; they offered me a chair;
Asked me politely to return next year:
But where shall we go today, my dear, but where shall we go today?
Came to a public meeting; the speaker got up and said:
"If we let them in, they will steal our daily bread":
He was talking of you and me, my dear, he was talking of you and me.

—W. H. AUDEN

CONTENTS

PROLOGUE

A World in Flux—Refugee Lens Investing in the Age of Trump: The Devastating Collapse of Humanitarian Support

Every human heart seeks a place to belong, yet for millions of people displaced by conflict, persecution, and climate disasters, this simple, basic human need is colliding with a collapsing humanitarian system, demanding bold new solutions. Whether a South Sudanese mother in Nairobi, a Syrian carpenter in Jordan, or a Ukrainian entrepreneur starting over in Charlottesville, Virginia, refugees carry hopes and aspirations as vivid as anyone's, but they face a world where traditional mechanisms of support are rapidly unraveling. In 2025, as we finalized this manuscript, over 123 million people have been torn from their homes, each a story of loss and resilience (UNHCR 2025). The systems meant to support them—humanitarian aid and development budgets—are buckling, nowhere more starkly than in the United States, where the US Agency for International Development (USAID) has been systematically dismantled, sending shockwaves through communities and organizations worldwide.

The second Trump administration's assault on USAID began on January 20, 2025, with an executive order freezing its $60 billion portfolio—over half of US foreign aid—for a ninety-day review to align with "America First" priorities (White House 2025). Staff were locked out of USAID's Washington, D.C., headquarters on February 1 and instructed to work remotely or collect belongings in 15-minute slots. By February 7, plans emerged to slash USAID's workforce from over 10,000 (including 8,000 direct hires and just under 2,000 contractors) to just 294 employees globally, a 97 percent cut, leaving only 12 staff in Africa and 8 in Asia (Landay et al. 2025). Since then, over just a few months, USAID has ceased to exist as an independent agency, its tattered remains folded under the State Department, with Secretary Marco Rubio as acting administrator. Of its 6,300 programs, only 500 survived the initial purge; 92 percent of contracts were terminated, including HIV/AIDS and malaria initiatives (Habeshian and Falconer 2025). Internal estimates warned of catastrophic impacts: 1 million children untreated for malnutrition, 160,000 malaria deaths, and 200,000 new polio cases over the next decade. J. Brian Atwood, a former USAID administrator, called it "outrageous," warning that "the mass termination of personnel would effectively kill an agency that has helped keep tens of millions of people around the world from dying" (Landay et al. 2025). An anonymous staffer described the chaos as "a madhouse. . . . People started leaving one by one as their access was cut off" (Bond 2025).

The cuts devastated faith-based and humanitarian organizations that were critical to refugee and conflict-affected communities. Catholic Relief Services (CRS), which relied on USAID for significant portions of its budget, lost funding for eleven of its thirteen international food aid programs by March 2025, affecting millions in regions like East Africa and the Middle East (Arnold 2025; Androwich 2025). The International Rescue Committee (IRC), with 42 percent of its 2025 budget ($650 million) from USAID, laid off thousands and suspended health services for 1.8 million people in Sudan, Yemen, and Syria (Loy 2025; In South Sudan, IRC's clinic serving 115,000 people with nutrition support closed, impacting families who had fled violence and relied on weekly food aid to keep their children alive. The Norwegian Refugee Council (NRC) halted aid for 1.5 million conflict-affected people in twenty countries, including a February 2025 distribution for fifty-seven thousand people in Ukraine's front line communities, leaving families without winter supplies (AL-Monitor 2025). The NGO Refugee Group (NRG) conducted a mid-year survey of 10 member organizations and 116 refugees in Kenya to assess the combined impact of US funding cuts—of the refugees polled, half said livelihoods support had reduced or stopped while 69.8 percent said it had become much more difficult to earn a livelihood, "I don't have any capital or cash to start a business." (NGO Refugee Group 2025). These organizations faced a "domino effect" as United Nations (UN) funding dwindled, disrupting safe spaces for refugee women and girls. (UNHCR 2025).

The human toll is profound. In Sudan, 80 percent of communal kitchens—feeding millions of people since the 2023 civil war—closed in early 2025, leaving families in Khartoum without daily meals (Plett Usher and Soy 2025). In Bangladesh's Cox's Bazar, home to over 1 million Rohingya refugees, many recovering from devastating monsoons, USAID cuts weakened disaster recovery operations and jeopardized the education of 230,000 children (UNHCR 2025). In Jordan, a Syrian refugee whose bakery we visited in 2022 employed five locals with a UNHCR microgrant; by April 2025, budget cuts crippled local economies, threatening small businesses like his and stretching local financial institutions (UNHCR 2025). A federal assault on diversity, equity, and inclusion (DEI) and environmental, social, and governance (ESG) initiatives—labeled "woke"—further chilled efforts, with a 34 percent drop in pro-ESG proposals that could impact the flow of resources to communities most affected by conflict and climate-related natural disasters (Green 2025).

HOPE THROUGH REFUGEE LENS INVESTING

Yet, in this crisis lies opportunity. *Banking on Belonging* argues that refugee lens investing (RLI)—channeling capital to refugee-led enterprises, companies supporting refugees, and the communities welcoming them—transforms tragedy into economic and social gain. With public aid faltering, private-sector ingenuity, rooted in displaced communities' grit, offers real economic potential and, more importantly, hope to those who seek belonging.

The Tent Partnership for Refugees, despite recent US policy shifts, is rallying global businesses. In June 2025, Gideon Maltz, Tent's executive director, announced that over five hundred companies, from Amazon to Uniqlo, had committed to hiring or training 100,000 refugees by 2027, building on a 2022 pledge of 22,725 US hires. While the Trump administration was slashing resources to displaced families, the pharmaceutical company Pfizer was busy hiring five hundred Ukrainian refugees across Europe for biotech and logistics roles, leveraging their skills to fill labor gaps. These five hundred firms, spanning twelve countries, have generated $1.2 billion in economic activity through refugee employment since 2022. Recruiters who work with refugees understand that hiring them is good for business. Tent, working with the Fiscal Policy Institute, conducted a study across firms employing refugees in four geographic areas across the United States and found that 73% of firms reported lower turnover rates, boosting firm profitability : "refugees are especially responsive to a welcoming environment…once they find it, they tend to stay with that employer" (Kallick and Roldan 2018).

There are other bright spots. The International Finance Corporation (IFC) launched a $35 million blended finance facility with Equity Bank for African communities that were welcoming refugees, alongside $2 billion in social bonds (IFC 2024). Australia's 2025–2026 budget allocates $5.1 billion in overseas direct assistance funding, with $2.157 billion for Pacific resilience, including refugee programs (Australian Government 2025). The UNHCR–Mercy Corps Refugee Finance Playbook, released in March 2025, enables credit for fifty thousand microentrepreneurs in Kenya and Jordan (Mercy Corps 2025).

In Poland, Ukrainian refugees have launched thousands of businesses, contributing millions of euros in taxes (UNHCR 2025). In Uganda, private programs have supported the entrepreneur Robert Okodia's WimRob honey business, scaling to employ thousands of refugees and bolster local markets by 2025 (Acumen Academy 2022). These hope spots, detailed in our chapters and also in appendix D, show that RLI thrives where policy fails.

Despite the Trump administration's unfortunate politicization of helping people in need, the private sector is continuing good work and pivoting as a response to the administration's attacks. Facing political backlash against diversity, equity, and inclusion (DEI) or environmental and social governance (ESG) practices, firms are rebranding programs as "inclusive excellence" and sustaining their commitments (Green 2025). The Global Impact Investing Network (GIIN) projects a $1.5 trillion market in 2025 for "inclusive investing," with RLI in healthcare and working-class funds (Hand et al. 2024). Faith-based investors, guided by principles like those in the Vatican's *Mensuram Bonam*, have a well-established interest in using blended finance to support refugee initiatives (Nicholls et al. 2022; Pontifical Academy of Social Sciences 2022) and, in our opinion, are well positioned to drive growth in RLI amidst the closure of government-funded humanitarian interventions.

As we explore hope spots from California to Jordan, *Banking on Belonging* argues that investing in refugees is a high-return strategy for resilient economies. When governments falter, private citizens, investors, and businesses must lead. As W. H. Auden's poem "Refugee Blues" implores, despite those who say, "there's no place for us," we can find room for all of us by investing in our shared humanity and building a future where belonging is a universal promise.

PREFACE

The two long and winding paths that led us to devote our professional lives to helping people who are forcibly removed from their homeland—refugees—may be different, but they both combine a deep sense of personal responsibility and the discipline to choose where to concentrate our efforts.

John is the adopted son of a father who fled Germany in the 1920s with so little means that he was quarantined at Ellis Island and later taken in by a schoolteacher, who took the personal responsibility to give him an opportunity in his new home country. His father was a refugee. His adopted mother was born in Baghdad, Iraq, and fled that collapsing nation at the end of British colonization to avoid political persecution. If not for John's adoption by these loving refugee parents, he might well have ended up as yet another displaced person in the foster care system. Instead, because his adopted family was embraced in a growing United States, the Kluge family went on to become one of the most successful and entrepreneurial families in America. John Werner Kluge, John's father, was the founder of Metromedia, which he sold to later become the Fox television network.

Christine's family was born into the Scots-Irish and Italian neighborhoods of Philadelphia. Her working-class family eventually moved to the historic countryside outside the city, and that is where she developed a deep appreciation for the natural world. As she learned more about habitat loss and climate change, she became an environmental justice advocate from a very early age, publishing op-eds in fifth grade and penning an environmental sustainability plan for her grade school. In the eighth grade, while being sick at home, she called into a local radio station to speak with the environmental and animal rights activist Jane Goodall, one of her heroines. In college, first in undergraduate studies and then in her doctoral studies, her academic interests broadened, influenced by violence and unrest in Africa. Genocide in Darfur, Sudan, in 2003 and massive human displacement caused by war in the Congo increased her growing interest in ameliorating the ravages of global political crises. Christine went to work supporting the Save Darfur Coalition, which launched a multifaceted worldwide advocacy campaign. Yet, despite generating a great deal of awareness and public support, it accomplished very little, so little that she later analyzed the mechanics of advocacy in a book entitled, *Failure and Hope: Fighting for the Rights of the Forcibly Displaced.* "[The] advocacy chain is broken at each level of governance when it comes to fighting for the rights of the forcibly displaced," she wrote. "For the advocacy causal chain of *Advocacy—Awareness—Action* to function there is one other requirement: leverage, political or economic."

Rather than recommend yet another advocacy campaign, she argued that concerned global citizens can mobilize economic leverage through person-to-person microfinance and crowdfunding campaigns. Corporate matches can further magnify that power. "I am suggesting that we mobilize the public to invest—invest in a new future for the displaced." Looking around for someone to do that, we decided to look in the mirror and try to do it ourselves.

So, two lives, two paths, and a united vision. What put us on this path together was a simple calculation: Where is my time best spent? An initial focus on ending genocide, for Christine, and building healthy sanitation systems, for John, led us both to the work of investing in safe and productive futures for the world's refugees.

Several principles guide our work and the arguments in this book. To be effective investors, we need to have a systems view. There are many smart and capable direct service providers, whether they be bed net manufacturers who help to prevent malaria or food service providers who feed the hungry. But they can only do so much if the wider system is broken. Today, our investments help to fund an ecosystem of providers, behavior change, policy change, and other strategies. We also ask, What are the gaps or opportunities that require the least effort to get the biggest impact? That is not to say be careful and cautious. On the contrary, a principle learned from John's father is this: Don't expect a big reward for a small risk. The greater the risk, often the greater the reward. This is why we have gone all out on this one pressing issue.

To begin, we reached three important conclusions: Refugee resettlement without economic integration is not a solution; closing our borders to refugees is not a solution; and unending and ever-expanding humanitarian aid is not a solution. We all benefit by looking for new and innovative solutions.

Our book, *Banking on Belonging*, is inspired by the practical notion of financial investment and the human value of belonging to and being embraced by a community or society. The reader will notice that at times we speak in the plural as "we" and "us." At other times we speak individually as "Christine" or

"John." But make no mistake, the book is our joint product and represents our combined experiences and beliefs.

Another note to readers: Our book focuses on the approximately 120 million persons who have been forcibly removed from their homes by violence, armed conflict, political persecution, and, increasingly, climate change. Our book is about refugees. It is not about the flawed and broken immigration problems facing the United States or any country. Our interest is in exploring and shining a light on new and innovative ways for helping the world's refugees to become contributors to their societies, communities, and economies. Our book envisions human flourishing for these people, not merely subsistence-level living. Our argument for the integration of lawfully vetted refugees is at once moral (it's the right thing to do) and utilitarian (it benefits the economies of those nations who receive them).

On New Year's Day 2025, *The Wall Street Journal* reported that a surge in global conflicts had gone largely unnoticed amid higher-profile wars in Ukraine and the Middle East. The newspaper reported that those tracking such conflicts have identified 28 state-based conflicts across 16 of Africa's 54 countries. Regardless of the cause or outcomes of these conflicts, there is only one certainty: Refugees from these conflicts will be knocking on the doors of peaceful nations. Whether your lens is a moral one or an economic one, there is reason to be prepared.

LOOKING FOR HOPE

This book is a journey through the refugee hope spots we have discovered around the world over the past nine years, as well as the despair spots, ultimately leading all the way back home to our family farm in Virginia. Everywhere we go, we meet and profile bold thinkers and doers from displaced backgrounds and their projects, showing how the larger movement is growing over time.

Chapter 2 presents new durable solutions to the endless waves of crisis that are massive and growing. When we began this work over a decade ago, there were 65 million people forcibly displaced from their homes due to violence, and every year we've seen that number steadily climb to now over 120 million. The conflicts are increasing, and with climate change, severe weather events, and increased competition over resources, the curve is projected to get steeper. Returning home is often no longer an option for decades, if ever. Resettlement to "third countries"—advanced economies that can more easily absorb refugees into their economies—has declined due to increased polarization and anti-immigrant and antirefugee politics. Incorporation into "countries of first asylum"—the countries where people find themselves when they stop and take a breath after running for their lives—is the best hope for stabilizing the lives of millions of family members. But capital holders and policymakers need to help incentivize a smoother transition.

Chapter 3 lays out the various ways in which creative impact investors, foundations, aid agencies, and others are doing just that all over the world, and it also presents the framework of refugee lens investing. Chapter 4 delves into the economic impact of integrating refugees into national, regional, and local economies.

Chapters 5 through 9 look at specific regions of the world. We begin with the United States, a messy inclusive economy created by various accidents of history that risks choking off the source of its own strength. From the wholesale bakery of an Iraqi refugee in San Diego to a refugee-focused real estate developer in Louisville, Kentucky, the country is full of unsung initiatives, refugee-powered businesses, and promising models. We take readers around all fifty US states and show that refugee resilience is alive and well in every corner of the country.

Chapter 6 examines the Middle East, a current epicenter of displacement that is also an essential site of highly original solutions. Jordan, in particular, has a long history of inclusion; an estimated one third of its population now consists of displaced peoples from the West Bank and Gaza and more recently of Syrians, Iraqis, Yemenis, and Sudanese, among others. We find a historic experiment in the works: the first time a country's status as a safe haven has been leveraged explicitly as a development opportunity. From a cutting-edge business accelerator to a rough-and-tumble refugee camp start-up, we meet the people who are making it happen.

Chapter 7 looks at the many waves of displacement coming from South and Central America into Mexico, a longtime "sending" country that is fast becoming a "receiving" one due to economic, demographic, and other changes. It's a transition with fundamental challenges but also extraordinary opportunities. At least 3 million displaced people are in Mexico, and many now want to stay. With its tradition of relative openness to immigrants and the relative ease of social integration, especially for other Spanish speakers, the country seems poised to become a model—if it can grapple with the complex dynamics of economic inclusion. People like Daniel Ruiz, a deportee from the United States, illustrate the possibilities of reinvention.

In chapter 8, we head to Africa, specifically the nexus of East African nations that are home to some of the world's most intractable conflicts as well as some of the largest and longest-running refugee camps and urban neighborhoods. Indeed, Uganda, Kenya, and Ethiopia each host far more refugees and forcibly displaced people than any Western nation, and by and large there is a remarkable degree of acceptance. Moreover, there are people like the Congolese refugee social entrepreneur Aimé Rebecca, who founded Patapia in Uganda, whose goal is to inspire and empower refugees to achieve economic independence. Patapia offers a unique combination of training, mentoring, access to the right resources, and financial services to make refugees more resilient and inspire them to create their own businesses.

Far from being just any destination for refugees, Europe, the focus of chapter 9, is now once again one of largest. Almost overnight, Poland has attempted to absorb millions of Ukrainian refugees, at least temporarily. The continent is also home to dynamic accelerators for refugee entrepreneurs, though many still face the familiar financing difficulties that savvy impact investors could help ameliorate. This chapter takes us on a tour of Europe and introduces the Temporary Protection Directive, an unprecedented policy response in which the European Union granted immediate right to work to refugees. It also describes the resilience of Ukrainian refugees.

In the conclusion, chapter 10, we outline how the wholesale attacks by the Trump administration on the humanitarian aid, development aid, and refugee relief sectors have rendered the strategies discussed in this book more important than ever. The demise of the US Agency for International Development (USAID), the gutting of the US refugee resettlement program, and the cutting of federal grants have put millions at risk. With public sectors abandoning the displaced at the very time they are needed most, the creative private-sector strategies we lay out become the only path forward. International governments certainly can play a crucial role in the struggle to help refugees realize their potential as doers and makers, but there are many different ways that actors of all kinds can engage. The problem of forced displacement is universal, but now so is the solution of economic inclusion. We believe that banking on belonging is the right bet.

BANKING ON BELONGING

1

ENDLESS CRISES

It began with a restaurant. No sign, no menu, no kitchen, and no table, but she called it a restaurant, and she couldn't have been more right. A restaurant embodies the will of one person to make food and sell it to another person. Over a small fire in a stick hut in a refugee camp in eastern Nepal, she made lentils and rice, and we were her customers. She was determined against all odds to make a living and, by extension, a home.

A decade later, the restaurant may no longer be there, but what remains is the drive and tenacity of the woman who ran it. We could only spend a moment with her, and she was just one of the approximately 100,000 Lhotshampa people displaced from Bhutan who were living in the floodplain of a river valley. By then the camps had been there for over twenty years, meaning that an entire generation had been born and raised in those leaky homes with mud floors, stick platforms for beds, no windows or doors, no privacy, pit latrines, and swarming insects, not to mention fires, harsh monsoon seasons, and cholera outbreaks.

The Nepali government would not allow these people to move freely, work, or ultimately even remain in the country. Bhutan, for all its talk of "gross national happiness," wouldn't take them back.

Some of the men worked illegally in India and sent back money, and some of the children crushed stones with their hands along the river and sold the materials to construction companies. A few men also worked illegally in the construction sector of the nearby town. But the vast majority of adults sat around all day, every day, completely dependent on aid—their lives in limbo, their extraordinary entrepreneurial potential unrealized.

This book is the story of how a defining tragedy of our time—that over 120 million people worldwide have been forced from their homes by violent conflicts—can become an unprecedented economic opportunity (UNHCR 2025). While media narratives focus on fear and vulnerability, forcibly displaced people everywhere are overcoming legal and social barriers to found and fuel businesses. They are today's true global citizens, a growing diaspora of natural innovators with key comparative advantages.

Through our research, we make the case for three investment strategies:

1. Supply: Accept and empower more qualifying refugees by adopting evidence-based immigration policies.
2. Demand: Adopt economic inclusion policies and practices that quickly and efficiently integrate these refugees into economically valuable roles, from start-ups to trades, and other priority employment opportunities.
3. Build public and political will to enable and sustain smart refugee inclusivity.

This book profiles dozens of refugees in countries around the world, mapping for the first time the new movement they are building in partnership with investors, businesspeople, policy makers, activists, and others. Every year and with every crisis millions more people are displaced, but the stories here show a way forward. With inclusive economies, everyone can join in and benefit from addressing one of the fundamental challenges of the twenty-first century: finding new homes and dignified livelihoods for those in need of refuge.

These forcibly displaced populations face a range of short-term and long-term challenges: homelessness, poverty, a lack of protection, limited access to basic services (health, education), restrictive social and legal rules, and lack of access to economic opportunities. What's more, host communities already struggle with their own challenges, and supporting displaced people can exacerbate existing issues and spark new tensions.

Globally, the gap between humanitarian needs and available funding is increasing. The number of refugees is growing even as much-needed funding to provide for and transition them is shrinking. The United Nations estimated that 305 million would need humanitarian aid in 2025 but that aid would reach only a third of them (United Nations 2024). As Tom Fletch, UN emergency relief coordinator and head of the UN Office for the Coordination of Humanitarian Affairs (OCHA), noted: "The world is on fire. . . . We are dealing with a polycrisis right now globally and it is the most vulnerable people in the world who are paying the price. We are dealing with the impact of conflicts—multiple conflicts—and crises of longer duration and of more intense ferocity" (United Nations 2024). Moreover, these humanitarian efforts—while critical—often do not address the longer-term, systemic challenges regarding employment, economic opportunity, and self-reliance. As the world confronts compounding health and economic crises, traditional, mostly publicly funded humanitarian aid is being redirected to address crises within donor governments' own borders, and the remaining funds are thinly spread across the most urgent needs, further reducing resources to address long-term systemic displacement and aid dependency at exactly the moment when those resources are needed more than ever.

For all the focus on unfolding refugee crises in Gaza, Ukraine, Venezuela, Sudan, Syria, and elsewhere, the vast majority of displaced people have been lingering in physical and economic insecurity for years, if not decades. Much of the humanitarian aid is understandably aimed at providing temporary shelter and lifesaving food and medicine instead of dealing with challenges like restrictive rules around movement or the ability to work, start a small business, or integrate into the economic life of the place where one finds oneself. Moreover, host communities already face struggles of their own and worry that support for the displaced will only make scarce resources scarcer.

For the displaced, a sense of "home"—being safe and settled in the place where one is living—remains elusive. At its core is livelihood, the ability to care for oneself and one's family through economic activity. When given the chance, the displaced show themselves again and again to be hard-working, entrepreneurial, and job-creating members of the communities they join. In the United States, for example, refugees have the highest rate of entrepreneurship (13 percent), and immigrant-owned businesses employ 8 million Americans—with a full 44 percent of *Fortune* 500 companies having been founded by immigrants or their children. In addition, when we invest in refugees and allow them to contribute economically, that rising tide can lift all boats, as refugee inflows have been shown to have a positive impact on local economies and small firms (Altindag et al. 2020). And refugees contribute to the tax base of their host countries: The American Immigration Council found that refugees contributed $25 billion in taxes in 2019 and were more likely than others to make long-term investments like owning homes and starting businesses. This rigorous report, based on data from tens of thousands of people, concludes that "refugees, despite the steepest odds, often manage to achieve the American dream" (AIC 2023).

Yet in most countries, refugees and migrants are legally barred from working, starting businesses, opening bank accounts, or even taking out microloans. In some countries, policies may technically allow some of these freedoms, but failures of administration and implementation result in de facto bans on economic life. When the displaced are dependent on aid because of antiwork policies, the result can be depression, illicit market activity, and tensions with host communities.

Stepping into that simple restaurant in Nepal's Beldangi Refugee Camp lit a spark that has stayed with us. At the time, Christine had been conducting research for nearly a decade in seven different conflict zones about the failures and limits of humanitarian intervention. Her book *Failure and Hope* (Mahoney 2016) gathered data on sixty-one protracted displacement crises and included in-depth interviews with over 170 humanitarian aid workers, government officials, and refugees. "Only" 60 million people were forcibly displaced worldwide at the time, a record number already back then that would grow by 50 percent in only the next few years. Research made clear that the traditional system of aid and camps was crumbling and that the way forward would have to be through new tools like social entrepreneurship, crowdfunding, and microfinance.

The question was how to do it, how to realize refugee potential in the face of so much need and at such a scale that a woman cooking food over a fire could be supported in her quest to make a living. An answer came in the form of the Refugee Investment Network (RIN), launched in 2018 by John, a systems entrepreneur and committed social justice activist—and the son of an economic migrant and entrepreneur. John's father would likely have faced displacement or worse if he had not left Germany in the 1920s, and the support of an extraordinary teacher when he reached to the United States was decisive for his upward mobility. This family history had a permanent impact on him.

John started RIN to get capital into the hands of refugee entrepreneurs by connecting them to investors, building up a new field around intentional refugee investment, and, most importantly, changing the narrative. People need to know that with economic integration comes social cohesion, family stabilization, and the ability for the displaced to become new neighbors and job creators rather than a "burden" as often claimed by anti-immigrant politicians.

Joining forces through RIN, we quickly recognized that all over the world there are "hope spots," as the legendary oceanographer "Her Deepness" Sylvia Earle describes key zones for ocean conservation. The hope spots for refugees are places where they can rebuild their lives and livelihoods, thanks to their skills and drive as well as a host of promising new strategies emerging to support them. So far, few of the hope spots are aware of or connected to one another, and there is a glaring lack of coordination among nonprofits, host governments, and the private sector (including employers, banks, microlenders, and international and national impact investors) around actively creating jobs, supporting refugee entrepreneurs, and changing policy.

It's not going to happen spontaneously. At a minimum, displaced people who are founding businesses need access to the same infrastructure of support that everyone else has. As we discuss later, that is not happening for a variety of reasons, including the scale of the problem and the fact that refugees need recognition and investment. For the first time ever, there are ways that ordinary people everywhere can invest in refugees and build a more inclusive world, but they need to know what they're investing in. Just as "gender lens investing"—finding opportunities in female founders, female-led companies, and companies with significant female leadership—has gained momentum in recent years, RIN's concept of "refugee lens investing" is spotlighting refugee-owned, -led, and -supporting businesses, as well as refugee funds and lending facilities.

The first priority is visibility. Refugees and forced migrants are investable, employable, and bankable. Investors are interested in putting capital to work for and with refugees, but there are concerns and challenges. Little has actually come from the pledge of over $1 billion in private investment capital made at the World Humanitarian Summit in 2016. Investors cite risk and a lack of viable investments or difficulty assessing them. Refugee entrepreneurs face risks of their own, negative biases from financial and lending institutions, linguistic and cultural hurdles, and lack of trust from host communities. Neither group, including those involved in aid and development, really speaks the same language. Everyone understands the "why" of taking on the global refugee crisis. The benefits are numerous, and the costs of not doing so are simply too great. What remain unanswered are the "how" and the "what."

THE CHALLENGE

Built in the wake of the Second World War for a very different world, the existing humanitarian system simply can't handle the chronic displacements of today's forever wars and failed states. The 1951 Convention Relating to the Status of Refugees was an international agreement on protecting the basic rights of refugees stemming from the wars in Europe in the first half of the 1900s. In 1967 the international agreement was amended, through the 1967 Protocol on the Status of Refugees, to remove the geographic and time-based limitations of the original agreement and apply it to people displaced by violence worldwide. States have the responsibility to protect their citizens, but when they are unable or unwilling to do so, that responsibility falls on the international community of states. Countries that are signatory to the 1951 Refugee Convention and the 1967 Protocol are obligated to protect refugees in their territories.

A basic right laid out in these international agreements is "nonrefoulment"—that refugees should not be returned to a country where they face threats to their life or freedom. However, the convention lays out a long list of additional basic rights, many of which are often not provided for even in signatory countries: for example, the right to decent work, education, and freedom of movement with the territory; the right to be issued civil, identity, and travel documents; and the right to social protection.

The number of people forcibly displaced worldwide has been steadily climbing since the 1990s and has picked up speed since 2012, with an additional 6 million people on average being forced to flee their homes every year. There are now over 123 million people living in limbo, unable to return home (UNHCR 2025). The United Nations monitors the numbers of the following groups: refugees (people who have fled across an international border due to a well-founded fear of being persecuted for reasons of race, religion, nationality, membership in a particular social group, or political opinion), Palestinian refugees (people who are under the care of a different UN agency called UNRWA—the United Nations Relief and Works Agency for Palestinian Refugees), asylum seekers (people who have left their country and entered another seeking international protection but have not yet been legally recognized as refugees), internally displaced persons (IDPs) (people who are fleeing war, violence, or persecution but have not crossed an international border), and finally other people in need of protection, including stateless people (those who have no recognized nationality) and returnees (refugees recently returning to their place of historical residence).

The numbers of people forcibly displaced from their homes is increasing, as is the duration of their displacement. Today refugees are forced to endure prolonged displacement of about twenty years: a lifetime. The huge numbers of displaced, the duration of their displacement, and the fact that they are not provided with many of the basic rights laid out in the refugee convention—all of this creates the situation in which we find ourselves: over a hundred million people suffering in limbo, their lives put on permanent hold, unable to support their families, live their dreams, or create opportunities for their children.

BUILDING A SOLUTION

Failure and Hope (Mahoney 2016) generated awareness of the problem through a book tour, the conference circuits, TED talks, op-eds, and media interviews, but it didn't seem like enough. With a problem as huge as millions of people living in limbo, just an idea wasn't sufficient. Luckily, there was another highlight that summer of 2016 in addition to the book publication: We were married on May 23. Just two weeks before our wedding, much to the confusion of our family and friends, we traveled to Istanbul, Turkey, to attend the World Humanitarian Summit, which brought together nine thousand participants representing 180 countries to "generate commitments to reduce suffering and deliver better for people caught in humanitarian crises, and to demonstrate support for a new Agenda for Humanity" (Agenda for Humanity 2016). It was a timely opportunity, perhaps not for getting married but certainly for pursuing a worthy idea.

There we met people working in nonprofits, international organizations, and multinational corporations. We shared the idea we were working on: to use microfinance pools and impact investing to support refugee entrepreneurs and simultaneously to incentivize host governments to allow the displaced to work. We posited that if we could raise significant pools of capital and spread those investments across refugees and their host communities, host governments could start seeing refugees as assets that contribute to their economies rather than burdens on their societies as they are often portrayed.

Interestingly, many people agreed. It's rare when an academic idea isn't met with "That will never work in the real world!" Instead, it seemed like an idea whose time had come. Humanitarian aid workers were deeply aware of how massive the needs were and how overstretched donor funding was becoming. The international organization staffers, similarly, saw an endlessly growing problem and a recognition that temporary shelters and food aid were simply no longer humane for families displaced for years. Private-sector actors too were waking up to the realization that they had a role to play—from employing the displaced, to creating products and services to improve their lives, to investing in displaced-led businesses. Some governments were also realizing that the refugee communities they were hosting were not going home anytime soon and that pathways to regularizing their economic participation might be in order. It is rare when nonprofits, for-profits, and governments are all in agreement, but this is what we were hearing in May 2016, throughout the exciting buzz of the World Humanitarian Summit and our meetings at the edges of the conference in Istanbul cafés and restaurants. We might be on to something; still, no one at the Humanitarian Summit seemed to be following up this idea—even if they thought it had merit.

The flight home was a life-changing moment. We were of course excited about our upcoming wedding, but our conversations in Istanbul had lit a fuse. Maybe the prewedding madness was taking hold, but on the plane flying back over the Atlantic, we decided to take Christine's idea from her book and bring it to life. For the remainder of the flight, we oscillated between discussing our vows and honeymoon plans and discussing what form our refugee investment solution should take. Should it be a nonprofit, a for-profit impact investing fund, a microfinance fund of funds, or a partnership with an existing microfinance institution (MFI)? We settled on creating a US-based for-profit company that would focus on raising funds and redeploying them to microfinance banks in countries that were hosting displaced communities, with the condition that half the funds be lent to refugees.

We were married on June 10, 2016, on John's family's historic farm in Charlottesville, Virginia, and shortly after we set off for our honeymoon in Italy. We seemed to have a pattern with airplanes and key moments, as on our return back to the States we learned that President Obama, on June 30, had announced a Call to Action for Private Sector Engagement on the Refugee Crisis (White House 2016), building on the momentum driven by fifteen companies—Accenture, Airbnb, Chobani, Coursera, Goldman Sachs, Google, HP, IBM, JPMorgan Chase & Co., LinkedIn, Microsoft, Mastercard, UPS, TripAdvisor, and Western Union—each of whom had taken various actions in support of refugees. As part of Obama's Call to Action, the White House announced the Partnership for Refugees, which at the time was a collaboration between the State Department and USA for UNHCR, the US fundraising arm of the UN Refugee Agency. The goal of this initiative was to spur other private-sector companies to make commitments and act in support of the world's refugees, particularly in the context of education, employment, and economic self-reliance. Despite being a Hail Mary at the tail end of Obama's last few months in office, this was a hopeful moment and to us another sign that we were on the right path at the right time. If only hope and optimism were enough to change paradigms!

After our honeymoon, we incorporated our new venture and started meeting with friends and people we respected from the business and humanitarian sectors to gain early feedback. The goal was to build the case that refugees were a good investment; they would stay in their new host community and build businesses with microloans, create value, and potentially open new jobs. We named the venture the Alight Fund and sketched out a logo featuring a bird alighting on a tree branch, symbolizing the respite we hoped displaced families would feel when they could finally settle into a life with more hope and more normalcy.[1]

We worked on our company's feasibility study using a mix of coursework, in-person and Skype interviews, and networking to map out what it might look like to bring the Alight Fund to global markets. Early feedback was promising. We reached out to the former ambassador Ryan Crocker, who enthusiastically responded to our blind email and likened our concept to the US government's economic investments in entrepreneurs in Iraq and Afghanistan, which were some of the most successful peace-building programs he'd seen in his time serving abroad. Sasha Chanoff, the executive director of RefugePoint, told us that "this is exactly what's needed right now." Sasha ended up becoming a mentor and a champion for the Alight Fund when John competed in the Hult Prize that year, an annual global student competition for ideas on solving pressing social issues such as food security, water access, energy, and education. John's team won the campus-wide Hult Prize competition at Babson and went on to compete with other polished ideas such as an uber-like tuk tuk start-up based in Pakistan. At this point we knew that more was needed, and we were determined to do more. Sometimes a good idea is just a good idea. We needed to put it into action.

Still, we had a bigger problem: In most of the world, what we were proposing was illegal. As we mentioned, while the 1951 Refugee Convention laid out the "right to a decent job," in most countries of the world, it is illegal for refugees to work, start a business, take out a microloan, or open a bank account. So we had to start our work in one of the few countries where refugees were legally allowed to work—Iraq. Especially in the semi-autonomous area of northern Iraq called the Kurdistan Region of Iraq (KRI), one is permitted to work as a refugee or asylum seeker with a residency permit and one does not need to separately obtain a work permit.

The Syrian war and refugee crisis had been going on for five years by that point, with 12.5 million already displaced from their homes. While the media focused more on the millions arriving on the shores of Europe, tens of thousands went the other direction—east into Iraq. Ninety percent of them settled in the KRI, where language and religious ties created a more welcoming and familiar environment for Kurdish Syrians. By 2024, of the over 270,000 refugees living in the KRI, 34 percent resided in nine refugee camps while 66 percent lived in urban settings, primarily in Erbil and also in Dohuk and Sulaymaniyah (UNHCR—Iraq 2024).

Not only was the refugee need high and those refugees granted the right to work, but at the time multiple US State Department documents reported over a dozen highly functioning MFIs in the region that were set up to deploy microfinance loans to Iraqi microentrepreneurs and that were funded by resources confiscated from Saddam Hussein during the US occupation.

We started working our networks to see if a field visit might be possible in the fall of 2016. It turned out that we could make this happen through the support of colleagues at Columbia University's Global Center in Istanbul, and we went about setting up interviews with aid organizations, government representatives, and US embassy staff; we also visited some of the nine refugee camps.

There was, however, another challenge. The autumn of 2016 also came to be what would later be known as the Battle for Mosul, a major battle to retake the city of Mosul from the Islamic State or ISIS that was initiated by Iraqi government forces and also involved allied forces such as the Kurdish regional government's Peshmerga soldiers. The battle evolved into a nine-month street fight in which Iraqi, Kurdish, and allied forces moved block by block to liberate the city, a fight described by some military commanders as the deadliest urban combat since World War II (Jones and Sarbil 2017). "Official figures only account for the bodies that have been found, saying 2,600 civilians died and 2,500 ISIS fighters were killed during the offensive to retake the city. . . . But investigations by the Associated Press and NPR estimate anywhere between 5,000 and 11,000 civilians were killed in the fighting. A former vice president of Iraq says Kurdish intelligence believes a staggering 40,000 perished here" (Ferguson 2018).

Our plane did a corkscrew landing into Erbil International Airport, about 50 miles from Mosul, to avoid being hit by antiaircraft fire. We both have felt, especially during our younger years, that we had to go where the work was, regardless of the dangers. It was only from being there—seeing things with our own eyes, talking with the people on the ground, and learning about their experiences in real time—that we could truly understand what was going on and feel the immediacy and magnitude of the problem and how critical it was to find immediate solutions.

Although it was important to do desk research to learn about the background of the conflict, the participants in the conflict, and the larger geopolitical forces at play, we also needed to do fieldwork. After conducting thorough background research, we studied all the key implementing partners—the nonprofits and national organizations aiding refugees and the internally displaced people on the front lines—and then went through weeks to months of emailing and phone calls to set up a first round of interviews, while also taking care of all the travel logistics, figuring out transport to remote areas, and getting travel and research permits when needed.

Once we were on the ground, travel was more challenging than traditional tourism. Getting to remote refugee camps often involved taking twelve-hour bus rides through mountains, hitching a ride with aid workers in UN SUVs over hard terrain, or from time to time riding on the back of a hired moped or renting a bike, as was required to get around on the Burmese border. But once we had traveled halfway around the world, twelve hours by bus, and another hour on a moped, interview subjects were surprisingly kind and generous with their time. We were there to understand what challenges they were facing, what solutions to their problems were working, and what type of help they needed, and we were fortunate to spend hundreds of hours learning from people doing incredibly difficult, heartbreaking, and desperately needed work. When landing in a small, chartered plane for aid workers on the Somali border or into the Kurdish region of Iraq, there was a palpable feeling of aliveness, that this was one of the most critical places on earth and we were in the middle of it. And yet, we simultaneously realized that at the same time dozens of crises just like this were burning worldwide, with hundreds of thousands of other people who had fled for their lives, and hundreds of other aid workers, government staff, and soldiers trying to hold the line in those places. The magnitude of the problem was nearly overwhelming.

After our plane safely landed in Mosul, we traveled throughout the region visiting aid organizations, government officials, embassy staff, Syrian refugee camps, Iraqi internal displacement camps, and Yazidi enclaves. The Yazidis are non-Arabs who adhere to Yazidism, a non-Muslim monotheistic religion originating in northern Iraq. When the Islamic State advanced into Iraq's northern Sinjar District, it began a campaign of violence again the Yazidis that many, including the United Nations, the United States, the European Union, and the government of the United Kingdom, say constituted genocide. The United Nations reported that

> Yazidi men and boys over twelve were separated from women and girls. ISIS groups executed men and older boys who refused to convert to Islam. Yazidi women and children were forcibly moved to holding sites. In one case, women aged over 60 were executed. Women and girls were sold as slaves, and subject to sexual violence. The total number of Yazidis captured, killed, and missing is uncertain. In 2017, the UN estimated more than 5,000 Yazidis were killed and 7,000 girls and women were forced into sex slavery. Up to 81 mass-graves in Sinjar have also been identified.
>
> (UK PARLIAMENT 2023)

Many of the women and girls who were able to escape ISIS enslavement and make their way to a refugee camp found themselves traumatized and rejected by their families because they were seen as tarnished (Ibrahim et al. 2018).

Nonprofits and KRI government initiatives in the Yazidi camps had created social enterprise models whereby the women could come and make handicrafts and earn some wages, and the sites doubled as a safe space to access psychosocial support. Nonprofits in the Syrian camps also were setting up carpentry-based social enterprises to help Syrian men develop and use their skills toward something productive and make some money to support their families. Bilateral government aid organizations were providing microgrants (with no expectation of repayment) for entrepreneurs to set up small shops in the camps, and those entrepreneurs were serving both Syrian refugees and local Iraqis who lived near the camps. Christian aid groups were helping communities organize savings and loan groups to support their small-business aspirations. A thriving market at the edge of the camp allowed refugees and locals to trade in housewares, vegetables, fruits, toys, clothes, and more. There was strong evidence that investing in refugee and host community entrepreneurs in this region could work.

There was one setback, however: The rosy reports done by consulting companies for the US State Department about a thriving microfinance sector proved false or incorrect at best. Many of the microfinance operators had left with all the funds confiscated from Saddam and earmarked for economic development. Few of those contractors had invested in training local lending officers or branch managers, so in addition to the capital that dried up, most of the knowledge left as well. Almost no operating MFIs were left, and the few that existed required proof of a government civil service job with the Iraqi government as collateral to get a loan. Moreover, because of fights over oil revenues between the government of the KRI and Baghdad and other economic challenges, there was little liquidity in the market. Even if we got investment into the hands of entrepreneurs, they would have a hard time finding customers with enough cash on hand to buy whatever they were selling. Without a pipeline of entrepreneurs and viable financial institutions to work with, we were back to square one. Our plans for raising funds in the United States and deploying them through local and trusted microfinance institutions went up in smoke. Or so we thought.

Feeling defeated and perhaps somewhat naive about the accuracy of large, government-funded research reports, we went home and did what anyone should do when feeling stuck—we looked for help and hoped for luck. We had a suspicion that if there was anyone with experience financing refugee entrepreneurs, they ought to be at the Social Capital Markets (SOCAP) conference taking place that October in San Francisco, since SOCAP bills itself as "the largest and most diverse impact investing community in the world." Regular attendees include major foundations like Rockefeller, W.K. Kellogg, Hilton, Omidyar Network, OPIC, Sorenson Impact Fund, and the Ford Foundation. By leveraging *Failure and Hope* and our Alight lending concept, we basically sent out a Bat-Signal, hoping someone would come find us. That someone turned out to be Lev Plaves, who at the time was the Middle East portfolio manager for Kiva.org (Kiva), the nonprofit microlending platform that by 2016 had provided over $1 billion with 0 percent interest in microfinance loans to entrepreneurs all over the world, including to displaced Palestinians living in the West Bank. Lev introduced himself on the conference networking app: "Sounds like we should talk." And so began our partnership with Kiva.

Kiva's model harnesses the goodwill of crowdfunding lenders—citizens who commit small increments of capital, such as $25 or $100, to microentrepreneurs whose financing campaigns are most often sourced and vetted by Kiva's trusted MFI partners operating in various emerging or underserved markets. Kiva's platform seemed so promising that Christine had given a TED talk in 2014 highlighting some of the first refugee lending

Kiva was doing. Lev shared that it had successfully provided loans not only to displaced Palestinians but also to some Iraqis. But in Iraq the problems echoed what we saw and heard firsthand in our visit to the KRI. What funds Kiva had deployed in Iraq seemed to have either disappeared or were somehow stuck in the country and couldn't (or wouldn't) be repatriated. So our conversation shifted to thinking about how to scale up Kiva's microlending program to refugee entrepreneurs in other, less volatile, refugee-hosting countries.

Lev shared that while Kiva's lending in the West Bank was working, MFI partners in other markets didn't see it as sufficient evidence that lending to displaced entrepreneurs could work. Most of them perceived refugees to be much higher risk; after all, in most cases they did not have a credit history, had very little (if any) collateral, and were displaced only in a "temporary" context, with the assumption that most refugees would return home at some point soon. "Why would I lend to a refugee to start his business if he's going to leave and go home before he can repay me?" was a common refrain. Like us, Lev knew these risks were only perceived risks, but for MFIs to change their mind, they would need data and evidence, and they would need it in more than one context. His idea, then, was to launch a larger pool of microfinance capital and extend Kiva's 0 percent interest loans to a portfolio of MFI partners in multiple countries, with few to no strings attached. The MFI partners would essentially have access to risk-free R&D capital to experiment with lending to displaced entrepreneurs. If the entrepreneurs repaid their loans, the MFIs would agree to expand their lending programs while providing Kiva with highly valuable data on refugee repayment rates. This idea was novel and deeply needed. But would Kiva support Lev's idea? How would Kiva pull this off, and how could we help to make it a success?

Our initial SOCAP conversation at Fort Mason in San Francisco was only the beginning. We agreed to stay in touch while Lev worked to get internal support from Kiva and buy-in from its MFI network to launch a multicountry crowd campaign for financing refugee microentrepreneurs. Just before this SOCAP conversation, the billionaire George Soros had publicly committed $500 million to invest in refugees to "inspire other investors to pursue the same mission." The media paid great attention to this announcement, and while it did not lead to a deluge of instantaneous coinvestment in refugees, it put the concept of investing in refugees front and center on the world stage. A month later, Convergence Blended Finance awarded a key grant to the Belgian investment firm Kois Invest to begin design work on an innovative new investment product supporting refugee livelihoods in Jordan and Lebanon. It took several years for this product to get out into the market, but in the end the bond was a success.

On November 5, 2016, Donald Trump won the US presidential election. Demonizing refugees and immigrants was a key theme. While much of the country was still coming to terms with the election outcome, we were invited to attend a meeting organized by the Obama administration's Partnership for Refugees. Had the election outcome been different, this meeting would have been a step forward. Instead, it felt like a wake. To preserve the still-early and unproven progress made in the previous few months, the White House transitioned the stewardship of the partnership to the private sector. Starting in the new year, the Partnership for Refugees would work closely with the Tent Alliance, a new group of businesses committed to supporting refugees and steered by the Turkish yogurt entrepreneur Hamdi Ulukaya. In many ways, this was great news. Despite the turn of politics, the work of engaging the private sector to support refugees would continue, except now with actual business expertise in more of a leadership role. Who better to engage and enlist other businesses than a philanthropically minded, successful immigrant businessman? Tent set a follow-up meeting date for the end of the following spring. Still, the room was filled with a sense of foreboding of what might come in January with the new administration.

However, we were busy that winter and didn't actually have much time to worry about the changing political landscape. John was completing his MBA coursework, and as a newly married couple, we were house-hunting—or, in our case, farm-hunting. John had started looking at properties online while in Boston, sending Christine online listings that she would then vet for us in person. The first property we looked at was a small farm close to Charlottesville, land that had been a vineyard in the 1970s and 1980s and before that was heavily logged for two hundred years dating back to Peter Jefferson (Thomas Jefferson's father); before that, it had been stewarded under the Monacan Nation. The soil was depleted, and the farm needed some serious repair. After visiting nearly fifteen properties, we closed on this farm; it would have future meaning for us and for the refugee issues we cared so much about.

In mid-May, despite spotty rural Wi-Fi, we received a message from Lev that Kiva was ready. We agreed to officially kick off our partnership by launching a Kiva refugee-supporting crowdlending campaign on June 20, World Refugee Day.[2] The campaign was codeveloped by Kiva and the Alight Fund. Lev shared that Kiva had already secured about $60,000 but wanted at least $250,000 in funds to match any loans contributed by the public. We agreed to help Kiva raise these resources and initially thought the match could be syndicated across Tent Alliance members. So far, the Tent Alliance members had done a great deal together (in terms of actionable and quantifiable projects), but there seemed to be interest in the employment and financial inclusion space to do something. Our thinking was that even if these businesses weren't engaged in microfinance, almost all the businesses would benefit from a shared "R&D" fund to explore best practices in supporting refugee, internally displaced, and host community entrepreneurs in different economic and political contexts. We agreed to endorse the Kiva campaign at the Tent Alliance meeting and to cofundraise with Kiva, setting up a syndicated match fund for Tent partners. If the launch proved successful, we could then develop a business case study to take to future investors or lenders to help scale Kiva's refugee lending efforts.

Kiva then called Tent to explore some of these ideas. Toward the end of May, Lev wrote saying they had discussed having Tent support the campaign but that the discussion "was more focused on what Tent themselves are doing and we did not talk about having the campaign officially endorsed or setting up a match fund for Tent partners." While Tent did not offer Kiva any official slot at the Tent meeting to present its campaign, Scarlet Cronin, at the time Tent's senior director for private-sector partnerships, generously agreed to include an invitation about our side event to its meeting attendees. Lev invited Kiva's then president and cofounder, Premal Shah, to colead our gathering. Now all we needed was a venue. Thankfully, one of our friends, Cameron Sinclair, the humanitarian response and social innovation lead for Airbnb, kindly offered us one of Airbnb's conference rooms at its San Francisco headquarters. On May 24, at 4:00 p.m. Pacific Standard Time, in a conference room at Airbnb's offices, we pitched Kiva's "World Refugee Fund." We kicked off the meeting by framing the World Refugee Fund as an opportunity that "will give corporations, foundations, and private philanthropists the opportunity to match 1:1 any lending on Kiva.org to displaced peoples and host communities from Lebanon to Colombia to Rwanda." Lev provided a deep dive review of Kiva's track record to date, including the fact that it had already successfully loaned over $2.6 million to refugees and IDPs. At the close of the meeting, the first interested backers included both Tent and Anne-Marie Grey, the executive director and CEO of USA for UNHCR, the UN's refugee agency.

Thanks to these founding partnerships, within a few weeks we had our match partners lined up. On June 20, 2017, Kiva's crowdfunding page for the World Refugee Fund went live. The next morning Lev texted us saying that we had not only hit our goal of $500,000 in loans but had doubled it. Within 24 hours, every refugee and IDP entrepreneur's loan listed on Kiva.org was fully subscribed, totaling over $1 million in fulfilled loans. This success quickly became the springboard for a larger campaign raising $9 million in refugee-supporting lending capital by the close of 2017 to help address the long-term needs of host communities and families displaced in the largest refugee crisis since World War II.

The World Refugee Day campaign proved two things. First, businesses and private-sector partners were interested in giving refugees and other displaced peoples access to credit and financial services that could in turn help create jobs and better livelihoods. Second, and perhaps even more importantly, the broader public believed in doing the same thing. If Kiva's model proved anything, it was that compassionate, everyday people can make a huge difference.

We were now faced with an important question. Having proved that there was market demand for durable solutions—at least from ordinary citizens—and that we could quickly mobilize financing for microenterprises, where would we go from here?

Deepening our partnership with Kiva and helping it expand its refugee loan portfolio and data collection efforts seemed obvious. But although microfinance is an important foundational layer of any market, not every refugee wants to be or should be a microentrepreneur. Many have dreams of building larger companies or creating organizations, while others simply want a good-paying and steady job. Others need critical essential services such as banking, childcare, housing, medical care, telecommunications, and education. Microfinance clearly had a role to play and needed to be expanded significantly, but there was more work to be done. Once again, we reached out for help.

This time, we called David Young, a friend we had met initially at the World Humanitarian Summit and whom we had befriended in our first year of exploring microfinance for refugees. David was a seasoned and senior partner at the Boston Consulting Group (BCG). He'd spent a decade as the COO for World Vision International and had returned to BCG to lead some of its consulting work with private-sector partners. David lived in Boston and had come to know us through conferences and many coffees in his home city. He was (and remains) tall, affable, sharp, and optimistic. He was very supportive of our work in those early days, so we asked him for advice. He was deeply familiar with World Vision's successful microlending programs (albeit to nondisplaced clients) and didn't think what we were proposing was farfetched. He also agreed that other layers of markets beyond microlending had to be marshaled, but he was frustrated by the lack of movement from the large development finance institutions and the lack of participation from private capital in supporting refugees. Most of what we had seen in the previous year from private business commitments supporting refugees came in the form of smaller corporate social responsibility projects or commitments that didn't seem to have teeth or substance behind them, never mind measurability. Even George Soros's $500 million commitment didn't appear to be moving, and as far as we knew, most of the funds deployed in those first nine months had gone to hiring staff and consultants to tell their investment committee how to spend George's money, not to investing in any refugee entrepreneurs or companies supporting them. Something had to change.

We decided to team up with David and BCG and gather a small but diverse group of staffers from the United Nations High Commissioner for Refugees (UNHCR), the World Bank, civil society organizations, private-sector foundations, investors, and philanthropists for a "Solutions Summit" in London. Just as at the World Humanitarian Summit, experts from several sectors agreed that we needed to engage private-sector capital to address the global displacement crisis. But how? The answer that emerged from deep conversations, ideations, and iterations was an "agile matchmaking organization." Because the World Bank, UNHCR, the International Monetary Fund (IMF), and other international organizations didn't operate at the level of the firm, they didn't feel that they were the right ones to lead this effort. The humanitarian sector had done terrific work in non-profit social enterprise models and some microfinance work, but its mission at the end of the day was providing lifesaving food, shelter, medicine, and protection, not private-sector facilitation. It didn't feel it had the business expertise to decide who was worthy of credit or investment. And the investors, while familiar with risk, felt that the risks of a war zone were too high. They didn't know how to quantify the risk of a refugee fleeing with a newly received loan, or the risk of nonrepayment because the shop of an entrepreneur borrower might be blown up, or the risk that a host government would be toppled and they couldn't get their money out. Complicating things further was a general state of distrust and lack of understanding between the humanitarians and the development and business communities. Some humanitarians felt that investors were trying to profit from people who were in a state of vulnerability, and some investors thought the humanitarians were bleeding heart do-gooders who couldn't recognize a balance sheet. They had different priorities. They measured success and failure differently. They even used different language (e.g., "beneficiaries" versus "customers"). There needed to be a new agile intermediary that could speak the language of all these key stakeholders and act as matchmaker, translator, dealmaker, and facilitator. We didn't know it at the time, but this was the birth of the Refugee Investment Network.

2

DURABLE SOLUTIONS

Durable solutions to the current refugee crisis are needed that catalyze investment. Despite negative perceptions surrounding migration, our research over the past fifteen years shows that forcibly displaced people are hardworking, entrepreneurial, employable, and creditworthy. As mentioned in Chapter 1, in the United States, refugees have the highest rate of entrepreneurship and immigrant-owned businesses employ millions of Americans. Investing in refugees can therefore generate returns that extend far beyond social and economic benefits to refugees themselves. Refugees and migrants are incredible contributors and partners to their new host communities if given the opportunity to engage in and contribute to their new economies.

Moreover, investors are interested in putting capital to work for and with refugees. However, our meetings and interviews with hundreds of investors, humanitarians, development finance professionals, entrepreneurs, and displaced people have made it clear that concerns remain—regarding both risk and finding a pipeline of viable investments—that limit investment in private-sector solutions to the displacement crisis.

Several challenges are currently inhibiting investment in refugee-founded and refugee-supporting enterprises and funds.

For starters, NGOs and venture capitalists speak different languages. On the supply side, investors and financiers often face challenges with identifying, assessing, and structuring deals in new and frontier markets. We certainly have experienced those challenges, for example, with innovative new technologies like toilets when solving water and sanitation problems. Venture capitalists want to understand the intellectual property landscape, who else is funding in this area, and what the deal flow is (investor-speak for a steady stream of new and novel approaches): Is there a steady stream of good ideas representing early-, middle-, and late-stage funds?

On the demand side, refugee entrepreneurs often face barriers such as perceived higher risks, negative biases of financial and lending institutions, language and cultural hurdles, and lack of trust from host communities. Humanitarian actors are more focused on short-term needs than on generating deal flow or on attracting new investors, while development banks tend to focus on deals that are often so large that they overlook newer businesses, which is where displaced founders would more likely show up. Lastly, none of these actors—investors, investees, and supporting partners—are known to speak the same figurative language or fully understand one another's interests or motives. In fact, we often found distrust between humanitarian organizations and development agencies and between public-sector officials and business executives.

To build a bridge between these stakeholders and to help accelerate the intentional deployment of impact investing and blended finance capital for solutions to global forced displacement, we eventually designed and launched the Refugee Investment Network (RIN). This work was modeled in part on John's experience in the early 2010s when he was coleading a search fund focused on scaling up access to clean water, sanitation, and hygiene. While there was plenty of interested capital looking for deal flow, the investment pipeline was severely underdeveloped. It was for this reason that John, and his then Swiss-American business partner at the time, Michael Lindenmayer, launched Toilet Hackers, an organization focused on accelerating and expanding the ecosystem of businesses and social enterprises working on sanitation in emerging markets. With grant support from the Bill and Melinda Gates Foundation, Toilet Hackers teamed up with the World Bank to launch the first Global Sanitation Hackathon (#SanHack), which was largely focused on tech-enabled solutions to sanitation and hygiene. Over the following years, Toilet Hackers helped to accelerate and support dozens of start-ups that were creating new hardware and software for dignified sanitation, handwashing, and menstrual health, as well as creative advocacy and behavioral change campaigns and partnerships with Sesame Street, UNICEF, the World Toilet Organization (the other WTO), Japan's leading toilet innovation companies LIXIL and Toto, and many others. Michael eventually became the entrepreneur-in-residence at the Toilet Board Coalition, a multinational coalition of businesses and social enterprises focused on expanding the global sanitation business ecosystem that was initially funded by Unilever, LIXIL, and Kimberly-Clark, while John went on to Babson to complete his MBA. The Toilet Board Coalition's flagship program, a business accelerator, provides business model coaching, corporate mentorship, and access to investment to Sanitation Economy entrepreneurs serving low-income markets. As of January 2025, the program had graduated eighty-eight small and medium sized enterprises (SMEs), impacting more than 5.7 million people daily and unlocking $40 million in finance. That model of ecosystem development made a deep impression on John.

As a specialized intermediary operating today, RIN does similar work, connecting investors with refugee-led and refugee-supporting ventures, building the field and community of refugee investment through research and technical assistance, and leveraging its community of capital to advocate for more inclusive refugee policies. RIN's ultimate goal is to create quality jobs, inclusive and equitable economic growth, and measurable improvements to the livelihoods of millions of refugees and host communities while changing the narrative of displacement from fear and burden to hope and contribution. But getting from idea to action was neither easy nor simple. At the time, we didn't even have a name for our new organization, never mind funding or a team to build it. We had an idea—maybe more than an idea—but as John's father used to tell him when he was a boy, "an idea not implemented is just an idea." So began our real start-up journey, as we set out to build our new organization.

THE VALUE OF PARTNERSHIP

Just as the original idea laid out in *Failure and Hope* (Mahoney 2016) wasn't enough, the revised idea of an "agile intermediary" also wasn't enough. To make this idea a reality required incubation, funding, and a team, but not just any team—one that could speak the three often-conflicting languages of policy, humanitarian ideals, and business, while also having expertise in getting nontraditional players to play well together. There's an art to building the types of organizations that require, by the nature of the challenges they work to address, actors from diverse perspectives coming together for a common purpose. To unlock innovation opportunities at scale, we needed creative policymaking partnerships of unlikely allies. We needed a revolution in collective action. And in this context, we also needed smarter resources: better and more innovative ways of financing humanitarian response, relief, rebuilding, and resilience. It was clear that this could not be done by any one partner or sector alone. Would it even be possible?

While there wasn't much precedent for this kind of disruption in the humanitarian sector, we found plenty of inspiration. Collective action between the public and private sectors had worked in other contexts, such as in fighting malaria. In 2000, malaria was considered one of the most significant obstacles to global development. How can an economy work when the workforce is sick? Even though malaria was treatable, interventions were neither expediently available nor affordable for everyone. Global stakeholders lacked a cohesive strategy. Finance gaps were commonplace. Few people at the time would have imagined much progress. Yet in 2006, the same year that the first White House Summit on Malaria was held, a small collective, led by the private equity legend Ray Chambers, helped launch Malaria No More (MNM), an innovative new organization with an audacious goal to end deaths from malaria in Africa by 2015.

In the years that followed, Malaria No More built innovative partnerships that helped distribute bed nets to more than 5 million people in seventeen African countries. It helped coordinate national governments and implementing partners to provide health education to over 20 million Africans; it launched a policy center that increased global commitments by over $3 billion annually; and working with the financial sector, it developed a bridge loan to ensure the timely delivery of health commodities to the countries that need them most. Between 2000 and 2015, incidents of malaria fell by 37 percent globally and death rates by 60 percent.

Malaria and global displacement are vastly different challenges, but what they require of us is quite similar: shifting our focus from short-term incremental progress to long-term transformational change. What Malaria No More set out to do in 2006—to end all deaths from malaria in Africa by 2015—was nearly impossible to achieve, yet it inspired an uncommon collective to join it on its mission, marshaling resources, fueling creativity, and sharing a new sense of possibility. John was familiar with the Malaria No More story and its success because he had traveled with the Malaria No More team to Senegal in 2011, along with the actor David Arquette, at the invitation of his friend Bob Pilon. There, the team helped distribute bed nets and spoke with village elders and parents who were leading the campaign to protect their communities.

One of the community leaders we met was a man named El Hadj Diop who showed us a photo of his daughter, Amy, who was killed by a mosquito at the age of eight. When she died, he dedicated his life to fighting malaria. He committed to making his entire village free of malaria deaths because he didn't want any other parent to experience the trauma and the loss he had endured. By asking medical professionals for guidance, he was able to learn about bed nets and preventive measures, and eventually he was successful in eradicating malaria deaths in his village. Soon a few people from neighboring villages started coming to him for help, and soon he had over sixty villages participating in his malaria prevention efforts. That's about fifty thousand people he stopped from dying. While it was El Hadj's initiative and his undying love for his daughter Amy that started his work, it was the partnership of Malaria No More and their actions together that made it possible for him to scale up his efforts. That experience and that story not only moved and inspired us but also left an impression of what is possible when different people and organizations start believing in a different future together. When the leaders at the Solutions Summit (see chapter 1) were looking for examples of successful collective action, this was a very good one.

At the summit, everyone agreed on the need for radically new cooperation and a strong facilitation mechanism. But there were opposing views on the scale of the entity. Our bias was to start small, test and experiment often, and iteratively grow whatever venture (or agile body) we built. This is basically the "lean start-up" approach to business, as outlined in Eric Ries's well-known book of the same title: create a minimum viable product (MVP), which Ries defines as the "version of a new product which allows a team to collect the maximum amount of validated learning about customers with the least effort," test your basic assumptions, and then rapidly improve or pivot your offerings based on the feedback you receive. This is often described as the Build-Measure-Learn loop. The lean start-up approach often requires fewer resources and makes it easier to confront unknowns. Starting any enterprise is littered with unknowns, especially something as tricky as a collective action endeavor. Babson teaches its students to start with what you already have (including what you know), calculate your affordable loss (or what you're willing to risk and put on the line), and then enlist others in your mission. That was at least the context we were approaching this from, and it seemed to be largely echoed by other summit participants like David and Lev, as well as by Sasha Chanoff of RefugePoint; Rebecca Marmot, the vice president of advocacy and partnerships for Unilever; and, to some extent, even Sean Hinton, the CEO of the Soros Economic Development Fund, who was enthusiastic and skeptical at the same time.

Our intention at this point was to put some meat on the bones of this concept and to start up an MVP of the organization.

David felt that we needed to get a deal or project under way first and then build an organization. We understood his point. It made sense to get something done, establish a track record, and then move forward from there. But we didn't work at BCG, and no one was paying our salaries to do this work. We had also been working on our own experiment with microfinance for over a year at that point, and we felt we had already achieved an early win with Kiva. Still, David is a persuasive friend, so we did both. We started sketching a more fleshed-out concept note about the agile facilitating body, thinking about potential thought and implementation partners, as well as those who might want to help fund a new, mostly unproven idea.

At the same time, we worked closely with David and his colleagues at BCG to put a deck together for an initial first deal—something tangible to get us away from wonky concepts, something that investors could sink their teeth into and invest in with real money. We needed something that could provide meaningful value to a humanitarian need, that would also support the long-term livelihoods of refugees and make business sense for investors and operators. The concept we landed on was based on Plumpy'Nut, a Ready-to-Use Therapeutic Food (RUTF) that was designed to treat severe acute malnutrition and that was invented and produced by Nutriset, a French company. In the Middle East, most RUTF is sourced from Nutriset and is imported. We knew from a colleague who led the World Food Program's (WFP) efforts in Jordan that if it could source a similar quality of a RUTF alternative that was manufactured in the region instead of having to import it, it would. The WFP said that it would be interested in being a buyer, but at least in 2016, there were no local alternatives. Rebecca Marmot said that Unilever (hypothetically) might be interested in being an operator of a manufacturing facility in Jordan for such a product, and she even suggested that we could use chickpeas instead of peanuts for the protein source. If the venture used chickpeas, it could not only manufacture a RUTF product but also produce hummus that could be exported to the EU. The factory could be financed through a blend of public and private capital and could integrate hiring opportunities for both Jordanians and Syrian refugees. It seemed like a great idea. Maybe it still is. But the WFP moved its headquarters to Saudi Arabia and our contact seemed no longer interested in a factory in Jordan.

We spent at least six months kicking this idea around. While it didn't develop into the tangible "first deal" that David wanted, it was a great exercise in thinking about (1) a legitimate need in the market, (2) value that could be delivered to both displaced and host country communities, and (3) how to leverage the existing strengths of a business like Unilever that had not considered a refugee-supporting manufacturing venture in this context before. This was not an off-the-shelf deal. It was a deal we tried to create, using what and who we knew, getting direct feedback from the market (from both WFP as a buyer and service provider and other organizations serving refugees in Jordan, like Mercy Corps), and testing it to the extent we could. We did this while thinking about how such a joint-venture partnership could support refugees by using a refugee "lens" throughout the process. Sometimes opportunities exist, like Kiva's, when a concept is already in motion and needs greater capital to scale. And sometimes need exists and an opportunity needs to be facilitated or designed and financed. But neither opportunity comes to fruition without a group of people committing to doing something very differently than the status quo. We would argue that both examples—Kiva's World Refugee Fund, which did come to fruition, and the chickpea RUTF factory that never was—require an entrepreneurial or lean mindset to at least attempt in any meaningful way.

A MERCHANT BANK OR SOMETHING ELSE?

The counterexample is the bigger, more fully resourced approach to building things that had at least a handful of advocates. In New York we met a man named Joel Bell who served as the chairman of the Chumir Foundation. He had far more experience than we did as a business executive, including time as former CEO of the Canada Development Investment Corporation and as the cofounder of Petro Canada, an oil and gas company with $5 billion in assets. And we seemed to bump into him frequently in meetings and conferences relating to the displacement crisis. Joel was obsessed with the idea of building a merchant bank to help the private sector participate in durable solutions for global forced displacement. In many ways, he was right about the functionality of the merchant bank: Someone had to help connect the dots, match needs with opportunities, unearth opportunities that lay dormant in markets reckoning with large-scale displacement, and help to structure and marshal the financing mechanisms for various refugee-supporting deals.

This was basically what the Solutions Summit was calling for as well, but the *form* of the entity was very different. Merchant banks are not small or nimble, nor are they agile. And typically, they cater to larger corporations and wealthy individuals rather than earlier-stage enterprises, which is not representative of the stakeholders we believed this market needed to be able to serve, to put it mildly. Still, the intention was there, and the merchant bank had, even in an overly clunky form, similar functionality to what we were proposing. We thought our idea of an agile facilitating body, backed by the expertise of the leaders at the Solutions Summit, might be a great MVP to the merchant bank, especially since to establish his bank concept Joel would need to invest or raise hundreds of millions of dollars versus a few thousand to get ours going. We asked Joel to consider funding us. He declined.

That was the start of our fundraising tour. We took our short little concept note and shopped it with dozens of foundations and high-net-worth donors. Many found it "interesting" and "innovative," but no one wanted to fund it, including several foundation colleagues who had met at the Solutions Summit and had verbally agreed how badly this concept was needed. We spent six months sending out proposals, making phone calls, conducting meetings, and networking at conferences in New York, Washington, D.C., Boston, and San Francisco, and we raised, as John's dad would say, "bupkis," or nothing.

But just when we were about to give up, we were introduced to Andrew Stern, who ran the Global Development Incubator (GDI). Andrew met us for coffee in Washington. He seemed intrigued by our idea of merging collective action with finance and impact investment, deal facilitation, and market research, all of which would lead to more durable solutions to support refugee livelihoods and well-being. This, Andrew told us, sounded a lot like a multistakeholder initiative (or MSI), which Andrew happened to know a thing or two about. In fact, the GDI organization specialized in incubating MSIs. As decades of previous research on collective action problems shows, getting humans to cooperate is difficult, and getting groups of humans to cooperate is even more so. He sent us an article he cowrote with two members of GDI's leadership team, Darin Kingston and Joanne Ke Edelman, that outlined what an MSI is and the risks (or perils, as they described them) of starting one, whether or not to set up an MSI, and a detailed outline of how to set one up.[1]

We couldn't believe our luck. We shared with Andrew and later Joanne our journey over the previous year and half.

They agreed that our solution set required the creation of an MSI and, importantly, that the time for this creation seemed to be now. Typically, MSIs have three main goals, regardless of their challenge: (1) build new markets or industries by bringing different people into the same tent, often through convenings and coordination; (2) mobilize new resources, whether financial or research- and evidence-based; and (3) gain policy and political support through advocacy and consensus building. The more time we spent with Andrew and Joanne, the more we felt that we were on the right path after all. We just needed some help, a team, and some funding. Knowing how hard it is to establish an MSI, Andrew suggested that Joanne be seconded, or loaned, to the new entity as our COO, a common practice in this space. He also suggested that we also bring in a copilot to help build the organization, someone who could complement our vision and think entrepreneurially but who had more direct experience building inside and outside of government. Thankfully, Andrew also had someone in mind.

Tim Docking started his career in the Peace Corps by volunteering in Mali, then served as a White House fellow who helped launch the US government's Millennium Challenge Corporation (MCC), and then built a career at IBM in the emerging markets funding group. Tim had strong credentials in government affairs and understood the mechanics of development finance. His unique profile included expertise in both public and private approaches to international development. While Tim and Joanne had not been focused on forced displacement, both got up to speed quickly. John and Tim, acting as comanaging directors, and Joanne as COO, were now working as a team, with Christine and Andrew serving as advisers. In time, Tim would become like an older, wiser brother and mentor to John, which is why, in 2022, when John wanted to step away from the management of RIN's operations to launch a new company embodying the work and lessons that we set out in this book, Tim was the obvious choice to take on the role of sole CEO. He has proven to be a capable executive for the organization, and we are grateful for Andrew's introduction.

Over the course of six months since our first meeting as a team, together we interviewed more than one hundred interested and concerned organizations and individuals from the capital, development, government, and humanitarian communities, including refugees and displaced people themselves, and validated a pressing need for an investment intermediary to make private investment possible in what we saw as an emerging market. We were in what GDI calls the prelaunch stage—building partnerships, designing our first products, and charting our course. We looked for both inspiration and direction in finding where we would focus our efforts, and how.

GENDER LENS INVESTING (GLI)

One of the people we reached out to for feedback was Suzanne Biegel, someone we knew from water and sanitation ventures in India and sub-Saharan Africa. Suzanne was a true champion for equity and social justice. She was a brilliant connector of ideas and people, a selfless and thoughtful mentor and collaborator, and a constant source of inspiration for those trying to make change in the world, even after she lost her valiant battle with metastatic lung cancer in September 2023. Long before John met her, Suzanne had been one of the driving forces behind the gender lens movement.

Gender lens investing (GLI) is the integration of gender analysis into a new or existing investment process for better social and financial outcomes. It's the act of intentionally deploying resources and strategies to improve gender equality and parity across a host of considerations. The key word is *intention*, as we know all too well that despite what some misguided economists say, markets do not correct biased power dynamics and inequities on their own. They require us to be intentional about making corrections, particularly when the inequities are severe. GenderSmart, an organization that Suzanne cofounded, described itself as encompassing "who is investing, what results occur, how investments and terms are structured, and how decisions are made. It covers gender, racial and ethnic diversity at the ownership level, governance, leadership, decision making, employment, value chains, and products, services, and customers. It is also about power dynamics and engagement" (2X Global 2025). A lens, including the gender lens or any impact lens for investment, enables one to see the world differently—to see opportunities and value where others do not; to understand that without that intentionality and a deliberate lens with which to see, we are often blind, both to these opportunities and to inequities, including our own part in them. But gender lens investing isn't only focused on correcting inequity; it's also backed by a deep reserve of data proving that investing with a gender lens isn't just the right thing but also the smart thing to do. Now, thanks to heroes like Suzanne, who led early market work, research, and field-building efforts to create a thriving global movement for gender equity, there are countless reasons for incorporating a gender lens into one's investment and business operating practices, as well as far more articulate and rich resources for learning about gender lens investing, some of which we list later in this book. What was important for us, and in the context of this book, is that while there is still a long way to go to achieve gender equity worldwide, gender lens investing was successful in taking root as a known and established practice within the field of impact investing. It was also a valuable model for how we might unlock not just millions but even billions of dollars of intentional investment supporting forcibly displaced people all around the world.

In January 2023, GenderSmart officially merged with the 2X Collaborative to become 2X Global, now the leading hub and community for all things regarding gender lens investing. This change evolved in part from an initiative developed at the US Development Finance Corporation (USDFC), formerly known as the Overseas Private Investment Corporation (OPIC), the only US government agency to return principal plus interest to the Federal Reserve. In May 2018, OPIC unveiled its global 2X Women's Initiative, which aimed to mobilize $1 billion in private investment in projects supporting women in emerging markets, "unlocking the multi-trillion-dollar investment opportunity that women represent." The 2X Women's Initiative developed simple but effective criteria for qualifying what makes or doesn't make a gender 2X investment (figure 2.1).

To unlock OPIC investment, businesses and funds needed to meet at least one of the criteria. OPIC's 2X Initiative became the foundation of the 2X Challenge, which was launched at the G7 Summit in 2018 as a commitment from the G7 development finance institutions (DFIs) to mobilize $3 billion in gender lens investments between 2018 and 2020. That first challenge blew through its original goal, raising an additional $11 billion. In 2021 at the G7 Summit in the United Kingdom, the DFIs set a new target of $15 billion, which was also surpassed with $16.3 billion over a 12-month period. As of 2024, more than $33.6 billion in gender lens investments have been mobilized under the 2X Challenge, which is why 2X and the gender lens movement became the model for what we wanted to achieve for refugees and forcibly displaced communities. It's also why we engaged not

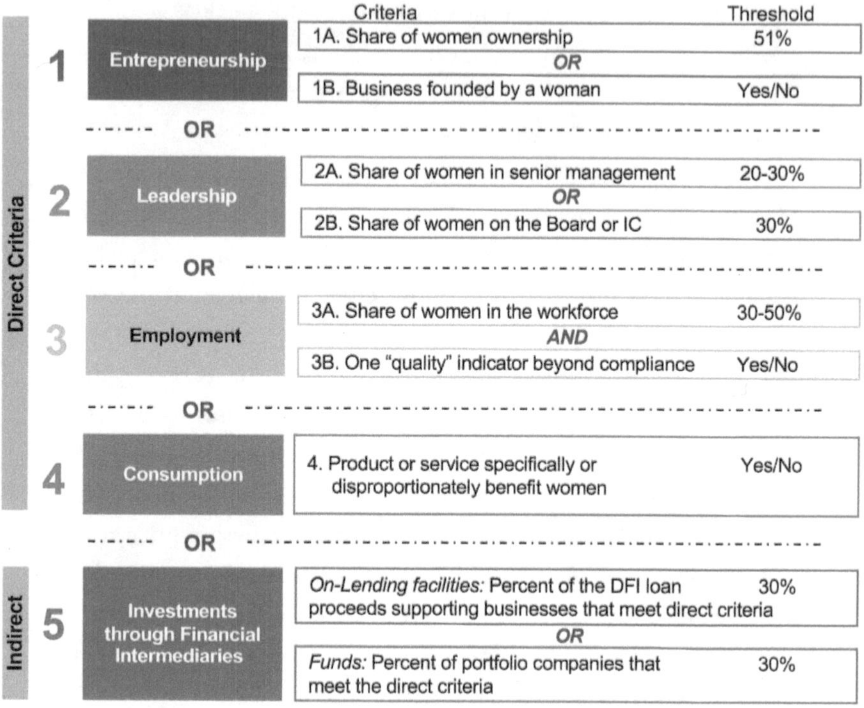

			Criteria	Threshold
Direct Criteria	1	Entrepreneurship	1A. Share of women ownership	51%
			OR	
			1B. Business founded by a woman	Yes/No
		OR		
	2	Leadership	2A. Share of women in senior management	20-30%
			OR	
			2B. Share of women on the Board or IC	30%
		OR		
	3	Employment	3A. Share of women in the workforce	30-50%
			AND	
			3B. One "quality" indicator beyond compliance	Yes/No
		OR		
	4	Consumption	4. Product or service specifically or disproportionately benefit women	Yes/No
		OR		
Indirect	5	Investments through Financial Intermediaries	*On-Lending facilities:* Percent of the DFI loan proceeds supporting businesses that meet direct criteria	30%
			OR	
			Funds: Percent of portfolio companies that meet the direct criteria	30%

FIGURE 2.1 Gender lens investing criteria.
DFI = development finance institution.

just Suzanne in our early design work, but also Mitchell Strauss, who was a leading voice for implementing socially responsible investment at OPIC, and David Bohigian, who in 2017 was executive vice president at OPIC and later became the acting president and CEO of OPIC, overseeing its transition into the now $60 billion behemoth that is the USDFC. It turned out that David Bohigian was also the grandson of refugees. Despite serving under the Trump administration, David and Mitchell both became great champions of our work and were instrumental in shaping our early thinking.

In fact, one of the first things we did was to design and build a criterion for investing with a lens to support refugees, largely by repurposing and recontextualizing the Gender 2X criteria. Now that we had a more concrete focus, we started identifying early potential supporters who believed in the need for systems change. Funders focused solely on direct service types of programs simply wouldn't get what we were trying to do. That is in part why we had such a challenging time raising funds before we found GDI: We were asking the wrong people. With Tim, Joanne, and the GDI team supporting us, we were able to secure some early, catalytic funding from the Boston philanthropist Barry Landry, the Patrick J. McGovern Foundation, and our friend Anne-Marie Grey at the USA for UNHCR, who had found significant value in their early introduction to Kiva and subsequent investment in it. With a couple hundred thousand dollars, we were "off to the races," naming "our agile facilitating body" the Refugee Investment Network, the first blended finance collaborative dedicated to creating long-term solutions to global forced migration. And with momentum often comes more momentum.

3

REFUGEE LENS INVESTING

In the previous chapter, we saw the gender lens as a smart framework and practice for making intentional investments and business decisions that measurably improve outcomes for women and girls, especially as those outcomes relate to equality, equity, and parity for everyone. Gender lens investing (GLI) was developed to help public and private investors across various asset classes use capital to close the gaps facing women and girls.

Lenses are important to investors, whether they invest in for-profit businesses or nonprofit causes. It is through a particular "lens" that investors can visualize the result they wish to see. Some bet on leadership, others on intellectual property, others on businesses that are working to lower carbon emissions. We invest in both businesses and NGOs that promote opportunity for refugees fleeing terrible situations.

Ours is "refugee lens investing" (RLI): a framework and practice to deploy capital and make business decisions to measurably improve outcomes for people who have been forcibly displaced and for the communities hosting them. These investments could be made at different stages of a community's displacement experience and could include the following:

- Investments that offset the risk of displacement in the first place (such as investment in climate resiliency)
- Investments that improve humanitarian response, capacity, and innovation during the first phase of a conflict
- Investments that improve economic integration when it is clear that the displacement is for the long term (such as those that improve access to housing, banking and financial services, childcare, healthcare, and livelihoods, as well as those that provide direct support of founders, who are often facing some of the most extreme forms of marginalization)

The Rockefeller Foundation and the Open Society Foundation soon joined our founding partners, and the Refugee Investment Network (RIN) fully developed the concept of "refugee lens investing." This type of investing offers untapped potential to generate positive social, cultural, and economic returns. The term *refugee* has a specific meaning under international law, which, under the 1951 Refugee Convention and later the 1967 Protocol, gives specific rights and protections to those who are forced to flee their country due to violence, persecution, or war. Internally displaced persons (IDPs) are people who have been forced to flee their home but have not crossed an international border and are therefore not afforded the same legal rights and protections. For the purposes of the refugee lens investor framework, and through consultation with refugee, IDP, immigrant, humanitarian, government, and investment representatives, RIN defines *refugees* broadly as a group of people who are externally or internally forcibly displaced, whether through armed or political conflict, ethnic tension, systemic discrimination, climate change or natural disaster, or the displacement of Indigenous communities. This group includes those legally recognized as refugees, asylum seekers, and IDPs, as well as stateless people and climate refugees.

Our initial landscape report, *Paradigm Shift* (Kluge et al. 2018), showed that increasing private-sector investment in the global displacement crisis requires creating a clear pathway for investment in businesses among displaced communities that deploys impact investing capital at the scope and scale demanded by the enormity of the challenge. Some investors already understand that this pathway is necessary. In the year following the World Humanitarian Summit in 2016, over $1 billion in private investment capital was pledged—some publicly, some privately—toward durable solutions to the crisis. As already pointed out, most investors and funders understand the "why" of taking on the global refugee crisis: The benefits are numerous, and the costs of not doing so are great. But only a tiny handful of deals have actually been capitalized.

The most direct way to support the forcibly displaced is to invest in the companies and funds that the displaced start or lead or that measurably improve their lives. In addition, investors are working to intentionally use capital to influence the national policies that so powerfully impact the lives and livelihoods of those forced to flee their homes.

The refugee lens designates six different types of refugee investments, each with specific baseline criteria for qualifying as a refugee lens investment (figure 3.1): R1: refugee-owned; R2: refugee-led; R3: refugee-supporting; R4: refugee-supporting and host-weighted; R5: lending facilities; and R6: refugee funds.

Just as the global displacement crisis continues to grow and the plight of displaced populations becomes more dire, refugee lens investors are becoming more sophisticated. We now see capital being actively deployed at all stages of human movement: (1) in companies and funds aimed at preventing future displacement; (2) in those seeking to support the displaced in the early stages of a displacement crisis; and (3) in those focused on the

An investment must meet the criteria of at least one of the following categories to be included as a Refugee Investment:	
Refugee-OWNED: Enterprise is at least:	A. 51% Refugee-Owned; OR
	B. 20% Refugee-Owned and have at least one refugee listed as a "key person" in operating documents.
Refugee-LED: Enterprise has:	A. At least one refugee in senior management (e.g., CEO, CFO or COO); OR
	B. A board with at least 33% refugee representation.
Refugee-SUPPORTING:	A project that provides or has the potential to provide a good or service that supports humanitarian efforts; or, an enterprise or investment that intentionally supports refugees through the development of infrastructure and services that buttress stability in disproportionately large displacement hosting cities/communities by providing infrastructure, jobs (a commitment of at least 20% of workforce), skills, products, or services to refugees that demonstrably improve the quality of refugee self-reliance, resiliency, health, education, or inclusion in financial markets.
Projects can also qualify as...	
Refugee-SUPPORTING, Host-weighted:	If they support host community businesses and the sponsor commits to adopt a policy to source at least 10% of all sub-contracting for the project from refugee-owned businesses. Deals must demonstrate either a minimum current percentage of refugee jobs or a commitment to increase their hiring within a reasonable timeframe to that level.
A Refugee LENDING FACILITY:	A debt instrument will be considered a Refugee Investment if refugee-owned/-led enterprises, refugee-supporting enterprises, or refugee borrowers will be the recipients of at least 25% of the loan proceeds.
Refugee FUNDS:	Private, alternative investment vehicles (e.g., private equity, venture capital, or portfolio structures deploying debt and/or equity) with investment strategies such as late-stage venture, growth equity, or expansion financing that have:
	A. A fund manager or general partner that is at least 20% Refugee-Owned or controlled; or
	B. Portfolio companies that are Refugee-Owned, Refugee-Led, or Refugee-Supporting (each term as described above) making up at least 33% of the vehicle's portfolio.
ALL Refugee Investments must take refugee protections into account including across the supply chain, identity protection, and other exploitative practices including working conditions. The above thresholds should not be absolute, and should not exclude Refugee Investments that have the potential to create sustainable or catalytic opportunities.	

FIGURE 3.1 The refugee lens.

long term, working to smooth economic inclusion and integration into formal economies for refugees who cannot return home.

The first category includes investments aimed at preventing displacement in the first place. The mixed migration flows to the Mexican borders throughout 2019 highlighted the role of climate change and related crop failures in forcing hundreds of thousands from their homes. High levels of generalized violence were driving people to flee, but failed coffee crops and leaf rust were also creating economic conditions that left families no choice but to move further north. Investments in companies that do work in climate adaptation and agriculture resilience will help farmers maintain their livelihoods and prevent migration. Similarly, while violence was driving large numbers of Venezuelans from their homes in 2019, economic collapse also was forcing millions to seek a better life across Venezuela's border. Economic development, microfinance, and nonpredatory small and medium-sized enterprise (SME) lending, when targeting at-risk-of-migration populations, can be an effective displacement prevention strategy when coupled with proven, smart policy interventions and diplomacy.

When violence or vulnerability leave people no choice but to flee, the first weeks and months in a new location can be traumatic. This is where the second category of investments in companies working to support an immediate humanitarian response comes in. Language barriers, lack of local knowledge, social networks, shelter, access to banking, and identification—all leave the displaced in incredibly vulnerable situations. Displaced people often find themselves victims of crime because of these vulnerabilities. Investments in innovations in safety, security, and shelter are all investments that can dramatically improve outcomes for the displaced, allowing them to get a stable footing while applying for asylum. Investments in technology that improves humanitarian effectiveness, as well as investments in innovative financing mechanisms that creatively expand emergency response capacity, are also new strategies to use capital to improve the humanitarian response stage of the displacement cycle.

Investments in longer-term economic inclusion and integration is a third important opportunity area for refugee lens investors. Returning home is not, and likely will not be, an option for millions of the world's displaced. Resettlement in a "third country," the term used for resettlement in countries like the United

States, Australia, or France, is also highly unlikely and during COVID-19 was nearly impossible. The vast majority of the world's displaced are residing in developing countries and will likely remain there for decades. Investments in companies and funds that help the displaced find a "durable solution" to their plight are critical. When an individual has lost everything, has suffered trauma and lost loved ones, and is starting from scratch, often in a new language, economic inclusion does not happen easily or organically. Investments in companies that are proactively working to provide the displaced with access to banking, housing, healthcare, childcare, and transportation hold some of the greatest promise in refugee lens investing. RIN refers to these as the "social determinants of work."

The displaced must have access to these key services before they can fully join their new communities and participate in the formal economy. While venture capitalists may not worry much about these types of social services when backing startup entrepreneurs in Silicon Valley, for impact investors seeking to invest in entrepreneurs and employees who have been forced to flee their homes, they are critical. Take, for example, the tens of thousands who have fled unspeakable violence in the Northern Triangle (Honduras, Guatemala, and Nicaragua). The United Nations High Commissioner for Refugees (UNHCR) has partnered with private-sector companies in Mexico to place these refugees into formal-sector jobs and to then secure them housing, healthcare, and childcare. These families have remarkable success rates; parents are employed, children are in school, and families are finding safe, solid footing for the first time in years.[1]

With at least six different types of refugee deals across three different stages of displacement, impact investors are developing a range of investment strategies to use capital to tackle the global displacement crisis. In addition, some are using divestment strategies to capital-starve participants in state-sponsored violence and abuse of the displaced.

Broadly speaking, refugee lens investing is an investment approach that seeks to turn the abstract idea of investing for the benefit of refugees into an intentional and functional investment strategy. The refugee lens is an intersectional impact thematic that investors can use to improve the lives of the displaced while also advancing any of the UN's seventeen Sustainable Development Goals (SDGs), such as gender equality (goal 5), reduced inequalities (goal 10), or sustainable cities and communities (goal 11), while simultaneously enhancing risk-adjusted returns.

Investors can pursue a range of more focused investment theses:

- Deploying a combination of agricultural crop insurance, direct investment in value-added agricultural exports, and infrastructure (like water and sanitation) for smallholder farmers, as well as supporting micro and SME diversification in emerging markets to improve community resilience and reduce the risk of community displacement. The US Development Finance Corporation (USDFC), Catholic Relief Services, and Acumen have all participated in deals that fit this model.
- Investing in sustainable fisheries and ecotourism to support host country economic development while creating pathways for refugee labor integration (currently being assessed by several investors focused on Mexico and Central America).
- Financing the social determinants of work in emerging markets. By providing investment and nonpredatory financing to existing small and growing businesses (SGBs) within the housing, financial services, transportation, and childcare sectors, investors can help local SGBs expand the targeting of their products and services to displaced communities, radically

improving the feasibility of pursuing formal employment and entrepreneurship.

- Investing in early-stage ventures that have high potential to improve humanitarian capacity or innovation. For example, NeedsList, a virtual marketplace software designed to match relief organizations responding to crisis and disaster with resources, closed on a $1 million seed round in 2019; the Swedish social enterprise Better Shelter, which spun out of a partnership incubated by IKEA and UNHCR, to date has provided over thirty thousand modular emergency and transitional shelters to more than forty countries; and the software developer training and outsourcing company Andela closed a $100 million series D round in 2017 led by Generation Investment Management.

APPLICATIONS OF THE REFUGEE LENS

In addition to investing at different stages of migration and different stages of company growth and maturity, impact investors are deploying capital across the capital continuum, using venture philanthropy to test new models and offset risk in emerging or postconflict markets. They deploy impact-first, concessionary capital to support the self-reliance of vulnerable communities in postconflict markets and use larger pools of more traditional, market rate–seeking capital to scale access to affordable housing, healthcare, and mobile banking. Investors, funders, and entrepreneurs have begun applying the refugee lens in a variety of ways in the two years since RIN's initial landscape report on refugee lens investing. These are by no means comprehensive but give insight into some emerging trends, theses, successes, and lessons from the field.

THE ROLE OF CATALYTIC CAPITAL

Despite the blind faith by many investors in the capitalist system, as evidenced by the gross inequality and extractive-based economies that exist in many countries around the world, unguided market forces alone do not make for a healthy, inclusive economy. Intentionality, sound policy, and systemic changes to the players who have power, hold capital, deploy resources, and can access the fundamental knowledge and networks that create upward mobility all play a role in building and growing an inclusive economy.

As we know from gender lens investing, which has been growing as an intentional community of practice for nearly twenty years, it is difficult to change deeply flawed systems and correct the entrenched biases within the capital community. It is particularly difficult when the holders of power (in this case, predominately older, white, Western males) are unwilling to surrender their power to achieve a more equitable world. The refugee lens requires no less commitment, intention, and courage than correcting the imbalances we see in disproportionate capital allocations to white, male-led companies versus companies led by women or Black, Indigenous, and people of color (BIPOC). As mentioned earlier, most displaced people fall into one, if not more, of these demographics. If intentionality, commitment, and accountability are the prerequisites to building refugee lens investment, courage and catalytic capital are the necessity.

The MacArthur Foundation defines *catalytic capital* as investment capital that is "patient, risk-tolerant, concessionary, and flexible than conventional capital". This type of capital is an essential tool to bridge gaps and achieve breadth and depth of impact, while complementing conventional investing (MacArthur Foundation 2020). In other words, without catalytic capital, certain investments—and by consequence of these investments, certain social and environmental goals essential to human flourishing—would not come to be. The MacArthur Foundation, the Rockefeller Foundation, and Omidyar Network have joined together as strategic partners to build the Catalytic Capital Consortium, "an investment, learning, and market development initiative bringing together leading impact investors who believe that greater, more effective use of catalytic capital is essential to realizing the full potential of the impact investing field, including its role in achieving the Sustainable Development Goals" (MacArthur Foundation 2020). For its part, MacArthur is investing $150 million on a matching basis in funds or intermediaries that demonstrate a powerful use of catalytic capital across diverse sectors and geographies, incentivizing additional investment and helping to build track records and scale for enterprises, fund managers, and markets.

Together the three foundations have committed to provide an initial $10 million in grants to "fuel learning and market development related to catalytic capital, helping to answer critical questions about the scope of the need for catalytic capital, when and how catalytic capital can be most effective, and what additional tools and practices are needed" (MacArthur Foundation 2020). This is precisely the kind of investment that RIN sees as necessary in growing the field and practice of refugee lens investment and in leveling the playing field for displaced communities everywhere. Catalytic capital, in this sense, is already being deployed to support displaced communities.

One of the key roles that catalytic grant capital can play is providing a rapid and adaptive response. Responding to needs in the market due to COVID-19, in June 2020 the World

Education Services (WES) announced $1.35 million in new grants across three organizations to advance career pathways for refugees and immigrants amid the pandemic:

- The Building Skills Partnership to develop and scale a new industry-recognized Infectious Disease Certification training program for building service workers
- The EdTech Center @ World Education to launch a new initiative, Equity in Learning, to build tools and networks that improve access to digital learning, training, and skill development programs for immigrant workers and immigrant-serving organizations
- The International Rescue Committee (IRC) to support and expand successful place-based career programs for refugees and immigrants

RIN saw two significant shifts in the funding environment because of the COVID-19 pandemic. The first was a retraction of resources from a geographic perspective. Some foundations and investors refocused their strategies so much that they began funding or investing only in projects and ventures within the municipality where they were based, as is the case with the Pershing Square Foundation. Others responded by funding only emergency-related programs: food, water, shelter, personal protective equipment, and legal aid. The problem is that these changes often mean that longer-term work, like systems change, is put on hold. World Education Services demonstrated a commitment to funding durable, long-term solutions despite an emergency. These programs will in fact enable future investment in and with refugee-led and refugee-supporting ventures. While the impact tail of these grants may be longer than a direct catalytic investment structured as a guarantee or as part of a capital stack, we consider these to be forms of catalytic capital investing.

Another example of a catalytic capital application of the refugee lens is Kiva's World Refugee Fund, mentioned in chapter 1. Kiva is a well-known nonprofit organization that allows people to lend money via the Internet to low-income entrepreneurs in seventy-seven countries through partner microfinance organizations. Kiva's mission is "to expand financial access to help underserved communities thrive." Kiva's refugee work illustrates the importance of having brave philanthropic capital move first to develop proof points that can unlock concessionary and market rate investing down the line.

Kiva began as a person-to-person microfinance platform where individuals could lend as little as $25 to microentrepreneurs across the world through Kiva's network of microfinance partners. In 2016 Kiva started lending specifically and proactively to refugees through its traditional crowdfunding platform. At first its microfinance partners on the ground were hesitant to lend to the displaced, fearing that they would flee and be at greater risk of default. However, Kiva.org raises capital for local microfinance institutions (MFIs) at 0 percent with individual "Internet lenders" taking on the risk of default. Because of its uniquely low-cost and risk-tolerant nature, Kiva funding—which included matching grant capital provided by a handful of family offices, private foundations, Tent, and the USA for UNHCR—allowed local MFIs to pilot refugee lending programs despite their risk concerns. That experiment showed that refugee borrowers are just as reliable as traditional microentrepreneurs. With more than $20 million loaned to over tens of thousands of refugees since the start of 2016, the microfinance crowdfunding platform Kiva has found that repayment rates for refugee loans are the same as those of nonrefugees.

INVESTMENTS IN REFUGEE-LED AND REFUGEE-SUPPORTING VENTURES: MICRO BUSINESSES AND SGBs

Having demonstrated the viability of refugee lending, Kiva has developed a new, for-profit investment fund (the first of any kind) to scale its proven refugee lending programs around the world. The Kiva Refugee Investment Fund (KRIF) is a $32.5 million, five-year closed-end fund consisting of $20 million in debt from the USDFC with a fixed coupon of 2.5 to 3.0 percent, $10 million in equity, and a variable rate of return targeted at 5.50 to 6.50 percent. As of June 2024, KRIF deployed $40.7 million and reached more than 51,400 borrowers. Investors that participated in KRIF included the family office Ceniarth; the faith-based investors Missionary Sisters of the Sacred Heart and the Mercy Partnership Fund; the Soros Economic Development Fund (SEDF), which provided an anchor investment of $5 million; and the USDFC, which provided up to 100 percent of the debt facility, depending on whether additional investors are seeking a debt placement ahead of their close. As can be the case with investments in emerging or frontier markets, a continuum of capital is needed to make this initiative truly succeed, and Kiva is actively raising additional grant support to underwrite technical assistance and cutting-edge impact reporting.

Other microfinance funds are starting to follow Kiva's leadership, though there remains some trepidation within various local markets regarding policy environments that are in many cases openly hostile to refugee inclusion. This is not to say that lending to refugees does not occur in these markets. Triodos Investment Management has provided capital (alongside Kiva) to the Lebanese MFI Al Majmoua, which is lending at a small scale to refugees. The US-based Developing World Markets

(DWM) and the Belgian impact investment firm Incofin Investment Management invested $3.2 million with internally displaced microentrepreneurs in the Caucuses through Georgia's leading nonbank financial institution, Crystal, among other geographies (Incofin 2019).

In the summer of 2019, DWM began developing a new private equity fund strategy and concept, the Displaced Communities Fund (DCF), with the objective of enhancing self-reliance and financial resilience among displaced communities, including with (1) refugees in protracted displacement; (2) IDPs; (3) vulnerable host communities; (4) at-risk source communities; and (5) vulnerable host communities. The intent was to make private equity investments in inclusive financial institutions (IFINs) and businesses currently serving or committing to serve displaced communities alongside host populations. These investments were enhanced by a technical assistance facility of up to 20 percent the fund size to support investment preparedness and to address readiness gaps in focus countries, as well as refugee lens adaptations to build displacement-inclusive products, services, business practices, and client financial literacy and skills. The DCF concept was approved for $15 million in financing by the European Investment Bank (EIB) in September 2023 with a total raise target of $50 million, potentially offering investors an opportunity to put larger tranches of capital to work supporting displaced communities with returns comparative to DWM's track record of over $2 billion invested to date (Swaminathan et al. 2020).

In other markets, lending to refugees has been slow to expand, not because of hostile policies but because of the high cost of capital and the lack of local financial intermediaries willing to lend at nonpredatory rates. This has largely been the case in Mexico, with some exceptions. If impact investors seek to deploy microfinance capital in markets where there are almost no financial intermediaries willing to lend at reasonable rates, they have a choice. They can either invest in building new institutions in those markets—likely something that would require both patient and concessionary capital—or place that capital in more favorable markets. Savvy impact investors and fund managers with a long-view mindset see significant opportunity in these market gaps. As we know, however, microfinance is but one layer of a market ecosystem. For an economy that is inclusive of refugees and migrants to be healthy, all layers of the market must be activated—micro firms, SMEs and SGBs, large firms, funds, lending instruments, and so forth—just as all forms of capital across the risk/return/impact spectrum must also be activated. Each market has its own gaps that serve as RLI opportunities.

In Mexico for example, we met with Karla Gallerdo, the visionary CEO of Viwala, an SME financing company that was built to address the missing middle of financing for impact-driven SMEs who need $30 to $250 thousand in financing, far below the ticket threshold that most Mexican venture capital firms offer. After their first three years of operations, Viwala's investments helped over 10,000 small farmers gain access to the economy, trained 25,000 young entrepreneurs, empowered over 70,000 women, provided over 80,000 people in rural communities with healthcare, and helped over 125,000 families gain access to affordable clean energy (Viwala 2023). Without early investment from New Ventures, USAID, and Pro Mujer, this work would not have been possible, which is why we call this catalytic capital.

Similarly, we would not have been able to prototype how we map refugee lens investing ecosystems were it not for catalytic capital. Since our approach and the concept for RLI mapping was new, very few funders were willing to fund our efforts. If the Dunn Family Charitable Foundation had not made an early grant investment enabling us to conduct our first market assessment on inclusive investment in Mexico, much of the work we do today to enable new investors, policymakers, and businesses to participate in RLI would simply not exist. While government, civil society, and the private sector recognize both a humanitarian urgency and a business case for creating long-term solutions to forced migration in Mexico (the "why"), stakeholders are seeking guidance on strategy and implementation (the "what" and the "how"). The Dunn grant has been instrumental in understanding how migration, investment, policy, and enterprise fit together in this market, which in turn allowed the RIN to attract this initial public investment. This is yet another example of catalytic capital at work and the importance of supporting specialized intermediaries.

For nearly a year and a half, the RIN was advising the Small Enterprise Assistance Fund (SEAF) in designing its Global Displaced Persons Fund (SGPF), which we hoped would become the first global equity and quasi-equity impact investment fund for creating value through SGB entrepreneurs focused on providing jobs, products, and services to the forcibly displaced and their host communities. SEAF is one of the most experienced global investment managers in the world, with a strong track record of investing in emerging and frontier market SMEs, several of which are historical refugee lens cases. The SGDPF concept was a multiregional fund focusing on five main regions with shared forced displacement dynamics: (1) Central America, Colombia, and the Caribbean; (2) the Maghreb and West Africa; (3) East Africa; (4) the Balkans, Levant, and Caucasus; and (5) the Association of Southeast Asian Nations (ASEAN) and Bangladesh. An interesting feature of the fund is that investors can opt out of specific regions.

The fund focused on five groups:

- Forcibly displaced–led businesses with significant ownership or representation in senior management
- Companies in sectors with a high prevalence of forcibly displaced people, especially in the labor force
- Businesses that provide vital products and services that cater disproportionately to the unmet needs of the forcibly displaced
- Companies that promote host community support via local supplier participation and job creation
- Companies that demonstrate a commitment to integration and empowerment for forcibly displaced people

SEAF believed that a significant improvement in the livelihood of at least 100,000 forced migrants globally would set the example for millions more, which is part of its impact thesis for creating a more sustainable shift in the reception of the forcibly displaced around the world. This number is critical, considering that RIN projections forecast 300 million people on the move in the next decade. To support and improve SGDPF's investment activity, SEAF created a proprietary lens rating tool inspired by RIN to identify investment candidates; track progress across nine vectors relating to displacement (including pay and labor protection, host community support or benefits, and diaspora connectedness and involvement); develop an actionable best practices framework; and leverage data to incentivize prorefugee policy reforms. SEAF was aiming for a first close of $30 million with a larger expected total fund size. Average deals were expected to be $1 million to $10 million and are targeting an internal rate of return (IRR) of over 12 percent per annum net. Unfortunately, the team that was leading the raise was trying to support too many funds at once. No one truly "owned" the SGDPF, and the project stalled. Still, it's worth mentioning for its innovative structure and scope as an equity and quasi-equity fund and as a lesson in how fund managers need to fully empower and equip their investment teams to succeed, particularly when taking new investment thematics or structures to market.

In the Middle East and North Africa (the MENA region), we see blended finance funds focusing on a single market, like GroFin's Nomou Jordan Fund (NJF), which is working to prove the single-geography model, though performance has struggled under the combined pressures of a stagnant GDP, drops in Jordan's stock market, lower consumer confidence and purchasing power, and a complicated and constricting right-to-work environment for refugees. NJF is a blended finance development fund that supports SMEs in Jordan, prioritizing women-owned, employment-intensive businesses as well as those that employ or are owned by refugees. The fund is a mix of equity (89 percent) and debt (11 percent) with 47 percent coming from public capital and 53 percent from private capital. By the third quarter of 2019, the fund had raised $26.8 million, including an early $8 million investment from the Open Society Foundation's (OSF) Economic Justice program as well as an additional $400,000 grant from OSF for technical assistance. Other investors include DFID, Norfund, KfW, the Dutch Good Growth Fund (DGGF), Anthos Capital, and the Lundin Foundation.

While NJF has a clear mission to support refugee-owned and refugee-supporting ventures, the $4.4 million in disbursements to refugee- and non-Jordanian-owned businesses represents only 20 percent of the total investment dispersed to SMEs (GroFin 2019). Given the difficult policy environment that limits refugee labor integration and entrepreneurship opportunities in Jordan, this is not too surprising. While RIN would like to see a higher percentage of capital going to refugee-owned businesses, it is encouraging to see that 45 percent of the total portfolio of businesses provide employment opportunities to the displaced.

The Ascend Venture Fund (AVF) unfortunately did not have as much success. In 2018 AVF showed promise as a single-market debt fund with a ride-along technical assistance vehicle (the Ascend Collaborative) providing concessionary capital to small and medium-sized Greek-owned enterprises that would create jobs for refugees, migrants, and vulnerable Greeks. With management from CNL Capital, Greece's leading SME debt fund, early philanthropic support from the Ikea Foundation, Coca-Cola Foundation, Libra Group, and Radcliffe Foundation, and an anchor investment from Radcliffe's principal Frank Giustra, AVF generated buzz amid early refugee lens investors as a potential model for country-focused refugee-supporting funds, but it struggled to complete its capital raise. Funds taking on the still-nascent thematic of refugee lens investing should be mindful of targeting their fund to a single geography, particularly when investors are already skeptical of a given market.

One of the other challenges we identified with Ascend's raise was that its fund manager, who was based in Greece, was seldom available in person for investor presentations and discussions (which largely occurred in the United States and Canada). Building trust and confidence with investors is essential, particularly when trying to do something new, innovative, and unproven. As brilliant and committed as a sponsoring foundation and technical assistance team might be, fund managers must be active and fully present during the raise process. Having a fund's anchor investor also fully engaged with the process would also be beneficial. Impact investors who are interested in refugee lens investing but who have not yet participated in their first refugee lens deal tend to be willing to try out a new geography, a new sector, or a new thematic, but never all three and rarely two of the three. This dynamic is exacerbated when interested investors are constrained in their access to fund managers and anchor investors.

Several enterprises and funds are using technology either to expand access to refugee employment or to enable it through secure payments, transactions, and savings. Even in the most remote regions affected by conflict, technology can help people on the move gain access to the global marketplace. Large multinational companies seek to engage what is often considered an overlooked workforce, wherever they may be. One fund in particular, Amplio Ventures, was focused on increasing remote refugee employment by investing in US and European companies with high growth potential that are (1) refugee-founded and -operated businesses (classified as R1 refugee lens ventures), (2) enterprises using a refugee workforce, (3) enterprises committed to using their resources to support refugees, and (4) enterprises whose product or service benefits refugees.

Amplio's stated interest derives from its cofounders' experience in building and operating a successful and highly profitable talent and recruiting firm, Amplio Recruiting, that placed thousands of resettled refugees into US manufacturing, advanced manufacturing, and hospitality jobs. As stated by its pitch documents, "businesses founded by refugees are materially more likely to succeed; refugee employees add tangible value to the companies they serve; and, as a market, the refugee community is growing year over year" (Amplio, Amplio deck via personal communication, May 5, 2020).

One such company that has garnered interest from Amplio was Valiu, a fintech start-up that provided unbanked migrants in Latin America same-day money transfers to their relatives back home for one-tenth of the current cost using crypto. Valiu's products were designed with an understanding of the unique financial challenges experienced by the forcibly displaced, especially the over 5 million Venezuelans seeking refugee across Latin America. Displaced Venezuelans are charged an average of 15 to 30 percent in fees every time they send money to provide for their families. "They live day-to-day and send home an average of USD $20/week. In a given month, they would send $80 home, but their families would only receive around $60" (Valiu 2019). Valiu hoped to capitalize on the Latin American remittances market, which sends and receives about two times more money than China (roughly $55 billion per year). Remittances to Venezuela from displaced family members in Colombia and Ecuador totaled around $6 million per year (World Bank Group 2017).

Valiu worked in the following way. A customer added a recipient bank, entered their amount to send, and chose their payment method (debit, credit, or cash tellers). Valiu received fiat money and used it to buy crypto assets in local markets. It then sold the crypto in the destination country in exchange for local fiat, which was then transferred from the crypto buyer to the recipient bank account. The process was safe, efficient, and cost-effective, which is more than can be said for most options currently available to those on the move. Amplio had secured early funding from the Walton Family and was continuing its raise. Both of Valiu's founders have since left the company and continue to advance careers in tech and crypto companies.

They are not the only investors who see potential in building safe and affordable financial transactions for refugees and migrants. Mercy Corps Ventures (MCV) signed a term sheet with Leaf Global Fintech, a global virtual bank helping refugees and migrants safely store and transport their money across borders. Leaf is based in the United States but has focused its product across five countries in Africa. By using Leaf, customers can avoid the risks of carrying their life's savings in cash, receive money conveniently and affordably from friends and family, and retain more of their wealth when crossing borders—drastically improving their ability to reestablish themselves in new communities. In its first two years of operations, Leaf received awards from SXSW, the National Science Foundation, the United Nations, and the Vatican; received a $225,000 Small Business Innovation Research (SBIR) grant and a $250,000 matching grant from the Colorado Office of Economic Development; and is now securing its first major investment capital from MCV, ParticleX, and the Berkeley Impact Fund.

Tim Rann, a partner at MCV, said, "We admire Leaf's proximity to its target customer segments, carefully aligning its product/tech design with local levels of digital and financial literacy. They remain one of the very few companies we are aware of that have linked USSD payments to the blockchain, which we believe could be a key innovation that broadens its application for inherently challenging segments of users (refugees, migrants, cross border traders)." Leaf's management team, Nat Robinson and Tori Samples, are both repeat founders who keep a good balance between developing a blockchain-based backend solution and building out customer acquisition and marketing channels. They've proven magnetism for resources and, critically, are strong at building partnerships (pivotal for their tech and regulatory compliance). MCV sees many synergies with other companies in its portfolio (it is an investor in Valiu), as well as an array of partnership opportunities with Mercy Corps's global field office network and partnerships (Celo, Libra, Ripple, Mastercard). The refugee lens overlaid with MCV's existing financial technology portfolio is exactly the kind of intersectionality other investors should consider when developing their own approach to refugee lens investing.

OUTCOMES- AND INCENTIVE-BASED INVESTING

Given the acute need for affordable housing, both within the United States and in urban markets abroad, there are many opportunities in the real estate and housing market, including rent-to-own interventions (to support wealth and asset building among refugee and migrant communities), nonpredatory home and land financing or trusts (the latter being especially critical in emerging markets with large agriculture-dependent displaced communities), and companies building solutions to guarantor or credit requirements. In Mexico, for example, all immigrants (not just refugees and migrants) are required to have a guarantor to secure an apartment lease. Often the employer or corporation of "expats" will sponsor their apartment, though even this practice has limits, given the requirement that guarantees are backed by hard (often land-based) assets.

The Mexico City–based property rental platform Homie raised $7 million from the private venture capital fund Equity International and Angel Ventures Pacific Alliance II. Homie acts as a guarantor for expats, circumventing the complicated bureaucratic process and difficulties of finding a guarantor for foreign renters. Although Homie has not begun targeting its services to the over forty-five distinct nationalities and cultures represented by refugees and migrants seeking a new home in Mexico, clearly its product would provide a valuable service. This is where refugee lens investors can play an instrumental role in incentivizing their portfolio companies to *become* refugee-supporting ventures. Providing companies with working capital that is conditional on the venture retargeting their services to support refugees and migrants is another, relatively direct way that investors can help expand this field.

Public and philanthropic funders, impact investors, and social enterprises are already working together in innovative ways to do exactly this. In recent years, the Swiss Development Agency (SDA), working with Roots of Impact (Roots), has pioneered the use of social impact incentives, or SIINCs. Roots defines a SIINC as "a funding instrument that rewards high-impact enterprises with time-limited premium payments for achieving social impact. The additional revenues enable them to improve profitability and attract investment to scale. Thus SIINC can effectively leverage public or philanthropic funds to catalyze private investment in underserved markets with high potential for positive impact" (Roots of Impact 2020). In essence, the SIINC aligns three different and essential stakeholders within a specific transaction: social enterprises, which with access to incentive-based financing are able to scale operations and impact; public and philanthropic funders, who seek to achieve positive impact outcomes; and impact investors seeking to enhance their social and financial returns on their investments.

A good example is SDA's inaugural SIINC with Clínicas del Azúcar (CdA), a social enterprise in Mexico specializing in low-cost diabetes treatments. SDA found significant promise in the CdA model; in its first six years of operation, it had become the largest private provider of specialized diabetes care in Mexico, with nine clinics reaching more than fifty thousand patients and with 95 percent experiencing access to specialized treatment for the first time in their lives. In addition, CdA offers its services at approximately 40 percent of the average price for private treatment.

Yet, despite its success, CdA was not offering its lifesaving services to clients at the base of the pyramid; the management team struggled to balance its commitment to serve everyone who needed its treatment (maintaining affordability) while attracting capital that would allow it to expand, which was also essential to reduce the cost of the treatment. "By providing payments for real impact achieved at the base of the pyramid, CdA was empowered to position itself as an innovator in diabetes care and a pioneer in prevention techniques. At the same time, CdA was able to achieve solid economic returns . . . while crowding in the right type of investors who supported their bold move into lower socio-economic groups" (Roots of Impact 2019). As the number one cause of mortality in Mexico, diabetes affects everyone, including refugees, migrants, Indigenous communities, and Mexican citizens deported from the United States. The CdA was not a refugee lens transaction itself, largely due to the lack of intentionality with regards to deploying these services to refugees and migrations, but RIN finds that the SIINC model and process have significant potential for refugee lens applications; hence its inclusion here.

ALTERNATIVE INVESTMENT STRUCTURES

As many impact investors across the world have found, sometimes social enterprises, especially those working with the most vulnerable communities, can benefit from alternative investment structures like cooperatives and revenue shares. An example of an investment in a creative business model that is targeted at preventing displacement and that also fulfills investors' environmental sustainability interests is Root Capital's investment in Ejido Verde. Ejido Verde is a sustainable pine resin company that builds income and wealth among the Indigenous communities of Michoacán. With deep industry-specific knowledge of the business-to-business (B2B) pine resin market, Ejido Verde is positioned to become a lead supplier in the $10 billion global pine chemicals industry. In addition to developing a stable supply chain of a critically important ingredient in products ranging from shoes to makeup, the company has created good-paying jobs for over two thousand people, has crafted a process that builds long-term wealth and connection-to-place for hundreds of families, and has sequestered 133,000 tons of carbon.

Ejido Verde's business model involves lending zero-interest loans to rural and Indigenous, autonomous, landowning communities (known as *ejidos*), and the communities pay back that loan in pine resin. This arrangement allows the Indigenous communities of Michoacán to maintain ownership of their land and invest in its long-term sustainable productivity.

This case is also an example of using different types of capital at different stages of growth. The project began with philanthropic capital from the Pinosa Group to run a number of experimental social reforestation projects. After piloting and testing several different models, Ejido Verde was transformed into an independent for-profit business with a long-term strategy to advance economic, social, and environmental prosperity for rural and Indigenous communities. After participating in RIN's migration programming and panel at the Foro Latinoamericano de Inversión de Impacto (FLII) in Merida, Mexico, in February 2020, Ejido Verde secured a $5 million investment from IDB Labs, the innovation laboratory of the Inter-American Development Bank (IDB) group.

Another case study that represents a cooperative model, is an example of catalytic capital, and has potential as a refugee lens investment is the Post Road Foundation (PRF). The lack of high-speed Internet in most rural communities limits their access to healthcare, education, twenty-first-century entrepreneurship, and high-paying jobs, a digital gap made even more acute by the

COVID-19 crisis. Rural communities without high-speed Internet are less healthy, have lower household incomes, and are losing young people to out-migration. Seth Hoedl, the cofounder and chief operating and science officer of PRF, shared that "the majority of rural America without high-speed internet gets its electricity from local electric cooperatives, established in the early 20th century. Today, 834 non-profit electric coops provide at-cost electric service to their member-owners. These coops own their own national support institutions, including CFC, a highly-rated, non-profit finance cooperative providing over $26B in low-cost loans to member coops." These electric cooperatives cannot directly finance the broadband Internet service because of their insufficient debt capacity and inability to raise equity capital.

That's where PRF comes in. Over its first year, it conducted five pilot studies of rural communities in the United States (two of which were Indigenous communities) to assess the market, demand, potential vendors, labor estimates, and potential feasibility of working with each cooperative community, all of which have informed the design of a financing model for high-speed, fiber optics Internet infrastructure through joint ventures with rural electric cooperatives. In partnership with the communities it hopes to serve, PRF is now developing a blended finance fund that uses subordinated first-loss equity from philanthropies and electric cooperatives to decrease risk and boost returns for senior equity investors. The fund's end goal is $200 million in total equity, including first-loss capital, that catalyzes $800 million joint-venture project debt from cooperatives and other lenders. Average ticket sizes will be $15 million to $20 million over a thirty-year term with commercial returns expected by year 10, although PRF intends to start smaller, likely at $10 million to $20 million or, as Hoedl shared, "ideally $60M—enough to do 2–3 cooperatives in the first round."

All of the work to date has been made possible through a catalytic grant from the Rockefeller Foundation's innovative finance team as part of its Zero Gap Initiative, which aims to tap into mainstream markets and investors to scale up investments into promising new finance vehicles that help to close the SDG funding gap. The Rockefeller Foundation's investment was close to $1 million, which for a deal of this size will be a profound return on investment in terms of the capital that PRF hopes to mobilize and the positive economic, social, and environmental impact this investment could have on the cooperative communities. Rockefeller's investment has also allowed PRF to develop a financial analysis tool that will help it work with the cooperatives.

Hoedl shared that many of the areas redlined for housing are also redlined for digital access. Redlining occurs when state, local, or federal governments or private businesses, either directly or through the selective raising of prices, refuse services based on race or ethnicity. It should be no surprise that many Indigenous communities across the United States have been targeted by redlining since the founding of the country.

The success of this investment is predicated on trust and partnership between PRF and the cooperatives, and the cooperatives own agency in the project. They own and operate the asset and have a strong community focus and participation. The cooperatives contribute part of the subordinated equity that also plays in how the investment is led by the community: "They're making a contribution, even if it is small." Lastly, the synergies between the communications of fiber and the electricity of the cooperative help to advance returns (such as extra revenue) and are also a marketing resource to speak to different audiences. Given the scale of PRF's offering, the impact and the returns it promises, this should be a compelling opportunity, particularly for larger institutional and faith-based investors. Again, without the early investment from the Rockefeller Fund, none of critical studies and relationship building that enabled PRF to design the fund concept would have been possible. This is a great example of a catalytic investment and one that could be beneficial to many Indigenous communities across the country.

DIVESTMENT

We have focused primarily on proactive investment in companies, funds, and instruments that are measurably improving the lives of the displaced or those at risk of forcible displacement. Divestment is another critically important tool that some sophisticated investors are using to support those fleeing for their lives. The impact investing expert Morgan Simon, founder of the Candide Group, teamed up with the NFL linebacker Derrick Morgan to use a divestment campaign to take on the detention of migrant families. They created the Real Money Moves (RMM) financial activism campaign to align money and justice. RMM strategically partnered with over thirty prominent athletes, activists, and actors to advocate against big banks financing private prisons and family detention centers.

Alongside the grassroots activism by the #FamiliesBelongTogether coalition and the #BackersofHate campaign, RMM leadership helped influence JPMorgan Chase, Wells Fargo, Bank of America, SunTrust, BNP Paribas, Barclays, Fifth Third Bank, and PNC to publicly commit to ending their financial ties to private prisons and detention centers. Thanks to their work, by the third quarter of 2019 private prison and detention companies lost $2.34 billion in future credit and loans, or 87.4 percent of their entire known pool of private financing (Simon

2019). As the cofounder Simon puts it, "We want everyone to reclaim power over their money and be able to say, 'if I'm depositing my money in the bank, I have a right to know where it spends the night and that it's supporting my values. I don't want to be building wealth for my family by locking up someone else's'" (Simon 2019).

As evidenced by the success of RMM, the importance and value of targeted divestment approaches cannot be understated and should be considered by every refugee and migration lens investor—or anyone, for that matter, who does not want to profit from the exploitation of marginalized communities. Understanding what is in our *existing* portfolios is a critical first step for any investor, asset manager, or foundation to consider in developing a refugee and migration lens strategy. It is relatively straightforward for investors to screen their index funds or shareholdings for direct financing of private prisons and detention centers like the GEO Group or CoreCivic; it is much like doing due diligence on other public companies or holdings where there are still major information asymmetries.

PUBLIC MARKETS

Refugee lens investing is still relatively new as an intentional impact investing thematic. As such, investment products and instruments have concentrated in these early years either within private offerings or within larger, multilateral institutions. Public markets and commercial investment offerings have yet to take root, though this situation will hopefully change in the coming year. As a signal of what might be coming, one can look to the Kellogg-Morgan Stanley Sustainable Investing Challenge, a competition of over three hundred students representing seventy-four graduate schools and fifty-six countries to challenge future leaders to develop innovative financial vehicles to help address environmental, social, and governance (ESG) challenges.

A team in the New York University Stern School of Business and Wagner School of Public Service proposed the Refugee ETF ("exchange-traded fund") a few years ago "as the first retail investment product designed to help drive economic integration of refugees. The ETF aimed to achieve its social and financial goals through investments in a global index comprised of listed companies with robust refugee-focused policies and initiatives" (Morgan Stanley 2020). Bringing this type of ETF to market would create a pathway for significant new inflows of capital. The team behind the ETF idea, Refugee Integration Insights (RII), started hiring data scientists to build out an index of refugee-supporting corporations. It expanded this dataset in 2022 to cover benchmark indices such as the S&P 500 and STOXX Europe 600 and to capture the growth of corporate action on behalf of Ukrainian refugees; the dataset includes research and analysis on over 1,800 global companies. Tim Docking continues to serve on RII's advisory board as it further develops its market research and offerings.

This chapter has introduced the concept of refugee lens investing and has highlighted some of the more promising, market-based, refugee-focused, and potential refugee-supporting investment opportunities in development since 2018.

There is a persistent horse-and-cart problem in this field: Although there are many bad government policies that disincentivize investment (e.g., rules barring refugees' right to work, right to bank, and right to entrepreneur), without private capital at the negotiating table, there is little economic leverage to incentivize policy change. This problem is another reason for investors to become active in this space. And while national policies may be challenging, as a macrotrend we see municipal and state government leaders much more willing to set inclusive policies for refugees and migrants. This is true in Kalobeyei and Kakuma, Kenya; Gaziantep, Turkey; and Tijuana and Merida, Mexico, with some exceptions in national leadership in Colombia and Ethiopia, which offer hopeful, if strained, models for other countries to follow.

As for "private-sector partnerships" in the humanitarian context, these still too often depend on the corporate social responsibility (CSR) interventions of large multinational companies, while foundations and nonprofit organizations often focus on various forms of short-term aid rather than durable, long-term solutions. While goodwill within business and allyship with displaced communities are helpful, they are not a strong enough vehicle to create systemic change. The impact of COVID-19 on donor government commitments to international development, particularly durable solutions to forced displacement, remains to be fully understood. What is clear is that we, as a global community, cannot afford a further retreat into nationalism and xenophobia. While private capital should take direction from displaced people, it first needs to make its offer of support heard and felt. This can best be done by executing on investments and demonstrating commitment, not by making more pledges or serving on panels. There has been far too much talk in the last two years by a limited pool of stakeholders; some have honored their commitments, but others have run perpetual cycles of reshuffling, consulting, and restrategizing, even while the numbers of people forcibly displaced continue to grow and entrepreneurs are starved of capital.

As a result, there remains a sizable gap between capital committed and capital deployed. Funds are still early in their development, and, where capital is being deployed, it is still too early to rigorously assess its impact on displaced communities. But this will come in time.

Developing a standard baseline for measuring the impact of effective investment, while also building off some existing frameworks and tools, will likely be an important next step. Equally important, particularly given the urgency of advancing equity and justice within capital and communities, is the unconditional support, training, and elevation of refugee and displaced fund managers, board members, and executives. We must also consider how to accelerate the work of building and growing this field by supporting intermediaries, advisory firms, and the ecosystem of incubators and accelerators that are creating the future refugee lens pipeline.

While the world may be facing compounding traumas of an unrelenting pandemic, economic inequality, and racial injustice, the resilience, generosity, and spirit of displaced people may be our deepest reserve of hope.

4

IT'S THE ECONOMY, GENIUS!

In the weeks just before Christmas 2024, the White House invited our Refugee Investment Network (RIN) to meet the president's policymakers within the migration bureau of the National Security Council (NSC). The meeting was held in the Eisenhower Executive Office Building, more commonly known as the Old Executive Office Building, or OEOB. Most White House staff work in this building, which is a short walk from the West Wing.

The OEOB's black-and-white checkerboard floor tiles were mostly silent that day except for small pockets of busyness here and there due to staff attrition and the holidays. Next door in the White House, large groups of visitors passed through the beautifully decorated hallways and stately rooms, but there, among the rank and file, the mood was somber. President Joe Biden would leave office in just a month. The appearance was more of a wake than a bustling nerve center. Still, the president's staff stood ready at their posts.

The plight of refugees has been a constant conversation inside these corridors of power since they were first constructed in the late nineteenth century. Whether Republican or Democrat, the president in power has made consequential decisions about the fate of refugees, something we will discuss more later.

But it seemed to us, on this December day, that the Biden administration was looking for something of a Hail Mary pass; perhaps outside interest groups like the RIN might bring forth eleventh-hour strategies or tactics that might spark a sudden breakthrough before President-Elect Donald Trump took office. We, too, were hopeful that the administration might offer a smart new initiative. We left wishing the meeting had happened years earlier.

Governmental and academic research has proven that the integration of refugees into the United States is a significant boon for the economy, business, and industry. The impact is multifaceted, as the following discussions show.

There are positive fiscal implications to the inclusion of refugees. From 2005 to 2009, refugees and asylees contributed a net fiscal benefit of $123.8 billion to the US economy, according to a Health and Human Services study entitled "The Fiscal Impact of Refugees and Asylees at the Federal, State, and Local Levels from 2005–2019." The federal government saw a net gain of $31.5 billion, while state and local governments collectively benefited by $92.3 billion (Ghertner et al. 2024). These figures underscore the substantial fiscal advantages of integrating refugees, as their economic activities generate significant tax revenues and reduce public expenditure over time. An American Immigration Council (AIC) study found that in 2019 refugees earned over $93.6 billion in household income and contributed $25 billion in taxes, leaving them with $68.6 billion in disposable income, or spending power, to use at US businesses (AIC 2023).

Refugees exhibit a remarkable entrepreneurial spirit, often surpassing other immigrant groups in their rate of business creation. The same AIC report noted: "The United States was home to nearly 188,000 refugee entrepreneurs in 2019. That means that 13 percent of refugees were entrepreneurs, compared to just 11.7 percent of non-refugee immigrants and 9 percent of the U.S.-born population. Refugee entrepreneurs also generated $5.1 billion in business income that year" (AIC 2023). This entrepreneurial drive not only fosters innovation but also creates jobs and stimulates local economies.

Then there are the labor market contributions. Refugees contribute to the labor market by filling essential roles in various industries. Their participation helps address labor shortages and supports the growth of key sectors. Studies have shown that refugees, after an initial period of adjustment, achieve employment rates that often exceed those of native-born citizens in the United States. For example, male refugees of working age had a 67 percent employment rate from 2009 to 2011, while native-born males had only a 60 percent employment rate during the same time period. Refugee women were just as likely as native-born women to be employed (Capps et al. 2015). This integration into the workforce is vital for sustaining economic growth and ensuring the competitiveness of US industries.

In its refugee employment report, the Private Sector for Refugees (PS4R) Platform of the World Bank points out the numerous economic and humanitarian advantages of hiring refugees in countries around the world:

- *Refugees fill vacancies.* When businesses need to fill vacancies, they often do not distinguish between refugees and local applicants. Businesses are primarily driven by economic considerations and look to secure the best employees at the lowest cost without triggering unnecessary delays. During economic upswings with labor market shortages, businesses may be more inclined to hire refugees. For example, significant labor shortages in Europe, such as in Poland and Denmark, are currently facilitating job opportunities for some Ukrainian refugees.

- *Hiring refugees allows companies to do "the right thing."* Some companies are motivated by corporate social responsibility (CSR) principles when they hire refugees. Larger, global companies are more likely to set strategic goals that align with humanitarian values because their greater budgets and communications departments can promote these values through hiring and philanthropy.
- *Refugees may be more productive and stay longer in a job.* Several researchers and practitioners suggest that refugees may be more productive than other employees because they are grateful for job opportunities after their past hardships. Some businesses observe that refugees are more loyal, resulting in longer tenure and reduced turnover. Although such data are emerging in certain country contexts, such as in Mexico, there is a need for additional quantitative data to firmly establish these points.
- *Refugees can help businesses expand their market reach and offer skills that boost revenues.* Refugees may expand business insight and reach into certain markets. Businesses with consumer-facing products tend to be more committed to supporting refugees because refugees represent potential customers. Branding efforts can help with customer expansion, and hiring refugees can diversify a company's employee skill set by, among other things, increasing its access to languages.

The World Bank PS4R report also importantly notes that while there are international legal frameworks to facilitate the legal participation of refugees in the labor force, many countries have failed to adopt those legal frameworks or have failed to pass national laws implementing their international commitments. When refugees lack access to legal employment, they are often forced to work informally, opening themselves to additional types of vulnerability and abuse. The countries that have been leaders in developing national legislation to legally incorporate refugees into their economies have been the best positioned to benefit from refugees' hard work, ingenuity, and business acumen (Chestnutt 2024).

Furthermore, refugees in inclusive economies benefit from investments in human capital such as job training and education, which have a positive impact on their long-term economic mobility. While initial outcomes may show lower wages and higher welfare use, refugees' economic prospects improve significantly over time. In "The Economic and Social Outcomes of Refugees in the United States," a study analyzing American Community Survey data, Evans and Fitzgerald (2017) found that after six years in the United States, refugees work at higher rates than native-born workers, contributing more in taxes than they receive in benefits. This upward mobility highlights the long-term economic benefits of supporting refugee integration.

Refugees can also support community revitalization. In many communities, the arrival of refugees has helped reverse population decline and economic stagnation. This dynamic is evident in many communities in the United States. When Christine was running after-school programs for newly arriving refugee families in Syracuse, New York, she quickly learned about the success stories of Bhutanese family members thriving in nearby Utica, New York. They were opening little corner shops selling treats and delicacies from Southeast Asia not found in big chain supermarkets. Smaller cities like Utica have experienced a renaissance due to the influx of refugees, who bring diversity, cultural enrichment, and economic vitality (Solman and Sachs 2016). These success stories demonstrate how refugee resettlement can transform struggling communities into thriving hubs of activity and growth. And, as Tran and Lara-García (2020) find in their study of five refugee groups in the United States—Bhutanese,

Burmese, Iraqis, Somalis, and Cubans—postmigration integration policies like language- or job-training programs go a long way in helping the displaced integrate more quickly and start being positive economic drivers for their new communities.

Buffalo has experienced a significant economic revival that is often labeled the "Refugee Renaissance." Refugees have been key drivers of this transformation, starting businesses that have revitalized neighborhoods and created jobs (Özgen 2020). For example, the West Side Bazaar, a small-business incubator, has become a hub for refugee entrepreneurs, offering a diverse array of products and services that attract both local people and tourists. "The Bazaar has restaurants featuring Egyptian, Congolese, Jamaican, American Soul food, Seafood Fusion, Thai and Korean cuisines. There is a retail booth that sells items from Sri Lanka, a retail booth that sells natural skincare products, and a bar that serves beer and wine on the first floor with additional booths for pop-up events" (WEDI 2025). The Westminster Economic Development Initiative (WEDI) that runs the incubator was started by a local Presbyterian church working to support the growing refugee population from Southeast Asia and the Middle East. Today it provides microloans and multifaceted support for the area's aspiring and early career entrepreneurs. As a leader of one of Buffalo's refugee support organizations, the Jewish Family Service, notes: "Buffalo wouldn't be on the rise without refugees—they're a huge economic driver" (Korfhage 2022). It's not accidental.

Clarkston, Georgia, has welcomed more than forty thousand refugees over the past forty years, transforming the once-fading community into a vibrant and prosperous area. Refugee-owned businesses ranging from restaurants to retail stores have flourished, contributing to the local economy and creating a unique cultural landscape. The success of these businesses has made Clarkston a model for refugee integration. As the mayor of Clarkston notes: "If you listen to how President Trump talks about refugees, you might assume our small town is impoverished and maybe even dangerous. But the opposite is true. Our new American residents are a vital piece of the fabric that makes Clarkston the vibrant community it is. They start businesses, volunteer at and run local organizations . . . and they are civically engaged." He adds that they've turned a "once-fading community, situated in the suburbs east of Atlanta, into a safer, more prosperous place for everyone" (Terry 2019).

North Dakota has led the nation in per capita refugee resettlement, and the economic impact has been substantial. First-generation refugees in North Dakota contribute positively to the economy, with an average cost-positive impact of approximately $3,250 per individual. This immediate return on investment highlights the economic benefits of refugee resettlement in the state. "In North Dakota, return on investment [for refugees] happens in the first generation, meaning there is never a time when immigrants are not contributing to North Dakota's economy," a Fargo city task force report found. "On average, a first-generation immigrant is cost positive in North Dakota by approximately $3,250 per individual" (Ingram 2018).

In an editorial for *The Wall Street Journal*, former Senator Phil Gramm (R-TX) wrote, "from 2000 to 2023, 40% of Nobel Prizes won by Americans in chemistry, medicine, and physics were won by immigrants. In 2023, that share was 67%. Forty-six percent of Fortune 500 companies were founded by immigrants or their children" (Gramm 2025). These companies produced $5.3 trillion in global revenue and employed 12.1 million workers worldwide (Hathaway 2017). Some of these immigrants came to the United States because they were forcibly displaced, making them what we call extreme entrepreneurs.

Alison Beard, in her article "The Case for Welcoming Immigrants," reviews book after book for the *Harvard Business Review* in which authors and researchers document how newcomers enrich economies and cultures (Beard 2022). She cites Jennifer D. Sciubba's *8 Billion and Counting* (2022), which argues that import and export of talent are critical for national prosperity; Tim Kane's *The Immigrant Superpower* (2021), which explores how immigrants enhance US power through brawn (labor), bravery (military service), and brains (innovation); Nancy Foner's *One Quarter of the Nation* (2022), a deeply researched book by one of America's leading immigration scholars that shows how immigrants have changed local economies, communities, and politics for the better; Ran Abramitzky and Leah Boustan's *Streets of Gold: America's Untold Story of Immigrant Success* (2022), which uses data and a decade of research to demonstrate that the children of immigrants from nearly every country, especially those of poor immigrants, do better economically than children of US-born residents (a pattern that has held for more than a century), that immigrants rapidly assimilate, that immigration changes the economy in unexpected positive ways and staves off the economic decline that is the consequence of an aging population, and that the dynamism that immigrants bring economies actually helps the US-born; and finally, Ali Noorani's *Crossing Borders: The Reconciliation of a Nation of Immigrants* (2022), which shows that the neediest are often the ones who will take the biggest risks and work the hardest to realize their new countries' fullest potential.

As mentioned in chapter 3, in 2018 we coauthored a report that is very much in line with this growing body of evidence. *Paradigm Shift* (Kluge et al. 2018) presents a market that is both hopeful and often overlooked because of the high perceived risks associated with investing in refugees. The report's data reveal that refugees are indeed employable, hardworking, creditworthy, and ultimately investable, facts that are already benefiting smart investors and their refugee partners.

Consider the story of Nyema Tubman and Richelieu Dennis, two friends who were displaced in the United States during a civil war in their home country of Liberia. Because they had to earn a living in New York, Nyema and Richelieu started a small soap company. Over twenty-six years they grew Sundial Brands into a $240 million portfolio of personal care brands employing over 3,500 Ghanaian women. Bain Capital became a minority investor in Sundial in 2015, and Unilever acquired Sundial in 2017. Sundial has now invested $50 million to start the New Voices Fund, investing $100 million to support and empower women of color entrepreneurs by providing capital and other resources to help them scale their businesses.

That same year, in 2018, the Center for Strategic and International Studies (CSIS) published a report entitled "Confronting the Global Forced Migration Crisis" (CSIS 2018). Its task force, on which John served, advanced several strategic ideas, including the importance of diversifying stakeholders: "The private sector should be motivated and incentivized to responsibly engage in ways that benefit the bottom line—in addition to corporate social responsibility, strategic gaps in business activities, investment, and private sector engagement should be addressed."

The economic impact—the market-oriented benefits—of accepting and integrating qualified refugees is nonpartisan. Every political party wants to see economic growth, whether it's national, regional, or local. And the positive economic impact has been demonstrated by research paper after research paper. Even Nobel Prize winners have studied the impact of refugees—David Card, Joshua Angrist, and Guido Imbens were awarded the Nobel Prize in economics in 2021 for their pioneering work on "natural experiments" that show real-world impacts of government policies, including migration. Their research has provided valuable insights into how migration, including refugee movements, affects labor markets and economies.

Daron Acemoglu, Simon Johnson, and James A. Robinson were awarded the Nobel Prize in economics in 2024 for their research on why some countries are rich and others poor and how societal institutions impact a country's prosperity. While their primary focus is on institutions and economic development, their work also touches on the broader implications of migration and refugee integration.

The World Bank has found that the benefits of integrating refugees into the labor market and host economy typically take years to materialize, but countries with a flexible labor market, strong investment climate, and a welcoming attitude to immigrants tend to see these inflows materialize faster. This finding is supported by the AIC's rigorously researched *Starting Anew: The Economic Impact of Refugees in America* (AIC 2023), which analyzes how recent refugees are contributing to the US economy. Using the five-year American Community Survey (ACS) from 2019, the authors identify a pool of nearly 2.4 million likely refugees based on their country of origin and year of arrival in the United States. They find the following:

- Refugees make significant contributions to the US economy as earners and taxpayers.
- While refugees receive initial assistance upon arriving in the United States, they see particularly sharp income increases in subsequent years.
- Refugees have an entrepreneurship rate that outshines even that of other immigrants.

- Refugees make particularly meaningful contributions to the economies of several large states.
- Even more than other immigrants, refugees take steps to lay down roots and build lives in America.

The University of Pennsylvania professor Guy Grossman has studied the relationship between refugee integration and development globally. His 2023 article with Zhou and Ge examined Uganda's inclusive refugee hosting policies (Zhou et al. 2023). Uganda's "self-reliance strategy" (SRS) allows refugees to self-settle, find employment, and start businesses. The authors note: "Large arrivals of refugees raise concerns about potential tensions with host communities, particularly if refugees are viewed as an out-group competing for limited material resources and crowding out public services. To address these concerns, calls have increased to allocate humanitarian aid in ways that also benefit host communities. This study tests whether the increased presence of refugees, when coupled with humanitarian aid, improves public service delivery for host communities and dampens potential social conflict." The authors' analysis combines geospatial data on refugee settlements with original longitudinal data on primary and secondary schools, road density, health clinics, and health utilization. They report two key findings: "First, even after the 2014 arrival of over 1 million South Sudanese refugees, host communities with greater refugee presence experienced substantial improvements in local development. Second, using public opinion data, we find no evidence that refugee presence has been associated with more negative attitudes towards migrants or migration policy." They conclude that inclusive refugee-hosting policies improve local development outcomes and prevent public opinion backlash.

Halfway around the world, Colombia has also seen an influx of refugees, in its case from Venezuela, in recent years due to unrest in its oil-rich neighbor. Our colleague Dany Bahar, who has studied the entrepreneurship that Colombia has enjoyed from integrating Venezuelan refugees, finds several things. "First, firms owned by foreigners, most of them Venezuelans, tend to be 10 to 20 percent more capitalized when founded, as compared to firms owned by locals within the same industry, geographic location, and year of registration. Second, while more intensive in capital, these firms owned by foreigners are just as likely to survive the first two and three years as firms owned by locals are" (Bahar et al. 2023).

A study published in *Nature* (Maxmen 2018), based on an analysis of thirty years of data from fifteen countries in Western Europe, suggests that refugees and migrants benefit their host nations' economies within five years of arrival. The study finds that soon after a spike in migration, the overall strength and sustainability of the country's economy improve and unemployment rates drop. Its conclusions contradict the idea that refugees place an excessive financial burden on a country by sucking up public resources.

The St. Louis Federal Reserve Bank has found that refugees can bolster future workforces (Bandyopadhyay and Bharadwaj 2018). Many nations that form the Organization for Economic Cooperation and Development (OECD) have aging populations, with substantial fractions of their populations exceeding fifty-five years old. As more of this population retires and people live longer on average, a corresponding number of younger people will have to move into the workforce to maintain a steady share of the working population for the entire nation. The Federal Reserve Bank found that this working-age population has to produce not only for itself but also for others, including the elderly and children. In this context, immigration can play a role, especially if the immigrants are of prime working or child-bearing age:

- First, immigrants can substitute for native workers who are retiring from the workforce.
- Second, working-age immigrants are likely to have children, who can contribute to the future workforce of the nation.

Integration improves, according to the OECD, when migrants stay longer (OECD 2015). Integration is a process that occurs over time. The longer immigrants reside in a host country, the more familiar they become with the way it functions, the more friends and acquaintances they make and—where it is an issue—the better they master the host country language. In European OECD countries, for example, an additional year of residence is associated with significant increases in immigrant employment rates and with lower rates of overqualification. However, the impact of the duration of stay varies across groups of migrants. Improvements that come with experience in the host country are particularly pronounced among refugees.

Sasha Chanoff, the leader of RefugeePoint, writes that on a local level refugees have revitalized American cities. Lewiston, Maine, drew national attention several years ago for a terrible tragedy. But it's also a bellwether town for the impact that refugees have on the local community and an important national example. In 2001 Somali refugees from across the United States began arriving in Lewiston, drawn by cheap rents and safe school opportunities. At that time, similar to today, antirefugee and anti-immigrant rhetoric emboldened xenophobia. A white supremacist group came to Lewiston to protest. But entrepreneurial Somalis saw a chance to open businesses in a town that had declined since the 1970s with the loss of the mill industry. Restaurants and shops took root in the decaying town center that residents referred to as the combat zone. Today Somalis are integrated and *Inc.* magazine named Lewiston one of the best places to do business in America.

This trend has been echoing in places across the United States and Europe. In every village and town, it seems, refugee families are starting new restaurants, cafés, bakeries, farms, groceries, cleaning services, salons, and boutiques. They are sparks of small businesses.

RESEARCH INTO ACTION

As mentioned in chapter 1, in June 2016 the Obama administration announced a call to action for the private sector—businesses large and small—to make new, measurable, and significant commitments "that will have a durable impact on refugees residing in countries of resettlement." Accenture, Airbnb, Chobani, Goldman Sachs, Microsoft, and others became the founding companies to stand with refugees. LinkedIn, for example, created a platform that serves as an entry point to connect newly settled refugees with employers who have committed to hiring them. Coursera, the largest open online education provider, created Coursera for Refugees, enabling an unlimited number of nonprofits that work with refugees to quickly build career skills and gain recognizable certificates for jobs.

Reflecting on our earlier experience with building an ecosystem for private investment in global sanitation, we knew that attracting new private investors in the refugee space required a well-articulated investment framework. Some investors would be happy to support those in refugee camps to make arts and crafts that gave hope and could attract buyers. Others believe in microfinance to help families, mostly women, start small start-ups. But many private investors want to invest in SMEs, or small to medium-sized enterprises, others are searching for larger companies that can provide employment for refugees, and still others are venture capital firms and private equity firms looking for real financial impact, price-to-earning (P/E) ratios. An aluminum and paint manufacturing company in Aqaba, Jordan, had an attractive P/E ratio *and* employed Syrians escaping from political violence.

RIN created a map of refugee investment opportunities that measurably improved the lives of the displaced, even if it wasn't yet using the terminology of refugee lens investing (RLI). The following companies were highlighted:

- A wastewater treatment company that supported refugees and is expected to have a total addressable market of $40 billion by 2026 and to grow at a compound annual growth rate of 11 percent. The rising global awareness of water pollution, rapid urbanization, and poor infrastructure for centralized treatment is expected to increase the demand for decentralized wastewater treatment in the MENA region.
- A women-owned business that produces hygiene paper tissues, disinfectant wipes, and cleaner wipes for all types of household purposes. The company was seeking an investment of $1.5 million to $2 million to boost production capacity and enter new markets, including markets hosting refugees. Key areas for this investment included factory space expansion, US market expansion, and exploration of elderly care products. Key opportunities included potential to hire and serve the displaced, more likely with an incentivizing refugee lens investment.

- AI Forte Solutions, a Canadian social enterprise that worked to develop telecommunication platforms as well as blockchain encrypted reference systems to be used by aid agencies, governments, and forcibly displaced people more broadly. Its impact thesis was to deliver technology products that serve the needs of development agencies, thereby better serving the beneficiaries, who are often the displaced.

Investment opportunities included direct services to reduce risks for displaced persons, humanitarian innovations to improve services to refugees, and strategies that advance economic integration (and therefore human flourishing).

Other large companies followed suit, perhaps inspired by Obama's Partnership for Refugees and by seeing the power of proactively incorporating the displaced. Amazon and other companies have pledged to hire thousands of refugees in Europe. In 2022 Arkansas-based Tyson Foods committed to hiring 2,500 refugees over three years. The company is providing these employees with professional skills training in English as a second language, financial literacy classes, and legal assistance. Hunt Oil Company, a nearly century-old exploration and production company with roots in east Texas, is an active member of the North Dakota Petroleum Council (NDPC). Hunt plays a role in the collective organization that represents various oil companies in the state. The NDPC not only advocates for the interests of its members but also fosters a collaborative environment that offers a wide range of programs and events to promote growth and responsible practices within the industry. One of those initiatives is the Bakken GROW program, named for the productive oil fields in North Dakota, Montana, and Canada. Bakken GROW was conceived in response to the influx of Ukrainian citizens into the United States. Its primary aim is to integrate Ukrainian nationals into the local oil and gas workforce.

Gideon Maltz, the CEO of Tent Partnership for Refugees, has reflected on the power of business to proactively incorporate the displaced into new economies. As explained in chapter 1, Tent took up the mantel of Obama's Partnership for Refugees once the first Trump administration came into office and State Department priorities changed. Tent is a coalition of more than four hundred global companies that connect refugees to jobs through hiring, training, and mentoring. "The most important role that businesses can play is facilitating and supporting the economic integration of refugees who may be displaced for a generation," Gideon told us. "And they can do this most effectively when they go beyond traditional philanthropy and engage refugees as economically productive employees, entrepreneurs, and customers."

In 2023, the Private Sector for Refugees (PS4R) Platform of the World Bank published a policy and research paper entitled *Refugee-Related Investment: Myth or Reality?*, which provides a nice framework of four types of refugee-related companies that measurably improve the lives of the displaced and that may be seeking investment:

> *Microenterprises and home-based businesses.* In many cases, barred from formal employment, refugees start firms, often informally, as a means of subsistence. Microenterprises are businesses with no or few employees (usually less than ten) and small capitalization relative to their country context. In some countries, these businesses can be operating from the home of the owner and on a very small scale. Others may be operating informally and consist only of the owner. Microenterprises need limited investments and often represent an entry

point for vulnerable segments of the population that wish to enter the private sector. When opportunity for scale exists, these businesses can grow and create significant numbers of jobs locally.

Small and medium-sized enterprises (SMEs). The definition of SME varies by country but usually refers to businesses of ten to one hundred employees. SMEs can have significant forward and backward linkages with other businesses locally, regionally, or globally, as well as a strong commercial interest to engage with other businesses and scale up. Together with microenterprises, these businesses form a significant part of the private sector in developing countries. They can include refugee-owned companies that began as microbusinesses and local companies that provide services to, or employ, refugees.

Global and regional businesses. Global and regional businesses have a strong regional or global reach, are often involved in trade (import and export), and are well integrated into local, regional, or global supply chains. They are usually strong market actors because they add significant value to products or services, provide services to other enterprises, and have large numbers of employees. Global and regional businesses can be SMEs or large businesses. This category covers global businesses and multinational corporations (MNCs) like IKEA, which trains and hires refugees to create as a mixture of environmental, social, and governance (ESG) and competitive advantage, as well as local or regional export-oriented companies that hire refugees or do business with refugee-owned companies.

Social enterprises (SEs). SEs are private organizations that harness business approaches to achieve social, environmental, and economic outcomes. What sets SEs apart from profit-driven enterprises is their unwavering pursuit of a social or environmental mission and their use of entrepreneurial and business

> activities to generate revenue while advancing these objectives. While some SEs may rely on subsidies, they are distinguished from charities or classic NGOs by their commitment to financially sustainable business models, even if not all achieve profitability—such as those supported by government revenue. SEs encompass both for-profit and nonprofit entities and often adopt "hybrid" structures that blend these models, representing a form of innovation from the status quo. Many SEs, whether refugee-supporting or refugee-owned, challenge traditional economic paradigms by integrating displaced communities into their operations.

The World Bank report provides a rich tapestry of international business case studies that span both developing and developed economies and that showcase how SEs can thrive amid diverse challenges. RIN, in collaboration with the Conrad N. Hilton Foundation, has furthered this effort with its Technical Assistance Playbook—a comprehensive resource designed to support SEs globally in scaling RLI. This playbook, detailed in appendix B, offers tailored technical assistance strategies, including sector-specific guidance for agriculture, fintech, and housing, alongside tools like risk assessment frameworks and capacity-building modules to overcome barriers such as lack of IDs, limited networks, or lack of access to finance. It draws on case studies from RIN's regional efforts, providing actionable steps for practitioners to integrate refugees into local economies—barriers ranging from the mundane, like obtaining an ID card or bank account, to the critical, like building professional contacts. This global applicability makes it a vital tool for fostering sustainable SE growth.

This practical approach inspired us to apply similar principles on our farm outside Charlottesville, Virginia, where we launched two small businesses—Wayflowering and Thistlerock Mead Company—that incorporate RLI ideas by hiring displaced individuals, sourcing from vulnerable communities, and reshaping the narrative around displacement. These ventures grow regenerative flowers, create immersive nature-based experiences, tend bee hives, and craft delicious mead, an ancient honey-based spirit. While Thistlerock Mead Company produces just over half the honey we use, we prioritize sourcing the remainder—along with fresh fruits, herbs, and other supplies—from local farms and protected classes, leveraging our purchasing power to provide steady economic support to emerging markets and communities at risk, including refugee-led and refugee-supporting organizations. Notably, the coffee beans for Thistlerock's coffee-mead blend come from 734 Coffee, a fair-trade enterprise founded by Manyang Kher, a Sudanese refugee who grew up in Gambela, Ethiopia, camps and later earned an international law degree from the University of Richmond. Reinvesting 80 percent of its profits, 734 Coffee funds over one hundred scholarships and educational initiatives for Sudanese refugees annually, exemplifying how SEs can drive both economic and social transformation.

5

THE UNITED STATES

From Her Beacon Hand Glows Worldwide Welcome

It is February 2025. We are thirty days and seventy-three executive orders into President Trump's second term. He has, through the blunt cudgel of Elon Musk's Department of Government Efficiency (DOGE), gutted several federal agencies, purging thousands of career civil servant jobs and deleting entire agency budgets, including most of the US government's international development funding. USAID is now on life support. The long-standing and historically bipartisan US Refugee Admissions Program (USRAP) is, for all intents and purposes, mothballed. And the Refugee Investment Network (RIN) just received a letter notifying it that two major US government grant awards for a significant part of our East Africa work have been suspended. For those of us who work on refugee issues, these are dark days. Yet we remain hopeful.

There have been many dark and painful periods in our distant and recent histories when our country, or our leaders, were openly hostile to those seeking refuge or those we saw as "the other." Examples include the forced displacement of Catholic Acadians prior to our country's founding, the genocide and forced displacement of indigenous Americans, the hatred toward German and Irish immigrants in the mid-nineteenth century, our inexcusable refusal to provide refuge to Jewish refugees fleeing the Nazis in the 1930s, the dislocation and internment of Japanese Americans during World War II, and more recently, President Trump's vilification of immigrants and refugees.

Yet over the last eighty years (notwithstanding the current administration), the United States has increasingly leaned toward a culture of belonging and inclusion, one that numerous Republican and Democrat administrations have advanced and formalized into (mostly) consistent policy that, at its heart, echoes the sentiments of the American poet Emma Lazarus's most famous lines:

> Give me your tired, your poor
> Your huddled masses yearning to breathe free

Lazarus, herself an advocate on behalf of Jewish refugees fleeing persecution in Russia, found a way to enshrine her empathy for people fleeing persecution and oppression into far more than a bronze plaque; it has become part of how many Americans—including the authors—see our values embodied in a physical form (Khan 2010). This sentiment is reflected perhaps best by the USRAP, which provided a safe haven and support to refugees who had fled their homes and helped them transition to life in the United States. It was also one of the few federal programs to enjoy consistent bipartisan support; a 2022 survey by Data for Progress found that over 70 percent of likely voters—across demographic indicators such as race, political affiliation, education, and age—strongly believed that the United States should have a refugee resettlement program, and "among voters who say they know someone who is a refugee, 89 percent support the U.S. refugee program" (Data for Progress 2022). The USRAP and its precursors were primarily humanitarian in nature, but their secondary role is foundational to the subject of this book: It created the enabling environment necessary for refugee lens investing (RLI) to take root.

Before the twentieth century, however, the United States had no formal refugee resettlement system. Immigration policies, primarily shaped by the Immigration Act of 1924, focused on quotas based on nationality rather than humanitarian concerns. The law severely restricted immigration, offering no provisions for those fleeing political or religious persecution. Although informal efforts by local communities and religious groups offered some support to people fleeing persecution, these were largely ad hoc efforts.

The end of World War II marked a turning point in US refugee policy, as millions of displaced people, particularly from Eastern Europe and Asia, needed resettlement. The Displaced Persons Act of 1948 was the first significant piece of legislation that addressed this crisis. It allowed for the admission of over 400,000 displaced persons into the United States, mainly Europeans displaced by the war (USCIS 2024). In the early 1950s, the Refugee Relief Act of 1953 continued efforts to resettle those fleeing communism in Eastern Europe, and later the Immigration and Nationality Act of 1965, which eliminated restrictive quotas, indirectly benefited refugees fleeing political unrest, allowing for a broader and more flexible immigration system.

A major shift occurred with the passage of the Refugee Act of 1980, which marked a transformative moment for US refugee resettlement policy. The act created the modern framework for refugee admission, making the United States a leader in global refugee protection. It was signed into law by President Jimmy Carter, who had long supported a more formal and systematic approach to refugee resettlement, particularly for those fleeing political persecution. Importantly, the Refugee Act did the following:

- Defined refugees as individuals outside their country due to fear of persecution based on race, religion, nationality, social group, or political opinion
- Established the Office of Refugee Resettlement (ORR) to manage the process of resettling refugees in the United States
- Authorized an annual cap on refugee admissions, with the understanding that this cap would be flexible depending on global conditions

This act paved the way for large numbers of refugees to be admitted to the United States, particularly those fleeing the Vietnam War, Cambodia, and Laos, as well as Soviet Jews, Cuban exiles, and others escaping communist regimes. The thousands of Vietnamese who fled their country by sea after the fall of the South Vietnamese government are perhaps the most publicly recognized group that was resettled under this policy.

The collapse of the Soviet Union and the end of the Cold War created new displacement crises, including those resulting from ethnic conflicts, wars, and genocide. The United States continued to be a primary destination for refugees fleeing areas such as Bosnia, Somalia, and Rwanda. The 1991 Immigration Act provided additional support for refugees and asylum seekers, acknowledging the United States's evolving role in global humanitarian efforts.

This was a period when the United States was leaning into the concept of belonging, at least for refugees. Secretary Madeleine Albright, US ambassador to the United Nations and herself a former refugee from Czechoslovakia, played a significant role in responding to the crises in places like the Balkans, advocating for international assistance for refugees and the displaced.

And then, on September 11, 2001, things began to shift. The terrorist attacks that day changed many aspects of American life, including US refugee and immigration policies. Citing national security concerns, President George W. Bush introduced stricter vetting processes for refugees. The Patriot Act of 2001 imposed additional hurdles for refugee admissions, including background checks and more intense security screenings. The United States also began to focus more on Iraqi refugees following the 2003 invasion of Iraq, but security measures made resettling refugees more complex. USRAP resettlement numbers dropped by about 50 percent, from 69,304 in 2001 to 27,110 in 2002, but started to climb above 50,000 by 2004 (Sridharan 2008).

During the Obama administration, the United States ramped up its refugee admissions, particularly in response to the Syrian civil war and the rise of the Islamic State (ISIS). Under President Obama, the refugee admissions cap was increased, reaching a high of 110,000 refugees in 2017. Responding to the needs of displaced populations in Syria, Iraq, South Sudan, and Central America, Obama emphasized the United States's humanitarian leadership.

It wasn't until President Trump's first term that the USRAP saw significant reductions—far more than the post-9/11 drop. The administration, which prioritized "America First" policies, slashed the refugee admissions cap, reducing it to 18,000 refugees in 2020, the lowest number since the refugee act's passage. Trump's administration also imposed even more stringent vetting procedures and reduced the number of countries eligible for resettlement. Kirstjen Nielsen, as secretary of the Department of Homeland Security (DHS), and Ken Cuccinelli, as acting director of US Citizenship and Immigration Services, played pivotal roles in implementing these restrictive policies, with Nielsen being remembered most for executing Trump's now-notorious "family separation" practices. For the record, we met with Nielsen after she stepped down from her DHS post to see if the administration might be open to exploring a "middle way" for addressing migration. After learning about the RIN's mission and approach, her comment was simply "I wish I met you while I was still running DHS." Suffice it to say, that conversation did not lead far.

When an administration drastically changes the numbers of refugees we resettle, either increasing or decreasing the numbers of people we help, it has a secondary impact beyond the obvious lives at stake: It impacts the long-term viability of the USRAP itself and has implications for the US economy. The USRAP didn't operate solely as a government program. It largely depended on a public-private partnership between the US government and nine voluntary resettlement agencies (VOLAGs): nonprofit organizations, many of them faith-based, that help the US government provide social services and financial and in-kind assistance to refugees who need to adjust to life in the United States and become self-reliant. They include groups like the Church World Service, the Lutheran Immigration and Refugee Service (LIRS), the International Rescue Committee (IRC), the Hebrew Immigrant Aid Society, and Catholic Charities USA.

A disproportionate amount of these organizations' budgets is linked directly to how many refugees they resettle in a given year. So, if an administration drastically changes the resettlement numbers for a given year, the agencies either struggle to staff up or have to cut their staff and programs significantly. The money is not designed to be a spigot that is turned on or off flippantly. Trump's first term in office came dangerously close to dissolving the "private" side of the public-private partnership enabling the USRAP.

Upon taking office, President Biden sought to reverse many of the Trump-era policies. Biden's administration raised the refugee admissions cap to 125,000 for fiscal year 2022, signaling a return to a more welcoming stance toward refugees (Global Refuge 2024). Under Biden, there was an increased emphasis on protecting Afghan refugees, including those who assisted US military forces during the war, and Ukrainian refugees, as part of a broader international humanitarian response to Russia's invasion. But despite the return to a higher admissions cap, it took the VOLAGs nearly the entirety of the Biden administration's four years to return their staffing and knowledge base to be able to manage larger resettlement numbers (Migration Policy Institute 2025). And in the first month of Trump's second term, they plummeted to zero.

While the future of the program remains uncertain, its legacy as a beacon of hope for displaced people and as a beloved program supported by a majority of Americans remains undeniable. In the context of our work, it is the foundation that paved the way for a vibrant domestic RLI market that we believe has tremendous potential for growth.

While the VOLAGs focus on helping resettled refugees transition into American life, much of their work concludes after a period of six months. The assumption, of course, is that refugees are resettled and will adapt into life in their new communities. It takes a while for any person to settle into a new community, never mind one that often involves a new language to learn and new cultures, norms, and systems. For many, this is just the start of navigating a new life, home, and career. In many ways, this is also where the work of RLI in the United States begins.

In 2019, we traveled to San Diego to accompany Kasra Movahedi, then executive director of the IRC's Center for Economic

Opportunity (cleverly acronymed "CEO"), to meet with several resettled refugees who were building new businesses. We met at the IRC offices before heading to our meetings. Kasra shared that there are at least three thousand refugee-led small and growing businesses (SGBs) in the United States, with an untold number of earlier-stage refugee-led enterprises as well as recently resettled refugees who want to *become* entrepreneurs. The IRC developed an innovative response to meet the needs of refugees who are seeking entrepreneurial paths in the United States. Kasra, through CEO, had been lending to refugee entrepreneur clients since 2003, initially through two field offices—San Diego and Phoenix—that combined to made over 2,500 loans totaling just under $3 million with a 94 percent repayment rate from 2004 to 2014. These lending assets have been transferred to CEO, an independent subsidiary and community development financial institution (CDFI) of the IRC that has since expanded to make the program accessible to all IRC locations in the United States.

Our first stop was Al Hamdani Sweets, a bakery owned by Nael and Manar al-Najjar, resettled Iraqi Christians, who fled their home in Baghdad after their church was bombed by the Islamic State following several years of increasing religious persecution and violence. As we arrived at their bakery, we looked through the windows at what seemed like hundreds of delicate golden pastries. As we entered, a scent of warm honey and pistachios lingered in the air. Mrs. Najjar stood behind the register with a warm smile as she handed a customer a large tray of sweets to take home. She welcomed us and offered us a tour of their kitchen. Not every entrepreneur we meet exudes joy, but with Mrs. Najjar, it was hard to miss. As she showed us the rows and rows (and rows) of baked delicacies being readied for the day's customers, she shared that she was expanding wholesale operations into four other states. "It wasn't easy, building this, but the IRC made it possible," she said. She referred in particular to some of their baking equipment that she had purchased with support from a savings program run by the IRC in coordination with CEO's loan program.

Key to CEO's model is that eligibility to apply for a loan is predicated on engagement with, at minimum, local IRC financial inclusion programming; most clients are engaged in multiple economic empowerment programs such as microenterprise, technical assistance, and workforce programs. This approach screens out a great deal of risk and situates their loans more as "tools" that can be deployed within a traditional social service setting and as one option among many other services that applicants may be receiving. While CEO is a subsidiary of the IRC, it has a surprising degree of independence and self-governance (including its own board of directors), which allows it to access capital markets and partnerships outside of traditional IRC grant structures. Mrs. Najjar and her husband are excellent CEO clients, but they aren't alone in this respect. What's unique is their relationship with their lender. There are over 1,400 CDFIs across the United States, so what made this one unique?

There's clearly something special about the way people access CEO's products. As Kasra said, "We have no customer acquisition costs." Another aspect of their work is improving credit scores. Many business lenders are focused on making business loans and getting around people with bad or no credit, but not enough are focused on moving peoples' credit scores. "Some have lowered the bar for this, but they haven't changed the bar or helped them navigate the US credit system. They might be looking at a conventional lending playbook—late fees and punitive APRs are part of the normative playbook which probably do a lot more harm than good when you're working with lower income disadvantaged populations."

We were inspired by the al-Najjar family, as well as by CEO's lending model. While CEO had been growing over the years, it still needed a significant capital injection to help it scale its lending services to refugee entrepreneurs. So the RIN partnered with CEO to create the RIN-CEO Social Impact Fund, which was designed to offer refugee borrowers capital to build credit, start businesses, buy cars, pay for workforce training, and support financial health. CEO offered investors returns of up to 2 percent for this first round of funding, with the intention of proving CEO's ability to expand and to deliver a modest return to investors, all of which would be essential for raising a follow-on, much larger round to scale its refugee lending in the United States. A 2 percent return is not exactly the most compelling rate of return (unless under negative interest rates), so CEO needed a unique match of capital. Working together with RIN, it was able to raise an initial $1.25 million from five investors: Cabrini Social Impact Investing, the Dunn Family Charitable Foundation, the Shapiro Foundation, Mercy Investment Services, and the Baltimore Community Foundation. The first round closed shortly after April 2020, propelling CEO's work forward.

But as COVID-19 accelerated and spread across the country, it became clear to CEO and RIN that providing additional debt to entrepreneurs already on the margins, even at highly concessional rates, would be an undue burden. CEO's investors have been extraordinarily responsive and adaptive, fulfilling their investment commitment but suspending the capital call until the economy stabilized. Refugee entrepreneurs were disproportionately affected by the pandemic and resulting economic shutdowns, with up to 50 percent facing immediate cash flow shortages and crippling impacts on their businesses. For most of these entrepreneurs, their businesses are the primary source of income for their families.

Responding to this problem, RIN launched the Refugee Entrepreneurs in COVID-19 Resilience Fund (RECOVR Fund), a campaign to support hundreds of refugee-led ventures with emergency cash grants through partnerships with four refugee-supporting accelerators, including the IRC's CEO. Ed Shapiro, principal of the Shapiro Foundation, made an anchor commitment to provide $250,000 in grant funding, earmarked to CEO, to help launch RECOVR, in addition to the investment commitment he made to the loan pool. The flexibility of being able to deploy both investment and grant capital, and the ability (and willingness) to adapt to rapidly changing market conditions, enabled CEO's investors to maintain their initial investment commitment—which in itself was catalytic—and in the case of Shapiro, to further empower CEO to serve its clients during an otherwise prohibitive economic environment, likely saving countless businesses from going under. CEO's adaptability, enabled by its leadership and flexible funding partners, positioned it well for long-term success. Through 2024, CEO made more than nine thousand loans totaling more than $35 million in refugee lens financing across more than thirty states.

According to Kasra, CEO's investment from private capital "has been great and the capacity to keep up momentum is there." In 2023 it brought in $10 million from different types of capital and grew from three employees to a team of twenty. It has received investment from many family offices and several foundations, including Hilton and PayPal, and is looking now toward banks and community foundations to help scale up these efforts. While the internal rate of return may not be beating the market, this remains an attractive investment for certain investors. For community foundations, it's a chance to increase their return on investment with investments they already have in their community by providing loans through CEO. For banks, there is a comfortable balance between banks and CDFIs for when borrowers have been successful but still can't qualify for a bank loan. These customers could partner with a CDFI like CEO to help them get ready for bank lending. For a bank, this is basic pipeline development.

The biggest challenge facing CEO today is that when Kasra or his colleagues speak to any investor, CEO demands concessionary rates. The maximum interest it pays is 3 percent. Kasra acknowledged that it's a tough argument to make, especially in a high-interest-rate environment, but "the way we can do this is by demonstrating the reach we have with our demographics, and, for high-net worth folks who are usually business minded, they get the impact we have. The economic model just makes a lot of sense."

Some of CEO's early funding came from a small program run through a business program at the ORR under Health and Human Services. This program, to date, is exclusively focused on entrepreneurship, but it could be expanded to include access to credit. It could serve, for example, as capital that resettlement organizations or communities could use to partner with CDFIs.

Entrepreneurs like the al-Najjar family are the backbone of the American economy. As part of the refugee lens taxonomy, providing them with working capital would be considered an R1 investment (a refugee-led company; see chapter 3). Not all R1 small businesses stay small, however. Take, for example, a scrappy little company manufacturing static memory chips in 1968. The third employee of that company, Andy Grove (born Gróf András István in Budapest, Hungary), came to the United States as a twenty-year-old refugee in 1956. Grove helped grow that company's annual revenue from $2,672 in 1968 to $20.8 billion in 1997, when he stepped down as chairman of the board (Sheridan 1997). That company, of course, is Intel. Or there is the legendary

Daniel Aaron, cofounder of Comcast, who fled Nazi Germany in 1937 and was able to navigate his new country as an orphan thanks to support from Pennsylvania's Jewish relief agencies and foster families (Aaron and Long 2001). There is Jan Koum, who fled then-communist Ukraine at the age of sixteen with his mother and had to live on food stamps just a few blocks away from the Mountain View, California, office that now houses his company, WhatsApp, which, as of December 2024, had a market cap of $1.3 billion (Rowan 2018). Then there's Alphabet's cofounder, Sergey Brin, whose family fled religious persecution in the Soviet Union in 1979. When Brin's family first settled into their new life in Maryland, they received support and assistance from one of the VOLAGs, HIAS, which received a $1 million gift from Brin forty years after welcoming him to the United States (Strom 2009). As of January 2026, Alphabet's market cap was $4 trillion, and it employed 187,103 full-time employees as of June 2025 (Elias 2026).

The United States is filled with Jans and Sergeys—or at least many entrepreneurs who have the potential to become like them with the right kind of support. Consider Adenah Bayoh, who had to flee her village at the age of nine after armed rebels invaded in the middle of the night. She fled first to Sierra Leone and then eventually resettled in Newark, New Jersey, where she attended public school and worked hard at McDonald's to pay her way through college. She recently became the first black woman to lead the development of a major affordable housing project in New Jersey and now manages a growing real estate portfolio and a series of restaurant franchises.

American investors are increasingly looking for displaced (and immigrant) founders and are building this effort into their investment thesis and strategy. Some investors are even looking for talent that is leaving oppressive and dangerous places.

Nick Davidov, a partner in Davidovs Venture Collective, has backed fourteen portfolio companies that, by 2022, were shutting down operations in Russia and moving elsewhere. One of those R1 companies is 3D Predict, a patented high-tech dental aligner led by CEO Marina Domracheva. Ms. Domracheva also received investment from One Way Ventures, which was founded by Semyon Dukach, the former director of Techstars Boston. Semyon noticed a trend that now describes the heart of its investing approach: "immigrant-led companies repeatedly outperform." Unshackled Ventures follows a similar thesis, having backed 145 immigrant founders with a total enterprise value of $3.5 billion across its portfolio. Sixty-six percent of its pre-seed investments have graduated to a seed round and have raised $31 million for every $1 million invested by Unshackled.

Whether growing multinational enterprises like Sergey Brin or building real estate portfolios like Ms. Bayoh, starting tech ventures like Ms. Domracheva, or SMEs like Manar al-Najjar, R1 entrepreneurs are great American businesspeople who are doing important work in our economy, and more investors would do well to develop more proactive strategies that include them in their portfolios. Similarly, capital providers like IRC's CEO, as a lending facility supporting refugee entrepreneurs (R5) or venture funds like One Way Ventures or Unshackled Ventures (R6), can benefit from the refugee lens by attracting values-aligned capital and deploying the refugee lens to their economic advantage. Consider the vast reserves of faith-based capital. In 2022, the Oxford Faith-Aligned Impact Finance Project (OxFAIF) published a staggering report mapping 360 separate organizations connected to religions across the world in the Abrahamic and Dharmic traditions, with identified total net assets valued at approximately $5 trillion (Nicholls et al. 2022). The potential is enormous, particularly given how many Christian and

Abrahamic faiths stress the importance of showing kindness and hospitality to strangers.

We've looked at some examples of refugee-led and refugee-financing companies. But what about companies that hire or provide products or services that support refugees (R3 or R4)? Innovations are under way in a number of sectors, particularly those that support social infrastructure—things that enable the economic integration of resettled refugees. This integration includes access to banking and credit, childcare, education, healthcare, job readiness, and housing.

Almost every refugee resettlement agency in the United States struggles to find enough affordable and quality housing for its resettled refugee clients. As new arrivals in the United States, refugees often face barriers to securing rental apartments or homes (never mind securing loans for home ownership) as the result of not having any credit history, significant assets for collateral, or an established network. Local resettlement agencies depend on long-standing relationships with local property managers to assist in providing their clients with their first housing opportunities. As national real estate firms and investors increasingly acquire and consolidate properties, they often seek to reduce their risk and improve efficiencies across their real estate portfolio. This move can translate to changes in who local property managers may or may not lease to and enforcement of regional or national Holdco policies, which have the effect of shrinking the pool of available housing for newly arrived refugees and migrants.

Launch Capital Partners (LCP), an impact investing private equity group, developed a multifamily affordable housing solution for refugees. LCP leases what it considers Class C properties to Class A tenants, and in doing so it has been able to strengthen refugee communities while increasing the investment value of

LCP properties. Remarkably, LCP is able to provide investors with the unique opportunity to earn market-rate returns while creating transformative social impact. There is nothing concessional about its offering; LCP has over a decade of experience in acquisitions and property management and currently owns and operates 450 units in Louisville, Kentucky, its first major property site. Since 2015, LCP has invested $1.7 million of its own capital and netted over 12 percent annual returns before property appreciation.

In 2019, LCP closed its $2.3 million Caspian Fund to invest in immigrant and refugee housing. In just over one year, Caspian increased investors' equity twofold and is now positioned to invest $1 million in Launch's new Aegean Fund, a fund of $7 to $10 million with a scheduled 2020 close. According to LCP, its new fund's net levered IRR is estimated to be 19 percent. LCP is able to keep its risk low and also support its refugee tenants by working closely with NGO partners at Refuge International, which mobilizes local church members to create intentional and transformative relationships between refugees and Louisville residents. They combine these efforts with one of LCP's subsidiaries that supports its tenants with job creation. The recipe of a relational property management strategy seems to be working. LCP CEO Jimmy Wright says, "Tenants become close to the resident managers, and this really strengthens the community as well as our operations. Rent payments were not affected at all by COVID-19 and we're at 100 percent capacity. If managers are looking at two clients, one who has a five-year work history with decent history, another who has no history and no credit, but who is vouched for by a resettlement agency, we'll take the latter every time. Refugees are the *most* vetted people who immigrate here."

LCP's business model is designed from the ground up to meet the specific needs of displaced clients. This purpose is what makes the venture so successful and what enables LCP to offer investors such competitive returns. LCP is constantly evaluating expansion to other refugee resettlement cities across the United States, as well as the potential to combine its model with Opportunity Zones. Wright mentioned Houston's Gulfton community as one potential expansion site ("the most diverse square mile in the United States"), as well as Clarkston, Georgia, and central Virginia. Many of LCP's investors are seasoned private equity professionals. Although 8 to 12 percent debt is seen as concessionary for some of them, "they do this for mission alignment. Others have invested with us for the return and the debt on the front end, which hasn't been concessionary. The industry would call it a hard-money loan." Most notably, LCP continues to have a high rate of reinvestment because its investors find they can achieve an impact with nonconcessionary returns.

The supply of affordable housing and housing designed with the nuances of meeting refugee and migrant needs has not kept pace with the enormous volume of demand. We need more firms like LCP in the market. Ideally these would be led by former refugees or immigrants themselves. In the meantime, impact investors in the housing sector, particularly those with exposure to large regional or national property management companies, should consider using their equity or debt positions to incentivize their portfolio companies to develop and enforce more inclusive housing policies for refugees and, following LCP's leadership, to suggest that local developers and management companies work closely with the nine resettlement agencies to attract clients, design lease arrangements that support their needs, and ensure that adequate wraparound services like those offered by LCP are put in place. Tim Docking, who has been advising LCP on behalf of RIN for a few years now, thinks that not only could this approach expand the housing market for refugees and migrants in the United States, but it would simultaneously expand the pool of clients for affordable housing developers while delivering competitive risk-adjusted returns for investors. This approach—tailoring specific development toward a refugee demographic customer base—is starting to spread to others.

We initially connected with Robert Foster, previously the director of Impact Investments at the San Diego Impact Investors Network, through our friend Kasra at CEO. Robert is now the managing director of Courage Housing, a real estate company in the state of Washington, where he is developing affordable and community-focused multifamily housing for refugees and new Americans. In our recent call in January 2025, he said his goal is "to develop ten thousand units for refugees." He's starting with forty-eight units, half dedicated to refugees and half dedicated for workforce units at or below 80 percent of area mean income (AMI), the income level that's used to determine eligibility for housing assistance programs. Robert was excited to share that he had completed an initial raise of $11.1 million for this first phase of the development, which is made up of $3.5 million in equity. His investors include a private investor interested in using his donor-advised fund (DAF), the Washington Trust Bank (also a lender on the project), a small federal grant, and even 1.46 acres of land donated by a public library that will be getting a new community center as part of the development project, for which they will receive a $10/year lease for one hundred years. The plan, Robert says, is to get a Housing and Urban Development (HUD) loan in three to four years and pay back the investors.

In the next few years, Robert plans to expand his housing for new Americans into five other markets—Puget Sound, Boise, Denver, Salt Lake, and Aurora, Colorado. He says that all of these markets have great growth potential "and a degree of climate resilience to them, as opposed to Florida and California which have real insurance risks." He's spoken with two of the VOLAGs as potential strategic partners in the development; both are apparently interested. We asked him about the intersection of real estate and refugee lens investing. "It's simple," he said. "This is an economic development opportunity for the United States. Refugees are really good for growth and the dream that is American. The essence of a great social enterprise means your idea becomes commonplace in thirty years. I want everyone to have criteria for seeing resettled refugees as the high-quality customers that they're hungry to have."

Both Launch and Courage Housing, as affordable housing developers, are what we'd call R3 refugee lens companies. These developers are directly providing critical social or "belonging" infrastructure to refugees so that they can economically integrate and contribute to their new home communities.

Sometimes there isn't a clear R3 or R4 business providing products or services directly to displaced communities, nor is there always an R1 or R2 company that offers a solution to a key problem in a community. When neither markets nor public policy delivers a solution to an urgent intractable problem, we need, as the Columbia University professor Georgia Levenson Keohane describes, "a more visible hand . . . concerted efforts by governments, multilateral agencies, philanthropies, and, increasingly, socially minded investors, to meet the needs and solve problems." When these stakeholders together develop a creative mechanism "to pay for investments in public goods and social and economic development, we call it innovative finance" (Keohane 2016).

KOIS Investments did this in Jordan with its livelihoods bond. But it also worked in Massachusetts. One of the people we met early on while we were still incubating the idea for the RIN was Andi Phillips, who at the time was exploring her next career decision after leading Goldman Sachs's $138 million social impact fund, which was a first of its kind for a US financial institution. Andi was developing a business plan for a new fund focused on innovative finance more broadly, at the same time we were exploring using innovative finance tools in the context of global forced migration.

While we didn't join our efforts, Andi's new company, Maycomb Capital, ended up participating in an exciting new impact bond, or pay-for-success model, led by the Commonwealth of Massachusetts, Jewish Vocational Services Boston (JVS), and Social Finance, the last led by Tracy Palandjian, a brilliant financial architect whom John also came to know while finishing his graduate work in Boston. The Commonwealth of Massachusetts was interested in increasing employment opportunities for English-language learners (social infrastructure that enables economic integration of refugees), but it did not want to take a risk with public funding to finance JVS's language learning and job readiness programs for new Americans resettled in the state.

In 2017, Tracy and her team at Social Finance launched the Massachusetts Pathways to Economic Advancement, a pay-for-success project that expanded education and employment opportunities for approximately two thousand immigrants and refugees in the Boston area. JVS, one of Boston's largest community-based workforce and adult education providers, gave vocational English-language classes that were integrated with job search assistance and coaching, thereby assisting limited English speakers in making successful transitions to employment, higher-wage jobs, and higher education. The commonwealth repaid investors when JVS successfully achieved positive outcomes for participants.

The Economic Mobility Corporation measured outcomes from the English for Advancement (EfA) track of the project via a randomized controlled trial (RCT), the first such study on the earnings impacts of a workforce development program for English-language learners. The study found that EfA resulted in a 7 percent increase in wages overall for participants and a 13 percent increase for individuals unaffected by the early pandemic labor market. The project was successful not just in delivering robust outcomes but also in providing a decent payback for its investors, which included, in addition to Maycomb, forty refugee lens impact investors such as the Living Cities Blended Catalyst Fund, Prudential Financial, the Barbara Bush Foundation for Family Legacy, Blue Haven Initiative, the Boston Foundation, the Boston Impact Initiative, ImpactAssets, the Inherent Foundation, the Kresge Foundation, the Shapiro Foundation, and the Sorenson Impact Foundation.

While there are countless opportunities for US-based impact investors to use creative financing to improve the prospects of new Americans at home, they can also be a force for good in the broader world. One of the more hopeful moments of building the RIN over the last few years came through a friendship we developed with Dave Bohigian, mentioned earlier in the book. It was an unlikely time for us to be entering into a collaboration with the US Development Finance Corporation (USDFC), given the Trump administration's actively hostile positioning toward refugees and immigrants, but life can be surprising. Dave's directive from the White House was to deploy US taxpayer dollars overseas, advance our development objectives, and return principle, plus interest, to the Department of Treasury. Dave was pragmatic. But perhaps as the grandson of a refugee, he understood at a very deep, human level what we were trying to do.

The Overseas Private Investment Corporation (OPIC) was already doing something similar through its 2X Women's Initiative, the framework of which we've already mentioned as our initial inspiration for the refugee lens. The 2X Initiative was a viable precedent that quickly accelerated from the US goal of mobilizing $1 billion in gender lens investments to something much bigger. Dave and Ivanka Trump toured South America together, promoting 2X investments with allies across the continent.

Sometime around Christmas of 2018, we asked Dave if he'd consider hosting a meeting at OPIC/USDFC on refugee lens investing. To our surprise, he said yes. It took a few months, but by March we had assembled a group of roughly twenty US investors who were interested in learning about our framework and exploring partnership opportunities. We brought our friend Manyang Kher with us, a gregarious and committed R1 entrepreneur who was resettled in Richmond, Virginia, and founded a coffee social enterprise called 734 Coffee to support displaced families from South Sudan (see chapter 4). Too many meetings in Washington occur where people discuss international development and forget about the people we need to serve. Two things of importance happened that day. First, Manyang completely charmed everyone and made a number of raving fans of 734 Coffee. Second, the meeting set in motion the USDFC's journey to becoming an active refugee lens investor.

Following that event, the US government invested in Kiva's Refugee Investment Fund (KRIF), providing $20 million in debt as the lead anchor for a $32 million round that closed in April 2021, and it also joined the IKEA Foundation, the Novo Nordisk Foundation, Norwegian Agency for Development Cooperation (Norad), and the Norwegian investment fund in a $9.8 million financing of KOIS's Development Impact Bond (DIB) for refugees in Jordan and Lebanon. The DIB, implemented by the Near East Foundation, was designed to fund a vocational, entrepreneurship- and resilience-building program supporting 4,380 refugee and host population trainees and to provide 3,400 business start-up grants in Jordan. Similar to the Massachusetts pay-for-success model, it brought unlikely partners together to fix a market failure. In this case, the bond would not have been possible without the coinvestment of the USDFC.

Over the last 250 years of the United States, while there have always been xenophobic voices against "the other," the arc of our history has been toward incorporating new neighbors, new ideas, and new innovations. Over the last ten years, we have seen important and proactive investment strategies to accelerate the economic incorporation and thriving of new Americans. As Peter Drucker, the famed father of modern management theory and a former refugee, once said, "Every single social and global issue of our day is a business opportunity in disguise." Yet these opportunities have not been developed on the scale we need, which is why it was so important to establish the RIN and facilitate the education and collaboration of impact-oriented investors.

6

THE MIDDLE EAST

From Haven to Hub

An hour's drive from one of the largest refugee camps in the world, there is a place for building almost anything.

Across 20,000-plus square feet of space—a clean area, an industrial area, and an outdoor area—we see every kind of machine that a modern maker might want. The clean area has 3D printers, a robotics lab, an electronics shop, and a design studio. The industrial area is humming with a wood shop, metal shop, molding shop, and laser cutter. In the outdoor area, which is the newest section, people can do whatever is needed to finish their prototypes in the open air.

We're at ShamalStart, one of the leading business accelerators in Jordan. The country has long been a hospitable haven for many different communities, but becoming a truly inclusive hub for the displaced is a higher-order challenge. Our team is here to assess the chances and move the dial if we can.

Ibrahim Faza, the manager taking us around, says that Shamal is located in Irbid because this is the area where many Syrian refugees have converged in the past decade. Despite all the skills and ideas they were bringing with them, some 70 percent were unemployed, not to mention half the local Jordanian population. In 2016, with funds from the European Union (EU), an Amman-based organization called Luminus, which provides technical and vocational education, partnered with the country's Royal Scientific Society to do something about it.

Ibrahim lays out the numbers: over 5,000 applications supported, over 1,000 boot camp trainings for entrepreneurs, 300 teams incubated, and 130 businesses created with 15 million euros in funding, which have resulted in over 500 high-level jobs. Start-ups incubated, accelerated, and launched here in just the past few years are now exporting products worth several million euros to the EU, the Gulf region, Japan, and the United States. Many are owned and led by refugees.

ShamalStart works, and not just in abstract numerical terms. Although initially designed for Syrian refugees, the program is also completely open to the Somali, Sudanese, Iraqi, Palestinian, Yemeni, and other refugee communities here. Nor does it ignore the host community; a major objective from the beginning has been to build bridges between local people and refugees, modeling how a truly inclusive economy could benefit all communities. With more direct funding, ShamalStart could have an exponential impact. It's essential to build more places like it.

The Fab Lab where we're standing is the first digital fabrication lab in Jordan (and one of the twenty largest in the world). People here make actual and very cool stuff focusing on early-stage manufacturing, though the spirit of innovation extends well beyond the visible and tangible. An example is the nontraditional venture capital fund that Ibrahim says is currently in the works. Refugee entrepreneurs have the drive and know-how, but the new fund will bring in different kinds of investors committed to direct mentoring and guidance, as well as novel and accessible forms of financing.

Here's how Shamal works. Anyone interested can try out its state-of-the-art tools and machines during open days and workshops. Those admitted to the program need a proof of concept, but it's collaborative and hands-on from there so that people can develop their ideas and access the market, discovering what actually works. Shamal helps as much as possible with the complexities of finding investors, building brands, and registering companies (usually through a Jordanian partner). Every start-up receives 15,000 euros in cash and 15,000 euros in kind, with organizations like the International Rescue Committee, UNICEF, and the Agency for Technical Cooperation and Development (ACTED) also sponsoring a select number of projects.

Take Darb, a start-up developed here in the Fab Lab that uses robotics to clean solar panels, which work great in deserts until the sand starts sticking. Named Jordan's best start-up in 2018, Darb landed a $200,000 investment through the Arab Bank and opened factories in Amman and Ayla. Now it's expanding to Saudi Arabia and possibly the southwestern United States. It's an ingenious concept brilliantly executed, hatched right here in the Fab Lab.

Just a few doors down is Teenah, a refugee start-up that supports Syrian women by designing and producing environmentally friendly tote bags. The first year there were just two of them setting up a minifactory as well as sales and management. In no time, they had exported over forty thousand bags to Europe and were making over 100,000 JOD (~$140,000) in revenue. Soon Teenah was employing twenty women in a much larger space that was provided rent-free in the nearby Irbid Development Zone.

In fact, ShamalStart is just one piece of a larger regional puzzle. Irbid is the second-largest urban area in Jordan, with over 2 million people. There are direct links by road both to Israel and to Syria, with the city of Daraa (an opposition stronghold heavily impacted by the war) less than 20 miles away. In the center of Irbid are five universities and two industrial zones.

After saying goodbye to Ibrahim, we drive just a few miles to one of those zones, the Al-Hassan Industrial Estate. There we meet Sanal Kumar, a driven and dynamic Indian entrepreneur whose company, Classic Fashion, is one of the largest apparel manufacturers in the Middle East. Kumar tells us that the company has 280 production lines, 12 factories, and 7 satellite factories around Jordan, doing over $800 million in annual revenue. Being based in Irbid's qualifying industrial zone (QIZ) allows the company to take advantage of advantageous free-trade agreements. Most of its clients are leading international suppliers and fashion brands in Europe and North America.

Although garment factory work is not glamorous, Classic Fashion employs thirty thousand people. According to local law, Kumar explains, at least 25 percent have to be Jordanian, but the rest can be migrants. Most of those people are Syrians, and there is an official goal for each production line to be at least 15 percent Syrian refugees; however, Kumar says there are barriers to Syrians securing the jobs like transportation and childcare and, as a result, there are thousands of displaced people nearby that could find jobs here on the Classic Fashion production lines but do not.

Nowhere is the urge to make a living stronger than at the Za'atari refugee camp, home to some eighty thousand people whose lives are largely on hold. Opened by the United Nations High Commissioner for Refugees (UNHCR) in 2012 to host 450 Syrians fleeing the early fighting, Za'atari swelled dramatically over the following year. Today this flat section of desert not far from Irbid is a city unto itself, complete with roads, schools, hospitals, and prefab metal shelters (which replaced the earlier tents).

Estimates vary, but it's believed that as many as 13 million Syrians have been displaced due to war. Over half fled the country, with neighboring Jordan the third most common destination after Turkey and Lebanon. At the very moment when regional conflict was already impacting the Jordanian economy, the country's population increased by over 13 percent, virtually overnight, thanks to the arrival of Syrian refugees in places like Za'atari. For perspective, this would be the equivalent of the United States welcoming over 44,213,000 refugees in one year. Officially there are 658,000 Syrian refugees in Jordan, but unofficially the number may be twice that.

Only in 2015, four years into the conflict, was this "refugee crisis" widely recognized outside the region, when over a million people from Syria, Afghanistan, Iraq, and sub-Saharan Africa arrived directly on European shores. They came first via the central Mediterranean, with an estimated three thousand drowning when the rickety boats of unscrupulous smugglers went down, and then soon came via the western Balkans. Europeans were completely unprepared to meet their own stated obligations to provide refuge, although in relative terms they were doing just a fraction of what Jordan and other regional host countries had been doing for years.

As the largest refugee camp in the Middle East and one of the largest in the world, Za'atari is a symbol of Jordan's spirit of generosity and tolerance, even though if suffers from many of the problems of the "camp model." No one doubts that humanitarian aid is a vital form of emergency response during the onset of a crisis. But camps like this were never meant to be permanent, and only since the 1980s have they become the default, replacing the enduring resettlement and integration options that refugees need.

The traumas people bring to Za'atari are beyond description. Syrian refugees in Jordan are disproportionately young, with nearly half under the age of fifteen. The average household has five family members, with the head of household more likely to be female. Most are relying on humanitarian assistance to meet their basic needs, and many feel forced to cope by cutting meals and sending their children off to work or marry early. What people need now is decent, stable employment.

If ShamalStart evokes exponential possibilities and Classic Fashion shows that there are nearby, scalable solutions, Za'atari is a testament to the drive and ambition of refugees even under the most difficult circumstances. On our way to meet with ten young Syrian refugees, we see the camp's famous "Shams Élysées." Punning off the famous Parisian boulevard and the Arabic name for Greater Syria (Shams), this street is the camp's bustling commercial heart. Only 4 percent of working-age refugees in Za'atari have work permits, but a whole unofficial microeconomy has grown up here spontaneously. For sale are cosmetics, textiles, pets, pharmaceuticals, and even black market construction materials like bricks and cement. Still hard to come by, at any price, is a sense of home.

Over the last century, few countries in the world have been as welcoming to refugees as Jordan. Today the displaced make up as much as one third of the population, with many having been effectively and smoothly integrated into Jordanian society. While the United States and other wealthy Western countries tout their generosity, small nations in tough neighborhoods like Jordan are actually doing most of the heavy lifting, with relatively little help.

Though there were earlier precedents, including Circassian and other Caucasian refugees who came fleeing Russian aggression, this history of Jordanian hospitality substantially began in 1948. That year's Arab-Israeli War, followed by the 1967 War, led to Jordan's hosting of approximately 2 million Palestinian refugees. Given the kingdom's annexation of the West Bank in 1950, most were able from the outset to become Jordanian citizens with full rights, but there are significant exceptions. Over 400,000 refugees continue to live in the country's ten Palestinian camps, and in particular those originally from Gaza have now been stateless for several generations. Moreover, a large percentage of Palestinians in Jordan live below the national poverty line and lack access to quality education and healthcare.

The last decade has seen Jordan become a key destination for asylum seekers, refugees, and migrants from Iraq, Sudan, Somalia, Yemen, Egypt, Pakistan, and of course, above all, Syria. Playing an important role is a broadly shared religion (Islam) and language (Arabic), not unlike the role of Catholicism and Spanish in the integration of Latin Americans in Mexico.

While camps like Za'atari are the public face of refugee life, the vast majority, including 81 percent of Syrians, actually live in Jordanian cities. No place has been more transformed by refugees and in turn transformative for them than the capital, Amman, with its population of over 4 million people and its intense concentration of educational, economic, and social opportunities. This extraordinarily diverse city is fast developing into a new kind of regional hub.

We've come to Amman to meet with Jordanian government officials, international experts, nonprofit leaders, and a whole range of others as we try to understand what does (and doesn't) make this refugee-powered nation work. At the same time, we're meeting with entrepreneurs in a range of industries to learn about their businesses and financing, to see what they need to open their doors to the displaced.

One day we're at a bookstore café with a local ecotourism expert, talking about the new Jordan Trail, which aims to draw hikers to the country's unique landscapes; the next, we're sitting down with a brigadier general who helps determine the government's refugee response plans. On the one hand, the minister of investment talks boldly about the importance of refugees and inclusive growth; on the other, a former insider at the Ministry of Interior tells us that policies and permissions in this sensitive area are always changing.

We talk to several UN agencies, the United States Agency for International Development (USAID), the British Embassy, and the Amman Chamber of Commerce. The politics are complicated in every direction, and the Jordanian government has to be careful about seeming to favor outsiders when its own citizens have so many pressing needs. Western governments and development agencies in Amman may be pressing Jordan to do more, substantively and vocally, but this pressure may have just as much to do with Western interest in keeping Middle Eastern refugees in the Middle East.

If one thing is clear, it's that few people are seeing the whole picture. With all the different efforts and individuals we encountered, Jordan *could* have just the right kind of emergent ecosystem to turn its status as a haven for the displaced into economic growth, ultimately benefiting everyone.

What the country needs is more people like Mary Nazzal, the founder of Landmark Hotels, a leading hospitality business. Taking time she doesn't have out of her crazy schedule, Mary whisks us around Amman and urges us to connect the dots. She tells us that she has had an unusual career that has been driven by "justice and fairness" on a trajectory from activism to lawyering to investing and business ownership.

Landmark, led by Mary, is committed to hiring refugees. There is no government assistance or encouragement involved—they just do it. As part of the UNHCR's civil society network, Landmark now also has an active presence in the camps, helping both Syrian and Gazan refugees launch social businesses. Gender fairness is a particular passion; Mary was included by *Forbes* in its list of "most powerful Arab women" because she is keenly aware of the social and cultural pressures that keep women from entering the workforce and starting businesses. "You have a community here interested in social enterprises," she says, "only in the last two years actually, and especially after Covid."

With Mary's help, we don't have to look far to find growing refugee-led and refugee-supporting businesses calling out for investment. One morning we drive on the outskirts of Amman down an unpaved alley past hardscrabble farms and a tent city to meet the hydroponics entrepreneurs behind Senara. Here in corrugated tin shacks young men are fabricating materials that will enable people to grow their own food in the most marginalized spaces, including in refugee camps. It's a classic example of what's known in Hindi as *jugaad*, the art of making things work as best you can with what you have.

Started by a refugee in the Gaza Refugee Camp in Jerash in 2019, Senara now has thirty full- and part-time employees who design and manufacture seven different hydroponic systems to install on rooftops, in gardens, or directly on agricultural lands. Senara not only sells the units but also provides training, subscription, and farming supplies to the buyers, as well as maintenance, technical, sales, and marketing support. Remarkably, it also runs a call center for an e-commerce company—whatever it takes to bring in sustainable incomes for families in the camp. Senara has ambitious growth plans, if it can get the financing it needs.

Also based in Jerash's Gaza camp and likewise creative and adaptable is Sitti Social Enterprise. Sitti started in 2014 when the Italian Agency for Development Cooperation held a soap-making workshop in the camp. At the end of the workshop, the women had hundreds of soap bars and the skills to keep going.

Today Sitti employs thirty-four people as soap makers, most of them refugees and sole providers in their households, while also hosting computer classes, English classes, and artisan training for many others. The soaps are sold globally, with over two hundred stores stocking the products in Canada alone. One of Sitti's founders tells us that an investment of as little as half a million dollars would be transformative, enabling Sitti to build a new factory to meet EU and Arab world product standards as well as establish a secondary base in the United States.

Just as remarkable and worthy of support, though on a smaller scale, are the home-based businesses that at least some refugees are able to run. Not everything can be a scalable start-up. Beekeeping, for example, is an ancient livelihood practice that remains very much a viable pathway for anyone to make income almost anywhere in the world, even people who are resettling or in limbo.

Suheir, a Syrian refugee we meet in Amman, started working with bees over thirty years ago. She learned from her father and later taught her husband and her son, and she brought these very portable skills with her when fleeing the war. After setting up hives on the roof with her landlord's support, she found that producing honey, wax, and propolis is convenient and enjoyable work. Suheir explains that her sales of 30 to 40 pounds of product per year go mostly to family and friends. While this can't cover all living expenses, the income has been crucial for supporting her daughter's education, including college fees now in Canada.

In many places, there is an ancient body of law and tradition protecting the right to raise bees—regardless of work permits, business licenses, or other modern-day bureaucratic regulations. Nor is it just a matter of money: Being with bees, people tell us, occupies the hands and the mind, filling traumatic times with a sense of clarity and purpose. We hear from the Beekeepers Union, the Beekeepers Association, and a range of ordinary beekeepers that although beekeeping in Jordan faces various challenges, there is serious potential for building an entire industry that is radically inclusive of whoever has the drive and skills and wants to be with the bees—both Jordanians and all those taking refuge in the country.

We also learned lessons from large-scale advanced manufacturing. The Daaboul brothers know what it's like to pull up roots and start again. In 2014 the brothers—Mutassem, Hassan, and Mumtaz—realized that the war in their native Syria wasn't going to end anytime soon. Their family business, Orbit Aluminum Industries, more than four decades old with two major factories in the country, was suffering. Orbit produces premium-quality painted aluminum coils that are used in a wide range of products with architectural, industrial, and transportation applications. Much of what they produce is for export, especially to the United States.

Mutassem tells us that the brothers were led to move their export-oriented operations to Aqaba because of its direct access to the port, tax incentives, and the fact that no custom duties are charged within the Aqaba Special Economic Zone (ASEZ). Another condition, however, was just as important to them: that they be allowed to hire Syrian refugees as well as Jordanians. As Canadian passport holders running a Singapore-based business, they are citizens of the world who are nonetheless deeply concerned with the fate of their fellow Syrians.

It took some negotiating, says Mutassem, with all the Syrian employees needing to undergo security clearance with Jordanian intelligence, as well as being registered with UNHCR. It required investment as well, with Orbit offering housing to its non-Jordanian employees and using its banking connections to establish bank accounts for them. From a roughly half-and-half split, the approximately two hundred employees are now roughly 60 percent Jordanian and 40 percent Syrian.

The company is committed to treating all employees equally, but there are limits to what it can do in the current environment. Some employees traveled to Syria to see family and for security reasons were not allowed to return; others were deeply distressed by not being able to attend the funerals of their relatives and friends there.

Although Orbit is a state-of-the-art manufacturing operation, capable of doing everything in-house, it battles with the high cost of logistics and energy in Jordan. Like any business owners, the brothers need investment: $100 to $120 million over four years, they estimate, for the serious expansion they would like to undertake. With new cold-rolling mills and hot-rolling mills and other machinery, they could employ hundreds more, with knock-on effects for families and communities that would spread far beyond the factory.

From Irbid to Aqaba, Jordan's special economic zones, with their business-friendly regulations and exemptions, have a vital role to play, not only in the country's economic growth but also in the employment of the displaced. In fact, it was this critical insight that led to the signing of the Jordan Compact in 2016, whereby Jordan and several Western donor governments pledged to turn the Syrian refugee crisis into a historic development opportunity for the country.

Everyone could agree that something had to be done. Even as hundreds of thousands of Syrians were arriving in Jordan, virtually none were being allowed to work legally in the country. The result was an informal market in which Syrians accepted lower wages and rates, thus competing directly with Jordanian nationals in certain, mainly lower-skilled professions. This is a dangerous recipe for social tension.

Together with pledges of donor support for the Jordanian economy, the Jordan Compact promised to create 200,000 jobs for Syrian refugees alongside Jordanians, with an emphasis on the special economic zones. Particular agriculture, construction, and home-based businesses such as food processing, handicrafts, and tailoring were in theory opened up to refugee workers. As of December 2020, the Jordanian government had issued work permits for over 215,000 Syrian refugees.

This is real progress. The trailblazing ideas behind the Jordan Compact deserve wider adoption and dovetail closely with our mission at the Refugee Investment Network (RIN). Yet the reality, so far at least, has been falling short. Academics, donors, and development agencies have led the process, with predictable implementation problems. Investors and companies that might have grounded and expanded on these goals were left on the sidelines. Nor were there sufficient community consultation and local follow-through.

Jordan has unquestionable strengths as a stable, business-friendly nation with a well-educated and talented population. The seven free-trade agreements signed by the government provide direct market access, particularly via the special economic zones, to some 1.5 billion consumers around the world. But growth has lagged behind expectations. The arrival of fresh talent from across the region could bring about a breakthrough.

Given Jordan's hospitable history, it's possible to imagine the government extending essential economic rights, even if political rights are not granted given the sensitivities. But for now there remain a host of different rules and challenges for different nationalities. Gazans, unlike other Palestinians in Jordan, are banned from owning assets, working in certain sectors, and receiving healthcare. Iraqis face limitations on work permits and legal status. Yemeni and Sudanese refugees can be deported at any time and for any reason, even if they possess valid documentation. Syrians deal every day with their own range of restrictions.

Beyond legal status, work permits, business licenses, and the like, there are even thornier issues like the lack of financing, the mismatch between jobs and skills, the dearth of matching and training programs, and cultural constraints. As refugees remain unemployed for longer and longer periods, the gaps in their knowledge and skills grow correspondingly. COVID-19 brought further challenges, as most refugees, being concentrated in crowded camps and poor urban settings with poor infrastructure and hygiene, had a higher risk of outbreaks. Without access to equipment and the Internet, virtual work is not even an option.

Yet everywhere we go in Jordan we meet driven and dedicated refugees. Just by coming here and mapping the terrain, we find an initial forty enterprises in the country with a significant refugee lens angle, what we would call a "use case"—Senara, Sitti, Daaboul, and others doing amazing, largely unrecognized things that are fundamentally altering refugee lives, day in and day out.

If one listens closely to government officials, investors, donors, and community members who want to move from humanitarianism to development, there is also a changing narrative. There are promising new financial instruments too, including microfinance initiatives like Kiva's, which has added Jordan to its loan portfolio, the KOIS DIB described in chapter 5, and a handful of local funds, including Anara Impact Capital, a new regionally focused fund—possibly the first impact investing fund focused exclusively on the MENA region—that has been developed by Alfanar Venture Philanthropy. Anara is led by Nafez Dakkak, who cofounded BLDR Ventures, a venture studio reimagining the future of work and learning, and who led the launch of Edraak, a Queen Rania Foundation (QRF) initiative and the largest Arabic open online education platform that is now serving nearly 10 million learners, including underserved communities across MENA.

When we first interviewed Alfanar, the design of Anara was still in development, but even then, it was clear that its team understood that, to best support underserved founders in the MENA region, particularly those with displaced experiences, the fund would have to be flexible in how it financed growing businesses, making available multiple financial instruments, including equity, debt, or a combination of both. In addition to investment capital, the fund would make available nondilutive technical assistance grants to help these businesses strengthen and scale their impact, operations, and revenue. It's this kind of thinking and innovation that will give refugee entrepreneurs and entrepreneurs serving the displaced longer-term support as they develop their businesses. If one thing is certain in Jordan, it's that the best strategy will include everyone—the way a good home has room for both hosts and guests.

7

LATIN AMERICA

A New Destination for the Displaced

Every day for at least the last three weeks, a migrant has been murdered in Tapachula. The crimes are being reported in the local press, full of lurid detail. But neither the state prosecutors, nor the attorney general, nor even the special prosecutor's office for migrant rights seems interested in solving the cases or tracking down the murderers. None of the civil society organizations in town, we are told, even have the wherewithal to document what is going on.

Our team is in Tapachula to speak to asylum seekers and those trying to help them, such as Salva Lacruz of the Fray Matías Human Rights Center, the leading migrant and refugee assistance center in this small Mexican city in the state of Chiapas, less than 10 miles from the Guatemalan border. A visit here immediately cuts through many of the myths that surround migration.

Until recently, few people outside the region had even heard of Tapachula. But it is now the gateway for refugees, where thousands of people are stuck and suffering in limbo. Like so many border towns the world over, Tapachula is suddenly on the front lines, forced into the role of first responder for forcibly displaced people from across the hemisphere and beyond.

The same is now true of Mexico itself, a longtime "sending" country that is fast becoming a "receiving" one because of economic, demographic, and other changes. It's a transition with fundamental challenges, but also extraordinary opportunities. At least 3 million displaced people are living in Mexico (including many displaced Mexicans from Chiapas, Guerrero, Sinaloa, and other states with high levels of violence), and an increasing number of those from elsewhere are not just passing through but want to stay. With its tradition of relative openness to immigrants and the relative ease of social integration, especially for other Spanish speakers, the country seems poised to become a model—if it can grapple with the complex dynamics of economic inclusion.

From Tapachula in the south to Tijuana on the US border, the Refugee Investment Network (RIN) has been assessing the country's progress and following in migrants' footsteps. Here in the south, basic safety is the most immediate issue. This city is one of Mexico's most dangerous, and migrants are particularly vulnerable. Some of the murders may be connected to local xenophobia and resentment toward the influx of non-Mexicans. Other cases are more personal. At the Casa de Refugiados in Mexico City, the staff later tell us that an estimated 40 percent of refugees and asylum seekers have seen the gang members that threated their lives in Mexico, often in Tapachula. Refuge, for so many, is elusive.

Then there are the perils of the journey itself. Many of the people converging on Mexico are from the "Northern Triangle" countries of Honduras, El Salvador, and Guatemala, which have never recovered from the civil wars of the 1980s and 1990s and are plagued by high crime rates, gang violence, drug trafficking, corruption, and severe poverty. Others are coming in record numbers from Nicaragua, Cuba, and Haiti. Still others trek on foot through the dangerous and roadless mountains and jungles of the Darien Gap to escape the poverty and violence of Colombia, Ecuador, and especially Venezuela, where full-scale socioeconomic collapse has been fueling one of the world's largest displacement crises. Still others are fleeing catastrophe in Africa, the Middle East, and Central Asia.

The exact numbers of refugees in Mexico are hard to determine because many do not apply for asylum in Mexico and have sought to continue north and apply for asylum in the United States. It is estimated that only between 2 percent and 10 percent of refugees arriving in Mexico apply for asylum in Mexico, suggesting that the official count of 164,699 registered asylum seekers between 2014 and 2019 could mean over 1.6 million actual refugees in the country.

Some have been traveling for months, if not years or lifetimes. Most still hope to make it to the United States, but first they have to make it through Tapachula. They can't cross the Rio Grande into Texas without crossing the Suchiate River into Mexico, where border guards are ready to intercept and detain them.

Although Tapachula has long been a place of crossings, Salva says that the Guatemala-Mexico border, like so many others, is more militarized than ever: There are no more rubber-tire rafts bringing dozens of people per hour across in broad daylight. People still cross, he adds, but either at night or in riskier areas upriver, where there may be a cartel presence.

In 2018, the caravans started coming. Conspiracy theories abound, but in fact very little is actually known about them, even their fluctuating numbers. The United Nations High Commissioner for Refugees (UNHCR) team in Tapachula estimated that some 400,000 people were irregularly crossing the border each year into Mexico. Another organization pointed out that there were sixty-one different irregular vehicular crossing points and a practically infinite number for those on foot. It was our understanding that the caravans were quasi- or fully organic, picking up people as they moved, with neither funds nor leadership—just desperate people with no choice but to leave home and seek safety in numbers.

By 2019, even apart from the caravans, at least a hundred people were entering Tapachula every day. But sometimes it was two or three times that—more in one year than in the entire previous decade, according to Salva, with large numbers of families and unaccompanied children. Humanitarian assistance operations like the Fray Matías Human Rights Center were strained to the breaking point.

Then it got worse. The US policy commonly known as "Remain in Mexico"—officially the "Migrant Protection Protocols" (MPP)—began requiring anyone seeking asylum in the United States to "remain in Mexico" while waiting for their asylum case to be heard. By forcing people to stay where they may face persecution, the policy violates the 1951 Convention Relating to the Status of Refugees, which the United States signed. Stated simply, it leaves people in danger.

The US Department of Homeland Security did not disclose the exact numbers of individuals subject to MPP since its inception, but according to the nonpartisan Transactional Records Access Clearinghouse (TRAC), at least seventy thousand people were returned to Mexico to await their asylum court hearings (AIC 2024). The Trump administration also significantly ramped up the activities of ICE (US Immigration and Customs Enforcement), resulting in large numbers of deportees from the United States: 2019 saw 1,013,539 removals, the highest number from all countries in a decade. However, it should be noted that the Trump administration's deportation numbers pale in comparison to the highs under the Bush W. and Clinton administrations (at 11,387,486 and 1,814,729, respectively). As Aarti Shahani, author of *Here We Are: American Dreams, American Nightmares*, notes: "Clinton's bills, by building a robust pipeline for mass deportation, created the legal architecture for present-day human-rights abuses at the border. Since their passage, the budget for deportation has exploded: from $1.9 billion in 1997 ($3 billion adjusted for inflation) to $21.1 billion by 2018" (Shahani 2019). In part due to the anti-immigrant stance of US policy and politics, and in part from the relatively improving economic conditions of Mexico, Mexico has transitioned from a transit country to a destination country for many refugees and forced migrants.

There has been intense US pressure on the Mexican government to hold back the refugees, whatever their situation might be. Many have been patiently waiting, but others feel they have little choice but to seek asylum from Mexico instead—an increasingly attractive option. In 2019, there were approximately eighty thousand applications from people seeking asylum in Mexico, triple the number from the previous year. It hasn't slowed down since, with the Mexican Commission for Refugee Assistance (COMAR) reporting over thirteen thousand in January 2023 alone, on track for a record. Generally, a majority of them have been handled by COMAR's office in Chiapas, which includes Tapachula. Of course, some abuse the process and still seek to enter the United States.

Long a place of crossings, Tapachula has become the choke point, if not a trap, for tens of thousands of stranded people. Most have to wait here for seven or eight months, says Salva, and the conditions are bleak. Those who can afford it rent overpriced and overcrowded rooms, anywhere they can find them in the urban area. Others make do in makeshift encampments.

For the city's employers, these migrants are easy prey, pressed to work 8- to 12-hour days for almost no money. Agricultural labor in and around the city, like picking fruit and growing coffee, is "semislavery," in Salva's words, sometimes earning as little as 20 pesos ($1) for a full day's work. For women, it's often sex work or bar work. Afro-descendant or African-origin migrants face racism and linguistic barriers to basic survival.

One day our team talks to some of the hundred or so people lined up outside COMAR's Tapachula office. A new arrival has thirty days to register with COMAR and file an asylum claim. It usually takes at least five weeks for COMAR to respond, and another two to four months for UNHCR to process the claim. That's why everyone we talk to has been living and working in Tapachula for six months or longer. Every month they receive a "cash-based intervention" from UNHCR amounting to 1,522 pesos ($76) per person, although rent seems to run about the same, if not higher. So wages are essential.

Those online are waiting to conduct their asylum interviews, receive news about their applications, or do the required weekly sign-in, which essentially keeps them trapped in the city. Nelson, like many here, is from Honduras. He's missing most of his right ear. He was an electrical engineer in Tegucigalpa, but here he earns 100 pesos ($5) a day working for a business he won't name. He's been staying in an apartment with his three children, ages seven, twelve, and seventeen, and the oldest is working in a restaurant. Maria Teresa, who is waiting with him, also has three children. All eight of them have been staying, and waiting, in a single apartment.

COMAR is key if Mexico is to become a destination for asylum seekers and refugees. Chronically underfunded, it relies on UNHCR funding for much of its work. Yet it's the official agency in charge of processing claims, and if COMAR processes claims efficiently and dispassionately people can get the papers to work. COMAR's approval is also necessary in order for the National Institute of Migration (INM) to grant permanent residency. Becoming a permanent resident is ultimately the only way that people like Nelson and Maria Teresa can get full employment and other rights, including a pathway to Mexican citizenship.

At least this new processing center is helping to speed things up. As Salva explains, Mexico's asylum process requires at least 3 hours of interviews to establish a well-founded fear of persecution based on gender, race, religion, politics, nationality, or social group membership. Those coming from countries considered to have generalized violence, like Honduras, Venezuela, and El Salvador, can be expedited thanks to the Cartagena Declaration. The very luckiest asylees, as we will see, are helped through the process and get the chance to go north.

For so many others, though, the frustration in Tapachula is boiling over. And not least among the 300,000-plus residents of the municipality, which stretches from the mountains of the Sierra Madre de Chiapas almost down to the Pacific. They have long faced challenges of their own: chronic violence, drug trafficking, and economic depression. Although there is a long multicultural history here—many Tapachulanos are Indigenous Mayans and Nahuas, while others descend from early-twentieth-century Chinese and German immigrants—the last few years have strained relations.

From the offices of aid organizations to asylees' homes and from the border crossing itself to a migrant shelter just on the other side, our team finds a region reeling from its newfound role in the crisis but nonetheless dependent on the mobility of people and goods. The city's minister for economy and tourism and other officials say that the last few years have come as a shock. They affirm that the city is welcoming but admit that many local people are leery of the newcomers. They themselves urgently need more and better housing, he emphasizes, never mind the migrants.

It's a familiar message in "host communities" around the world, and the clear solution is to invest simultaneously in both migrants and the local people who host them. UNHCR's office here has taken a small step by providing supplies to six local schools, as well as health and education support. At the same time, it is trying to get powerful organizations like the United Nations Development Programme (UNDP) and the World Bank to prioritize Tapachula and similar communities in their project planning.

But fundamentally it's business, investment, and employment opportunities that will make a difference, and Tapachula, like so many host communities, is full of them. The conversation quickly turns specific, focusing on tuna processors, car parts manufacturing, medical tourism, agricultural research and development, house building, and cruise ships. Sixty-one centavos of every peso spent in Tapachula, the officials say, comes from Central America, following a transportation and business corridor that they see stretching as far north as San Diego.

On the one hand, no one doubts that migrants are already huge contributors to the local economy, informally and indirectly. Targeted investments here could have a powerful economic and social impact. Instead of being exploited and in limbo, all the talented and driven people now showing up on the city's doorstep could actually catalyze development while starting to regain a sense of "home."

The officials tell the story of a Nigerian asylum seeker, a trained biologist, whom they had managed to match with Flora Habitacional, a locally based firm doing agricultural research.

Then he disappeared—dragged by INM into a detention center for migrants simply because he was walking around town without his documents on him. It took several days to find him and free him. For all the potential in Tapachula, there is a long way to go.

Further north, the story is more hopeful.

A POLICY CONTEXT SUPPORTIVE OF REFUGEE LENS INVESTING

Mexico has been a global leader in the shift toward more innovative approaches to the growing phenomenon of forced displacement. It is signatory to both the 1951 Convention Relating to the Status of Refugees and the 1967 Protocol, as well as the 1954 Convention Relating to the Status of Stateless Persons. The Mexican government is one of the leading states in an initiative to develop a regional application of the Comprehensive Refugee Response Framework (CRRF), a key contribution to the adoption of the Global Compact on Refugees in 2018 (UNHCR 2018c). This regional initiative, known as the Comprehensive Regional Protection and Solutions Framework (MIRPS, in Spanish), is much more forward thinking and welcoming to asylum seekers than we see in many other countries around the world. The MIRPS is a regional cooperation framework between countries of origin, transit, and destination that promotes shared responsibility mechanisms, strengthens protection, and enhances solutions for refugees, asylum seekers, internally displaced persons (IDPs), and returnees with protection needs (UNHCR 2018c).

Importantly, individuals who are granted asylum in Mexico are allowed to legally work and access health services, schools, and other social safety net services. Asylum seekers to the United States being forced to remain in Mexico by way of the MPP policy are also allowed to legally work according to Mexican policy. Mexican legislation "guarantees all children on Mexican soil the right to enroll in state schools, regardless of their immigration status and the fact that access to education is a fundamental human right" (UNHCR 2018b).

In addition to being signatory to the 1951 convention and 1967 Protocol on the Status of Refugees, Mexico adopted the broader refugee definition laid out in the Cartagena Declaration of 1984 to also include "persons who have fled their country because their lives, safety or freedom have been threatened by generalized violence, foreign aggression, internal conflicts, massive violation of human rights or other circumstances which have seriously disturbed public order" (Reed-Hurtado 2013). Mexico is the only country in Latin America whose executive branch has gone even further and adopted a regulatory framework in the form of the 2011 Law on Refugees, Complementary Protection, and Political Asylum to guide implementation of this broader definition (Reed-Hurtado 2013). The UNHCR also considers Mexico's 2015 establishment of the Special Unit for the Investigation of Crimes Against Migrant Persons with the Attorney General's Office (PGR) an important positive development for a more hospitable environment for migrants.

While the Mexican refugee agency COMAR lacks the funding and staffing needed to face the rising displacement figures, the head of COMAR, Andres Ramirez, spent twenty-eight years with the UNHCR prior to joining the administration of President Andrés Manuel López Obrador. It may be due to this experience that COMAR is collaborating with the UNHCR on one of the most innovative and effective refugee integration programs in the world.

For years COMAR and the UNHCR have been working to identify asylum seekers in the south of Mexico and relocate them to areas of higher economic activity, providing wraparound services to help stabilize families in new homes with access to services and enrolling children in school. The program has been an incredible success, with families moving into full employment in the formal sector, paying taxes, contributing to their new local economies, and having 100 percent full enrollment of school-age children.

Mexico is in many ways an ideal case in which the global impact investment community can invest to measurably improve the lives of millions of displaced people and the communities hosting them.

REFUGEE LENS INVESTING IN ACTION

As a critical first step to help catalyze investment, we conducted a refugee-focused market assessment to identify refugee lens investment opportunities in Mexico, high-impact investment opportunities that could become refugee lens investments (RLIs), and pathways by which investors could continue to identify future deal flows through accelerators and entrepreneurial support organizations. These investments would allow the companies to scale and support more refugees.

It is important to note that refugee lens impact investors have the power to encourage high-impact social enterprises and enterprises serving the poor and to become RLI opportunities through conditional impact investing, which is the offer of investment on certain conditions—in this case, on the company hiring or serving the displaced. In our market assessment research, we were looking for both refugee lens companies and those that could become RLIs with the right impact investing incentives.

The ultimate goal is to accelerate the growth of a robust entrepreneurial ecosystem that fosters new high-impact venture creation and scalability and the expansion of employment, workforce development, and skills matching, thus creating thousands of jobs, enriching the entrepreneurship ecosystem in Mexico, and reducing unemployment and displacement. The assessment methodology used here is meant to be holistic and provide results that can inform numerous investment and development approaches. We had a three-pronged approach:

- Identify high-potential sectors, geographies, and investment opportunities in Mexico that were ripe for investment
- Within these segments, further develop and prioritize high-potential, market-based "refugee investment opportunities" (defined later) with the highest likelihood of positively impacting the displaced through services, employment, or corporate leadership
- Assess the political, economic, and social enabling environment and identify any barriers to RLIs as well as strategies to overcome them

Our market assessment approach is a first of its kind that aims to support the development of entrepreneurial and investment ecosystems for inclusive growth. Because the goal of our work is to build thriving economies inclusive of the forcibly displaced, a traditional market assessment is insufficient. Market opportunities and available capital must be assessed through a system-of-systems approach—considering the intersection of entrepreneurial and investment ecosystems with national policy systems and the international humanitarian aid system.

Desk research and the RIN network were used to identify an original interviewee list. Snowball sampling was used in the field to identify additional investors, entrepreneurs, policymakers, academics, and humanitarian organizations supporting refugees and migrants. In all we interviewed 225 respondents as part of this research. The majority of interviews were in-person one-on-one and small-group interviews conducted during two months of fieldwork in Mexico in late 2019. Experts and participants in the Mexican investment and entrepreneurial ecosystems, as well as officials and aid organizations working on the front lines of the displacement crisis, shared their nuanced local knowledge of the current situation and solutions to move forward to unlock private capital in service of displaced communities.

In addition to in-depth interviews, we created a database of 114 start-ups supported by entrepreneurial support organizations such as Impact Hub Mexico, Ashoka, ANDE (Aspen Network of Development Entrepreneurs), Endeavor, and Sistema B (Latin America's B Corp network). This database has detailed information about each start-up, including investment type, location, potential refugee impact, and whether the investment would be targeted at the prevention, response, or integration stage. We also analyzed over 150 social enterprises pitched as part of the Unreasonable Mexico competitions to assess the potential "refugee use cases" for these companies' products and services.

Doing fieldwork is often a gift, and getting to taste the creations of incredible entrepreneur chefs is one of the highlights. We set off first through Mexico City, where we get the blue corn pizza topped with Oaxacan grasshoppers soaked in salt and lime. The place is Pixza, a cool spot in Mexico City's Roma Norte neighborhood. Go there for dinner and you might think it's just another delicious and original restaurant in a city that's famous for them. But there's more to it than the flavors and the atmosphere, which is why we're here.

Pixza, says its founder Alejandro Souza, is "a social empowerment platform disguised as a pizzeria that offers the world's first and only pizza made of blue corn with 100 percent Mexican ingredients." It's also part of Sistema B, the Latin American arm of the global B Corp movement, reflecting state-of-the-art standards in terms of social and environmental impact. How many restaurants have a director of impact? Pixza has expansion plans and is ripe for investment.

Everyone who works here, says Regina (the director of impact), is a vulnerable young adult, generally between the ages of seventeen and twenty-seven, who is at risk of being abandoned by society. From the waiters to the line cooks, they have struggled with homelessness, abandonment by their families, lack of formal education, drug abuse, and criminal records. Now some are migrants and refugees.

Cristian is a nineteen-year-old gay refugee who fled Honduras last year because his brother beat him and there were no jobs. He crossed into Mexico not far from Tapachula, received a humanitarian visa, and arrived in Mexico City, where he contacted UNHCR. An officer there put him in touch with INTRARE, a nonprofit that focuses on social and economic integration, and INTRARE introduced him to Pixza.

Mexico City is starting to feel like home, Cristian says, a place where he can establish a meaningful life free of violence and threats. He applied for asylum a year ago, hoping for permanent residency in Mexico, but COMAR is still processing those applications. "Why go to the United States if you can improve your life by being in Mexico?," he says. "Not everything is about money." He dreams of becoming an actor.

Like other Pixza employees, Cristian is not just slinging grasshopper pizzas but also engaging in a larger process that is much more holistic and transformative. Run by the restaurant, Agents of Change is a "multidimensional empowerment program" for employees that lasts eighteen months, involves four phases, and focuses on fully setting people up in their personal and professional lives.

Nor is Pixza alone. INTRARE was founded in 2018 by Hannah Töpler to bridge the gap between refugees and the companies wanting to hire them. It also vets the companies in terms of security and fair employment, constantly monitoring to avoid those just looking for cheap labor. At the same time, INTRARE provides mentoring and psychological support to help people like Cristian find their way in the city.

This is intensely personal, one-on-one work, with some twenty-five refugees helped so far, Hannah tells us. The staff currently work pro bono. Funding is from wherever they can find it: the German Development Agency (Hannah is a German citizen who came to Mexico City in 2017) or an auction held by a local artist. She is particularly proud of persuading AT&T to hire a relatively well-educated Honduran refugee who is now thriving at the company and making well over the average Mexican salary.

Before any of this can happen, however, someone just arriving needs a place to stay. CAFEMIN is one of the few places they can go. One day we pull up to its colorful brick building, covered in murals, on a side street in a residential neighborhood in the north of the city. We walk by radiant altars full of fruit, candles, and images—traditional offerings, known as *ofrendas*, for the Day of the Dead. A welcome sign promises shelter, protection, integration, and promotion. CAFEMIN is an acronym, in Spanish, that translates to Shelter for the Training and Empowerment of Migrant and Refugee Women.

Catholic nuns are in charge, as they are at many of the other twenty-plus shelters across Mexico that form a vital network for migrants, who trust the church more than any government or nonprofit. In recent years, these shelters have been strained far beyond their original capacity, at times laying out mattresses anywhere there's space and accommodating four times the number originally envisioned.

Every year CAFEMIN provides shelter to some four hundred female forced migrants, their children, and unaccompanied minors for short- to medium-term stays. It also runs a kitchen, bakery, and café where migrants can build skills for employment. A catering business with growth potential puts a little money back into the shelter. The larger network of which CAFEMIN is a part has started a shared intake form for migrants, respecting their time and focusing on their skills and assets. Many here are from Guatemala and Nicaragua.

Mexico City may be at the heart of much that is Mexican, but historically it was not on the migrant route north to the US border. Now, as the country becomes a key new destination for the displaced, the city is gradually growing a new infrastructure to support them, beginning with efforts like Pixza, INTRARE, and CAFEMIN.

No one knows how many of the estimated 3 million displaced people in Mexico are staying in the capital, but the number is likely to be substantial. With a population over 21 million and as one of the largest cities in the world, Mexico City is an economic powerhouse that accounts for a quarter of Mexico's entire GDP (~$500 billion) and produces 130,000 university graduates every year.

It's a city with millions of jobs, but also countless opportunities for entrepreneurs. Displaced entrepreneurs and founders are themselves leading companies here that employ and support other displaced people. They in turn need support to do this. There is already a burgeoning social entrepreneurial and impact investing ecosystem in CDMX. While we're in the city, we meet with over a dozen entrepreneurs, with roots all over the world, who are deeply committed to social justice.

At the center of the action is Impact Hub Mexico City, which is part of the global network of Impact Hubs and helps dozens of social entrepreneurs every year with coworking space, capacity-building trainings, and networking opportunities. Many of the companies it's creating serve at-risk populations through education, job training, STEM development, tech careers, access to clean water, access to healthcare, and more.

Direct investment in refugees and their businesses would be a natural fit here. Hola Code, founded in 2017 and led by a deportee displaced from the United States, is a living example. With its office just over a mile from Pixza, Hola Code is a social enterprise that offers five-month coding bootcamps for migrants that prepare them for work in the tech sector. The program costs nothing (and even provides a monthly stipend) until the graduate has secured a full-time job. Some four hundred Mexican and Central American migrants seeking refuge in Mexico apply every month. Employment rates for Hola Code graduates are over 90 percent.

There are other examples and similar possibilities in the growing tech hub of Guadalajara and in cities across the country. At the national level, the Mexican government expresses justifiable pride in its history of welcoming persecuted people from around the world by granting them political asylum or refugee status. A long history of diversity and openness, which should be much better known, is setting the stage for Mexico to be a model.

The current crisis that brings large numbers of Central Americans and now other migrants began in 2014, but it's far from the only time that Mexico has been an important host country. Russian dissidents fleeing the Soviet Union arrived beginning in the 1920s, most famously including Leon Trotsky, whose Mexico City home is today both a museum and an organization promoting the right to asylum. Spanish Republicans escaping Franco's Spain began coming in the late 1930s, and in the 1950s it was Guatemalans following the fall of democratically elected president Jacobo Arbenz. In the 1970s came those seeking asylum from dictatorships in Uruguay, Brazil, Chile, and Argentina. Soon after, there were more than forty thousand refugees from civil wars in El Salvador and Guatemala, with many returning voluntarily in the 1990s.

This remarkable history, worthy of celebration, has been matched by Mexico's commitments at a global level in addressing forced displacement. Mexico has signed the 1951 Convention Relating to the Status of Refugees and the 1967 Protocol, as well as the 1954 Convention Relating to the Status of Stateless Persons. It adopted the broader refugee definition laid out in the Cartagena Declaration of 1984. It is one of the leading states that is running with the Global Compact on Refugees at a regional level by developing a MIRPS that is among the most forward-thinking and welcoming to asylum seekers in the world. MIRPS stands for Marco Integral Regional Para la Proteccion y Saluciones—or the Comprehensive Regional Protection and Solutions Framework.

There is powerful national legislation as well, such as the 2011 Law on Refugees, Complementary Protection, and Political Asylum (UNHCR 2018c). Mexican legislation also guarantees all children on Mexican soil the right to enroll in state schools, regardless of their immigration status, and grants access to education as a fundamental human right (Government of Mexico 1917).

Crucially, as we've seen, those granted asylum in Mexico can work legally as well as access health services, schools, and other social safety net services. This is also true for those stranded here by the US "Remain in Mexico" policy. Mexico's Secretariat of Foreign Affairs (SRE) and a number of its business leaders realize that there is an opportunity to attract long-term strategic growth capital to the country by including the displaced in economic development projects. This is where RIN comes in.

In April 2019, working with Mexico's SRE, we convened a group of leading Mexican business leaders to explore a potential partnership that would promote investments supporting the implementation of the Mexican government's development priorities and that would leverage the collaborative power and resources of business, government, civil society, and displaced communities. This effort, which we formally announced at the Milken Global Conference as the Initiative for Inclusive Investment in Mexico (3IM), is a cross-sector, cross-border partnership, led by the RIN with support from the SRE and other partners, to attract long-term strategic growth capital for investments in Mexico through the inclusion of displaced people in economic development projects.

As a key first step to help catalyze investment, we expanded our field research to identify RLI opportunities in Mexico, seeking high-impact investment opportunities that could become RLIs. Our ultimate goal with 3IM was to accelerate the growth of a robust entrepreneurial ecosystem fostering new high-impact venture creation and scalability and to expand employment, workforce development, and skills matching, thus creating thousands of jobs, enriching the entrepreneurship ecosystem in Mexico, and reducing unemployment and displacement.

To drive investment dollars toward RLIs, we need to identify a baseline of local market investors. Impact investing and blended finance are growing the region. In 2023 ANDE interviewed ninety-two Latin American firms making impact investments across Latin America that collectively managed $3.4 billion in assets under management (AUM). The Latin America Venture Capital Association (LAVCA), on the other hand, reported a record high of $29.4 billion invested in the region in 2021 (LAVCA 2022). Of the firms included in ANDE's study, roughly 30 percent have active portfolio investments in Mexico.

Table 7.1 lists some of the companies we met with: impact investors, venture capital investors, and institutional investors located in Mexico and located abroad but investing in Mexico that are investing in high-impact sectors like financial inclusion, health, education, and agriculture. Every one of these companies could be incentivized to invest in ways that increase the

Table 7.1 A sample of Mexico-focused investors investing in impact-oriented companies, including refugee lens enterprises

o Promotora Social México	o VIWALA
o Adobe Capital	o Oikocredit (microlender)
o CO Capital (Tania Rodriguez)	o Concreces
o DILA Capital	o Jaguar Ventures
o Angel Ventures	o Fomento Social Banamex
o Redwood Ventures	o Salud Fácil
o ALL Venture Partners	o Amafore
o EcoEnterprises Fund	o Redwood
o FEMSA	o Rampa Evolution of H/F
o Financiera Sustentable de México (microlender)	o Sonen Capital
	o Village Capital
o El Buen Socio (socent lender)	o Root Capital
o SVX México (advisory)	o Kaya Impacto (advisory)

economic integration of the displaced when supported with identifying deal flow of companies that measurably improve the lives of the displaced. There are already hundreds of millions of dollars of impact-oriented investing being put to work in Mexico, providing a strong foundation to build on. In addition, with nonprofit support getting the displaced ready for work and investment (for refugee entrepreneurs), there is a ready and waiting investment community with which to partner.

Like major cities everywhere, Mexico City is a quintessential site for these efforts. Partly as a result of its diversity, the capital has strongly progressive human rights protections built into its legislation. In principle, migrants should be able to access any benefit offered by Mexico City authorities. There is even a law on *interculturalidad* (interculturalness) that explicitly creates a "big tent" for all the city's migrants, including Central Americans, "returnees" from the United States, and others.

The reality is more troubling. Everyone we talk to reports that migrants' access to labor, housing rights, education, health, and other social services is lacking. Part of the reason is clearly discrimination, but migrants also lack familiarity with key programs, and officials often demand paperwork that migrants don't have. Rural migrants from other parts of Mexico also face major barriers, but those from other countries are even less likely to get help and attention. A massive, complex city like this one can be liberating and catalyzing but also daunting, overwhelming, and profoundly alienating.

So much has been written about "the border," meaning the US-Mexico border, as if it were the only border in the area. In reality, the two countries are profoundly imbricated and interrelated at every level, with global flows of forced displacement passing with great complexity through both and with many patterns and directions of migration. One of Mexico's most dynamic industrial and commercial centers is just a three-plus-hour drive south of Texas: the greater Monterrey area and the city of Saltillo.

We have come to Saltillo, capital of the state of Coahuila, to visit a unique experiment, a program for refugees unlike any other in the world. For nearly a decade, COMAR and UNHCR have identified qualified asylum seekers in southern Mexico, especially Tapachula, and have brought them north for formal-sector jobs with access to schools and the health system. They call it the Relocation, Employment, and Local Integration Program, and it's a runaway success.

It is critical that the displaced must have access to some key factors before they can successfully integrate into their new communities and economies, and chief among those needs are housing, healthcare, and access to education and childcare for their families. Thankfully, a number of exemplary organizations are working on the front lines of the displacement crisis, working to provide these prerequisites for economic integration alongside the UNHCR.

Saltillo is where it started, but the model is now spreading to other UNHCR resettlement cities: Mexico City, Guadalajara, Monterrey, Puebla, and San Luis Potosi. In total, more than ten thousand refugees since 2016 have had the chance to start over in Mexico as entrepreneurs, managers, and factory workers through the program. And it's scaling up rapidly, with more than half of those having come to Saltillo in the last few years.

The staff at UNHCR's Saltillo office explain how the program works. While migrants come to poor and crowded entry ports like Tapachula, there are many more opportunities in northern manufacturing boomtowns like this one. UNHCR ushers families through the COMAR asylum process, helps secure their temporary residency paperwork, and relocates them.

It ensures that the families have housing in their new city, that their children are enrolled in school, and that they can access the wraparound services they need, including a year of psychosocial support.

Then UNHCR arranges one other critical component for successful integration: a formal-sector job with a major manufacturing company. In fact, the office works with a wide range of thirty-five different employers, which is crucial because the refugees in Saltillo come from diverse employment backgrounds, from having few skills to having recognized professional qualifications.

A hotel in downtown Saltillo is where people are brought first, partly because it's close to the Ministry of Health, where newly resettled refugees are immediately signed up for Seguro Popular, Mexico's public health insurance program. (Health is an immediate concern because most of the refugees come from Tapachula and points south and so have never experienced cold like that of northern Mexico.)

That's Monday. On Tuesday, there are legal services for those without status and a small employment fair. On Wednesday and Thursday, there are full-on job fairs, with guaranteed options. Friday is for exploring housing options and taking a workplace exam. Saturday and Sunday are set aside for activities with children. Refugees receive two weeks of support from UNHCR; by then, salaries are kicking in.

Our team heads to Palliser, a Canadian-owned furniture manufacturer that has been operating in Saltillo for over two decades and is one of the partnering employers. We visit the shop floor to meet some of the employees. Palliser has employed twenty-two refugees, though some have left to reunite with or visit family members elsewhere. The company provides training for a career at the factory and offers significant opportunities for promotion and advancement tied to job performance. This is skilled artisanal labor, requiring attention to detail. A Honduran worker who left home because of the gangs and the lack of opportunity says he is happy working at Palliser and living in Saltillo. He is focused on the task at hand, making a frame for a piece of a furniture.

Another key employer here is Mabe, a company founded in Mexico City nearly eighty years ago by two refugee entrepreneurs escaping the turmoil of post–civil war Spain. The firm is now one of the largest appliance makers in the world and has hired one hundred refugees and asylum seekers as part of the program.

One of them is Melvin from El Salvador. He, his wife Claudia, and their toddler son (a Mexican citizen) were in Tapachula for two years, where they saw the gang members threatening their lives and thus qualified for the relocation program. Our team meets them at their modest two-bedroom home on a quiet street in Saltillo. They have their own furniture, a TV, a well-stocked kitchen, and a place behind the house where they can wash and dry laundry—all achieved in a year. They are extremely happy, they say, to be living in Saltillo and working at Mabe, since stability (not the American Dream) is what they were searching for.

Around 85 percent of program participants stay in the city they relocate to, putting down roots with their families. Some, like the Salvadoran cab driver Alberto Rivas who worked and saved and now has a small fleet, create their own businesses. All pay taxes, contribute to their new local economies, and enroll their school-age children at an unbelievable 100 percent rate. Ten percent move to other cities in Mexico, while only a small remaining number go to the United States or elsewhere. Something deeply right is happening here.

Just in terms of the payroll taxes the migrants pay, the program is bringing in more money than the Mexican government spends every year on COMAR. UNHCR foots the bill, and it can be intensive and expensive to match migrants' skills with companies' needs on a one-by-one basis. While Mabe may be one of the most innovative and effective refugee integration programs in the world, it needs sustained funding to continue and grow. Better yet, private investment could build on its success, helping the displaced access capital, banking, affordable housing, and further employment opportunities.

The need is only increasing. It's still only a small percentage of refugees entering Mexico who apply for asylum in the country, but US policy under the Trump administration has changed things. Suddenly the United States has ramped up border patrol, cracked down on border crossing, and essentially frozen the refugee and asylum process. In 2018, the Department of Justice and the Department of Homeland Security launched their "zero tolerance" policy, "increasing misdemeanor illegal entry prosecutions across the entire southwest border" (Buchanan et al. 2021). Thousands of children were taken from their parents at the border, while Customs and Border Patrol (CBP) knew it lacked the ability to track, let alone reunite, children with their parents. In June a federal court deemed the policy illegal and ruled that the practice of family separations "shocks the conscience" and violates the constitutional right to family integrity (Buchanan et al. 2021). At the beginning of 2021 there were still over six hundred children who were not reunited with their families after years of separation (Hesson and Holland 2021). Experts say the trauma inflicted by the family separation policy will have negative ramifications for years, if not the entire lives of the children and their families. Many speculate that the brutality of this policy may have also increased the number of refugees seeking asylum in Mexico. Divesting from the border, including all the companies that benefit from it, may be an important strategy to fight this militarization, but the fight will be a long one.

In the other direction, the United States is now deporting, on average, some 200,000 Mexican citizens found to be in the United States irregularly. Many have lived nearly their entire lives as Americans, have grown up completely American, and barely know Mexico. In certain respects, deportation turns them into refugees facing social, linguistic, and other barriers as they enter Mexico from the north.

Some, like the deported veteran Daniel Ruiz, are defying the odds and dramatically reinventing themselves. Brought to the United States as a baby and deported at twenty-two on marijuana charges because he wasn't a citizen, Ruiz found his way to working in a call center and ultimately managed to open his own center. He now employs hundreds, including many fellow deportees, through several enterprises including his venture, EZ Call Center.

Tijuana, where Ruiz settled, is an economic hot spot full of entrepreneurs and with deep links to neighboring San Diego; it is one of the most populated border regions on the planet. Yet the city is also a place of desperation and displacement. Putting those thoughts together, Ruiz opened a place right at the border for both migrants and deportees to stop by and use free phones and computers. Soon he was putting in bathrooms, showers, and lockers, as well as giving out clothing and food. He started a business that makes promotional items while also providing professional training. He plows profits back into Deportados Unidos de México (United Deportees of Mexico), a nonprofit he started for people who are facing what he faced—"to put an end," he says, "to the suffering of being deported."

But again, this is a good example of where business and entrepreneurs are also working alongside civil society organizations. Otros Dreams en Acción (ODA), for example, is a nonprofit organization dedicated to mutual support and political action for and by those who grew up in the United States and now find themselves in Mexico due to deportation, the deportation of a family member, or the threat of deportation. When the United States deports citizens born in Mexico, it often drops them off on the Mexican side of the border, with no resources, no contacts, and no paperwork. Thus the thousands of people brought to the United States as children and deported as adults lack basic paperwork like birth certificates, identity cards, and tax identification, which makes it difficult to secure housing, employment, bank accounts, and more. ODA supports recently deported individuals, helping them navigate the complex Mexican bureaucratic process to secure the paperwork needed to begin building a life in Mexico. Their work is an essential bridge to bring people closer to economic integration.

Similarly, back in Mexico City, we met with CAFEMIN (mentioned earlier), a nonprofit shelter run by Catholic nuns. In addition to providing food and shelter to female forced migrants, their children, and unaccompanied minors for short to medium stays, it is also creating opportunities for the displaced to build their skill sets while in Mexico City. CAFEMIN runs a bakery café where the women can learn how to bake breads and pastries and the various aspects of running a small business. In addition, it has a catering arm that provides more opportunities for job training, skill building, and confidence building. The staff of CAFEMIN tell us that many of the migrants they meet are from agriculture backgrounds and the skills they gain through CAFEMIN's bakery café and catering operation are transferable to wherever they ultimately settle. CAFEMIN is just one of dozens of shelters providing housing throughout Mexico on the migrant route. The more opportunities shelters can create for skill building during migrants' stay, the better.

Further east, we also find clever innovation taking root in the Yucatán. The Government of the City of Mérida may perhaps be one of the most progressive municipal governments in the world when it comes to planning for the incorporation of migrants and the displaced. Mérida, the capital of the Mexican state of the Yucatán, had a population of just over 1 million in 2020 and the population continues to grow, with predictions that it may be at 2 million by 2030. It is popular with expats and migrants drawn by the rich Mayan history, culture, beauty, weather, and security (it has registered as one of the safest cities in North America); the population of non-Yucatecans topped seventy thousand in 2020 (*Yucatán Magazine* 2019). Developers and local officials have been working to further revise state and local policy to draw more real estate investment (*Yucatan Times* 2019). In addition to expats and internal migrants from other parts of Mexico, the region is starting to see more refugees from Honduras, Venezuela, and Guatemala. The City of Mérida has developed a plan to help direct those migrants toward services and jobs, proactively preparing before a large displacement event rather than reacting to a crisis once it arrives.

Although the scale of displacement is large in Mexico, there are nonprofits, local government bodies, and national and international collaborations proactively working to economically integrate the displaced. With this social infrastructure support, refugees in Mexico are better able to take advantage of their right to work and offers of employment by the private sector, and they are also in a better position to start businesses.

Throughout the country, we discovered active RLI opportunities (R1 through R5; see chapter 3) as well as social enterprises serving low-income Mexican citizens that could easily transition to become displaced-serving companies if refugee lens impact investors provided conditional investments. A number of growth sectors and investment themes emerged as promising, including technology, affordable housing, financial services and banking, and sustainable fisheries, agriculture, and forestry. RLI could be the carrot to incentivize companies to broaden their employee, borrower, and customer base.

We found several companies in Mexico that focused on preventing displacement, assisting refugees during emergencies, and supporting displaced people in long-term economic and social integration. One example of an indigenous-owned and displacement-preventing company is the R1 venture Ejido Verde, introduced in chapter 3.

As a purpose-driven, triple-bottom-line company, Ejido Verde's regenerative agroforestry model provides environmentally beneficial solutions—in this case, sustainably harvested pine resin—while creating transformative wealth for rural and indigenous, autonomous, landowning communities (known as *ejidos*). Their model ensures that low-income forest community producers capture most of the wealth creation for the harvest processing and scale of resin products, as well as maintain ownership of the land, which prevents displacement of these indigenous communities. When we interviewed Ejido Verde, its CEO, Shawn Paul, shared that it had secured financing from the Inter-American Development Bank fund IDB Invest and was positioning for an additional capital raise from Mexico's growing impact investing community.

Or consider Échale, a well-established affordable housing social enterprise that helps people living in poverty to become owners of their own homes or helps them to renovate and improve the ones they have to achieve a decent and safe standard.

It has worked to rebuild communities of internally displaced Mexicans and internally displaced indigenous communities, initially following the devastation of regional earthquakes and disasters. With a long and successful track record of raising philanthropic dollars and providing microloans to families to build their homes, it was launching a for-profit lending facility to take on private-sector capital and expand its reach.

But refugee lens companies aren't always so obvious in their impact. As we were traveling near Tijuana, we found ourselves at a gas station that was wrapped in fresh hot pink paint and displayed a logo of three professional and confident female cartoon characters. We noticed that all of the employees at the station were women. We learned later that Rendichicas employs a 98 percent female workforce, many of whom are migrants or are displaced, while simultaneously creating a safer gas station experience for female customers. In a country where gender-based violence is a significant problem, this business model, even though it is a petrol station, makes a compelling case as an impact investment.

We identified scores of companies that were solving real challenges across the country; some were clearly serving vulnerable communities, while others had innovations that had real potential to do so. Of the 114 high-impact social enterprises that we analyzed that were supported by entrepreneurial support organizations such as Impact Hub Mexico, Ashoka, ANDE, Endeavor, and Sistema B, we found that 66 percent of the companies had "refugee use cases"; that is, refugees, IDPs, deportees, and migrants could directly benefit from their products and services or could be incorporated into their labor forces given the right incentives. We also analyzed over 150 social enterprises pitched as part of the Unreasonable Mexico competitions to assess the potential "refugee use cases" for these companies' products and services. Nearly 100 percent of the social enterprise concepts and companies could measurably improve the lives of the forcibly displaced or become displaced-hiring firms if provided the correct incentives by refugee lens impact investors.

Regional Entrepreneurial Ecosystem Highlight: Mexico City (CDMX)

We did fieldwork in the geographies with the most promise for impact investment: Mexico City, Guadalajara, Monterrey, Tijuana and Mérida, and the Yucatán Peninsula. The first three are the three largest cities in Mexico, Tijuana is the sixth-largest city but an important economic engine on the border and a continuation of metro San Diego in California, and Mérida is the safest city in Mexico and voted one of the safest cities in the Americas. Security is a concern for investors looking to invest in Mexico. The US State Department prohibits travel for its employees to the states of Colima, Guerrero, Michoacán, Sinaloa, and Tamaulipas due to crime and kidnapping and advises caution when traveling to a dozen other states (US Department of State 2019).

Mexico City's metropolitan area, with a population of around 23 million, accounts for about 22 percent (or roughly a quarter) of Mexico's national GDP, estimated at $401 billion in recent data (Wikipedia 2026). The city is a major hub for education, with universities contributing to Mexico's nationwide output of 130,000 engineers and technicians annually (Egusa 2018). It has been the regional seat of power since its founding as the Aztec capital of Tenochtitlan in 1325, with temples razed by the Spanish conquistadors now lying beneath its historic center.

Being the largest city in Mexico, this economic engine not only means millions of jobs, but also opportunities for entrepreneurs. Just like entrepreneurs everywhere, refugee entrepreneurs and founders who are leading companies that can hire and support the displaced can benefit from entrepreneurial support organizations. There is a growing social entrepreneurial and impact investing ecosystem in CDMX. First, Impact Hub Mexico City, part of the global network of Impact Hubs, hosts dozens of social entrepreneurs every year with coworking space, providing capacity-building trainings and network opportunities. Many of these companies are serving at-risk populations in the fields of education, job training, STEM development, tech careers, access to clean water, access to healthcare, and more.

We met with over a dozen entrepreneurs, many non-Mexican nationals that were committed to measurably improving the lives of the poor. Most of their companies could easily pivot to serving the displaced and develop into an RLI. Unreasonable Mexico and the network of campuses of Tec de Monterrey work to seed and support new social enterprises throughout Mexico. ANDE and Endeavor Mexico and Latin America help scale social enterprises and take them to the next level, creating more high-quality jobs and more impact. Another network supporting the social business community is Sistema B, the Latin American arm of the global B Corp movement. This network helps highlight socially and environmentally mission-driven companies to international clients and investors.

Regional Entrepreneurial Ecosystem Highlight: Guadalajara, Jalisco

With more than 4.7 million residents, metro Guadalajara is the second-largest city in Mexico and is now known as Mexico's "Silicon Valley." Motorola opened manufacturing operations in 1968, followed by IBM, HP, Intel, Oracle, Toshiba, Amazon, and many more. There are now over seven hundred electronics manufacturing and information technology companies throughout the state of Jalisco that combine to make the tech sector the largest area of activity for Jalisco's economy, constituting over 60 percent of the state's trade exports (StartupBlink 2016).

Jalisco benefits from a well-educated population. Sixteen technology institutes and twelve universities graduate more than eight thousand technical and engineering students every year (StartupBlink 2018). There are over thirty tech-related communities "holding educational and networking events each week just for the sake of sharing best practices and success cases—that alone has helped to inspire, educate and connect more people to work together and efficiently and then give back to the new entrants" (StartupBlink 2018). iTuesday and Makers GDL hold monthly meetings and have hundreds of participants and thousands of followers. There are also a number of incubators and accelerators in Guadalajara:

- Tec Lean Accelerator—Run by one of the top private universities in Latin America, Tec de Monterrey, this incubator helps start-ups develop their business plan and financials.
- Ashoka, Changemaker Hub—Started in 2011, and also run by Tec de Monterrey, the Changemaker Hub runs cohorts every year and focuses on strengthening the impact models of social entrepreneurs.
- Reto Zapopan—One of the largest accelerators in the city. Managed by the municipality of Zapopan (a city that essentially merges with Guadalajara), it offers office space, mentoring, and access to funds.
- HF Coop MX—More than an incubator, this is a cooperative of start-ups combined with world-class mentors, office spaces for start-ups, and support for international growth. It is the first HF incubator out of Silicon Valley.

All of these provide clear pathways for impact investors interested in RLI to monitor new companies and identify opportunities. These entrepreneurial support organizations provide a strong support network for displaced entrepreneurs, especially those with higher levels of educational background like many of the refugees from Venezuela.

In addition to the entrepreneurial communities, incubators, accelerators, and top universities, policymakers are also supportive of Guadalajara's tech boom. Jalisco was the first Latin American state government to create a Department of Science and Innovation, and one of the first ministries to have a designated directorate on social innovation.

Bismarck Lepe, a Mexican American, Stanford-trained serial entrepreneur, grew his first company in Guadalajara and sold it to an Australian telecoms giant for $410 million. He started a second, Wizeline, as well as StartupGDL, with the goal of importing great ideas from Silicon Valley while growing top-notch jobs for Guadalajara-based developers. "You're starting to get the second or third generation of technologists who have experience build[ing] scalable products," he says. "And it's not only the talented people that are there, but the ones we can attract to live there" (Selee 2018). Wizeline now has employees from Egypt, France, Ecuador, Colombia, China, New Zealand, and the United States working at its Guadalajara offices . These home-grown tech companies could offer high-paying jobs for displaced individuals who know how to code or have access to software development training companies. The bilingual community of "deportees" could especially benefit from the tech boom in the Guadalajara ecosystem.

Lastly, the Guadalajara tech ecosystem presents numerous examples of fintech, edtech, and other solutions that could expand its customer base to proactively serve the displaced.

Consider, for example Yotepresto, a marketplace lending platform that connects individuals and institutional investors to borrowers applying for a personal loan. This platform democratizes access to capital and could measurably improve the lives of refugees who are seeking working capital to rebuild their livelihoods. The local venture capital fund Redwood and the international impact investing firm Village Capital have both invested in Yotepresto to achieve financial return along with social impact.

The main goal of our work in Mexico was to map its entrepreneurial and investment ecosystems through the lens of refugee empowerment, refugee entrepreneurship, and refugee employment. Our research has shown that there are several promising pathways for impact investors that want to invest with a refugee lens. Investing in refugee entrepreneurs, investing in companies that are measurably improving the lives of the displaced, and investing in firms that are proactively hiring refugees are all routes by which-private sector actors can help the displaced integrate into their new communities and dramatically improve their lives. The groundbreaking economic integration program being run by the Government of Mexico via the refugee agency COMAR, in partnership with UNHCR, has shown the power of private-sector engagement in the global refugee crisis. Since 2016, tens of thousands of refugees have started over in Mexico as entrepreneurs, managers, and factory workers through the program (USA for UNHCR 2021).

Former Reuters correspondent and UNHCR global website editor Tim Gaynor notes: "In Saltillo, a manufacturing boomtown in northern Mexico, Salvadoran cab driver Alberto Rivas saw an opportunity. He bought a taxi and worked long hours to shuttle residents around the city where factories and assembly plants make everything from trucks, cars and auto parts to home appliances and furniture. Drawing on his savings, he then bought two more cars and now employs drivers from Mexico and Central America to work around the clock. 'There are great opportunities here if you are hard-working, enterprising and want to do things the right way,' says Alberto, a refugee who was driven to flee his home country" (Gaynor 2021). This Salvadoran refugee entrepreneur started a company, created jobs, and established a solid financial footing for himself and his wife and children.

This type of economic integration is the critical first step to rebuilding a sense of belonging. Aid organizations and refugee lens investors have a role to play in helping the displaced access capital, banking, and affordable housing and identify employment opportunities.

8

EAST AFRICA

A Refugee Investing Success Story in the Making

Over one third of all forcibly displaced people are concentrated in sub-Saharan Africa. When Christine was doing fieldwork in the late 2000s in East Africa, there were already nearly 10 million displaced. The hot spots were the conflict in Somalia, which drove refugees into Kenya; the violence of the Lord's Resistance Army (LRA), which drove massive internal displacement in Uganda; and the ongoing conflict in Sudan, which is driving internal and cross-border displacement. While we have continued our research, writing, and advocacy over the past decade, the number of displaced individuals has skyrocketed in this region to now over 44 million people due to ongoing crises in the Democratic Republic of Congo, Nigeria, Mali, Somalia, and South Sudan. The situation has been further exacerbated by violent conflicts erupting in Ethiopia, Mozambique, Burkina Faso, and Niger. These challenges have turned the displacement crisis in Africa into a deepening and widening tragedy that affects at least thirty-seven of the fifty-five countries on the continent. Africa hosts three quarters of all new internal displacements (Mbiyozo 2023).

Natural disasters and disputes over resources like water and land have exacerbated the immense humanitarian crisis. In recognition of the magnitude of the problem, the African Union declared 2019 as the Year of Refugees, Returnees, and Internally Displaced Persons. The urgent call for durable solutions to forced displacement resonated throughout the continent. In the Greater Horn of Africa, a series of destabilizing social and climatic shocks have forced millions of people to leave their homes. Despite having four of the world's fastest-growing economies, the region is plagued by socioeconomic disparity and increasing hardships. The devastating impact of the COVID-19 pandemic and recent outbreaks of violent conflicts in Ethiopia and Mozambique, along with persistent droughts, floods, famines, and locust infestations, have further complicated the already tragic conditions faced by the long-term displaced.

The dozens of protracted crises on the continent urgently require a new approach that focuses on investing and incentivizing the quick and smooth integration of refugees into the new economies in which they find themselves. Luckily, a number of forward-thinking entrepreneurs and investors are leading the way. We had the opportunity to travel to Nairobi, Kenya, in the fall of 2022 (this time with our five-year-old in tow) to attend the world's first global Refugee Lens Investing Summit. Co-organized by the Refugee Investment Network (RIN) and Acumen, the summit convened one hundred key stakeholders from sixty-eight organizations representing the emerging refugee lens ecosystem in East Africa, including representatives from social enterprises, impact investors, philanthropic foundations, donor governments, and humanitarian and technical experts. Roughly a third of the attendees were representatives from refugee lens investment (RLI) businesses, 40 percent were investors or funders, and the rest were from ecosystem organizations.

It was inspirational to hear investment pitches from companies that were building scalable business models that are tackling displacement, from agribusinesses that were providing farmers with quality seeds in Ethiopia, and from edtech and fintech companies that were lowering the barrier of entry for the forcibly displaced. It was also remarkable to hear from forward-thinking foundations and bilateral development agencies like the IKEA Foundation, the Hilton Foundation, and the Swiss Development Cooperation, which are moving the needle on how we think about responding to the global displacement crisis. Lastly, we felt we needed to pinch ourselves because the movement had come a long way since the World Humanitarian Summit in 2016, when this was all just an idea. Now a global summit on refugee lens investing was being convened, and during coffee breaks microfinance professionals were saying how they had traveled through multiple counties to learn the latest developments in refugee lens investing from some of the world's leading organizations in impact investing!

Acumen, a global nonprofit that was founded by the University of Virginia alumna Jacqueline Novogratz in 2001, is changing the way the world tackles poverty by investing in sustainable businesses, leaders, and ideas. The organization's mission is to use the power of entrepreneurship to build a world in which everyone has the opportunity to live with dignity. Novogratz's concept of "patient capital," which was shared with the world through one of the most-watched TED talks, was a new middle way between the zero returns from philanthropic giving and the expectations of outsized returns seen in traditional investing. Patient capital investments are investments made in social impact companies with the patience and support to help those companies succeed, scale, and magnify their impact.

Over the past two decades, Acumen has raised hundreds of millions of dollars in philanthropic capital and invested it in early-stage companies whose products and services enable the poor to transform their lives. It launched Acumen Academy to build the capacity of social entrepreneurs. After building out a proven model, Acumen was able to also launch Acumen Capital Partners, a for-profit subsidiary of the nonprofit Acumen that allows impact investing funds that are seeking a return alongside their impact. This subsidiary makes investments to scale catalytic companies that are solving the problems of poverty. Acumen has been able to mobilize hundreds of millions more in impact capital through this for-profit vehicle.

Acumen Accelerators is a network of investment accelerators that support entrepreneurs and early-stage start-ups through a combination of education, mentoring, networking, and investing. Acumen has many types of accelerators designed to address specific issues and geographical regions: Pakistan Agriculture, Green Growth Accelerator, Gender Equity and Advancement Accelerator, and more. These accelerators help to refine business models, accelerate social impact, gain feedback from peers and Acumen staff, and build relationships with like-minded social innovators. In 2022 Acumen launched its Accelerator for Ventures Serving Displaced People to refine and develop scalable business models that advance sustainable livelihoods for forcibly displaced populations in East Africa. Fourteen teams from East Africa were selected for Acumen Academy's accelerator; collectively, they employed 819 people and worked with 86,000 Forcibly Displaced Persons (75 percent of which are women) and 38,500 host community members (of which around 71 percent are women) across Kenya, Uganda, and Ethiopia.

In October 2023, Joy Gikandi, the program lead at Acumen Academy East Africa, helped showcase the work of some of the entrepreneurs in Acumen's refugee accelerator, such as Patapia, whose goal is to inspire and empower refugees to achieve economic independence. Patapia offers a unique combination of training, mentoring, access to the right resources, and financial services to make refugees more resilient and inspire them to create their own businesses. Aime Rebecca, the CEO of Patapia, said, "We designed Patapia so that refugees can access financing without collateral, and by becoming a bank for the unbanked, Patapia is creating a first step for the future. We dream of creating a world where refugees are self-sustainable, and together, we can get there" (YGC Recoupling Awards 2022).

William Tinyefuza, the cofounder and COO of Turaco Valley Foods, shared the founding story of his company, a social enterprise focused on investing in smallholder farmers within refugee-hosting areas to strengthen their ability to improve productivity and income. The company provides free mobile agro-advisory services, distributes key agro-inputs, and demonstrates best agronomics practices on its own farm. Turaco ensures that 70 percent of its raw materials come directly from refugee farmers and 30 percent come from host communities, and it purchases them at 5 to 10 percent above the market rate.

Pelerė Group Limited is another social enterprise company that supports displaced communities in the agricultural sector. Pelerė manufactures and sells organic cosmetic and personal care products made from Shea nuts and provides training and employment to forcibly displaced persons who act as product suppliers (Acumen Academy 2022). Employees receive training in growing raw materials as well as instruction in producing the final products sold to consumers. Sandra Letio, the managing director and founder, says that "sharing a cohort with others who have dedicated their life's work to supporting refugees and their host communities has been highly significant." While witnessing her colleagues' triumphs and hearing their ideas, Sandra was able to soak up valuable new information, improve her business skill set, and ultimately work through her own learning curves (Acumen Academy 2022).

Many of these entrepreneurs work to empower other entrepreneurs as a strategy to promote self-reliance among refugees. Kakuma Ventures is a platform that supports African refugees in becoming entrepreneurs who manage WiFi hot spots in the Kakuma Refugee Camp. Kakuma is in the northwest of Kenya and was originally founded in 1992 to house the "lost boys of Sudan." As conflicts have changed, different populations have fled to Kakuma for safety, and today over 280,000 refugees reside there, hailing from South Sudan, Somalia, Ethiopia, and the Democratic Republic of Congo.

The company's goal is to bring solar-powered Internet access to one of the world's largest refugee camps. Innocent Tshilombo, the cofounder and managing director, explains that "Kakuma Ventures provides cheap internet, which allows customers to save up to 70 percent of their costs. We've been able to connect more than 1,500 people to the Internet" (Ashden 2022). It has also educated over four hundred students and trained more than sixty young people in computing and solar engineering skills. Its business model is scalable and sustainable: "Entrepreneurs buy a solar home system and WiFi equipment on credit from the organization, then sell internet subscriptions to their neighbors. Money from these subscriptions is held by Kakuma Ventures to pay off the cost of the equipment after which the subscriptions generate an income for the entrepreneur. The organization has also recently launched a digital listing platform for businesses based in the camp, allowing them to trade online" (Ashden 2022).

In addition to celebrating, networking, and connecting these types of refugee lens companies with investors, the Refuge Lens Investing Summit was also aimed at changing the negative narrative promoted by antirefugee politicians. This type of rhetoric is found all over the world: If there is a nation hosting the displaced, there is always a contingent of politically motivated government officials and candidates disparaging the migrants. Part of the RIN's and the summit's mandate was to hold up the stories of displaced entrepreneurs as value makers and job creators.

Another goal was to build the field of refugee lens investing and raise awareness of opportunities and "hope spots" from the global participants in the joint RLI project. One major initiative is RIN's partnership with Economist Impact (part of the *Economist* magazine family), called the Refugee Opportunity Index (ROI). The aim of this initiative is to measure the extent to which a country's policy environment enables access to economic opportunities for refugees and forced migrants. This index compares policies on refugees across ten countries in East Africa (Ethiopia, Kenya, and Uganda) and Latin America and the Caribbean (Belize, Colombia, Chile, Costa Rica, the Dominican Republic, Ecuador, and Peru) against a set of forty-five qualitative and quantitative indicators organized into three categories—(1) admission, integration, and resettlement; (2) basic rights and access to services; and (3) employment conditions)—and thirteen subcategories (Economist Impact 2023). The goal of the ROI is twofold: "1. To equip policymakers with actionable and relevant data to identify pathways for improvement in refugee policies and programs; and 2. To inform private sector stakeholders—and investors in particular—about opportunities and constraints that refugees face to incentivize investments in refugee value chains and refugees as entrepreneurs" (Economist Impact 2023). The ROI explores how countries are developing an inclusive enabling environment for refugees to reach their full economic potential through legislation, policies, programs, and practices.

The ROI assigns equal weight to all categories and subcategories. Within the subcategories, more weight is applied to indicators that assess the de facto environment than those that assess the de jure environment. The information for de facto indicators is obtained through interviews with stakeholders in each country. This attention to the difference between de jure and de facto is a critically important innovation and evolution. Academic work has looked at the rules on the books, but often even if policies are in place, they are not being implemented on the ground due to a lack of capacity, will, or both.

In the first ROI report, which was focused on Latin America and the Caribbean, the *Economist* team found the following:

- Government action is most evident in providing basic rights and access to services for refugees and other displaced persons.
- All countries in the index strongly support entrepreneurship, and most offer good job-seeking support. However, country performance varies greatly depending on employment conditions for refugees.
- Across the Latin American region, nonrefugee displaced persons suffer from greater restrictions on their rights and freedoms. Many policies, programs, and legislative arrangements are limited to those with official refugee status.
- Because governments in the region do not regularly collect and publish data on the economic status of refugees, they do not always tailor policies to the specific needs of these groups.
- Bureaucratic and discriminatory practices hinder refugees and displaced persons from meeting their economic potential.

The Refugee Lens Investing Summit in Nairobi gave participants a glimpse into the indicators for Ethiopia, Kenya, and Uganda. As with many places in the world, the policies on the books don't always match the reality on the ground.

We now make a deep dive into the challenges and opportunities the displaced face in one East African country, Uganda, which in 2025 was hosting the highest number of refugees in Africa. Uganda has some of the most progressive displacement policies in the world. Since the neutralization of the LRA in 2017, most of the 1.5 million people internally displaced have been able to return home. However, Uganda struggles with the capacity to serve the 1.9 million refugees from South Sudan, the Democratic Republic of the Congo, Somalia, Eritrea, and Burundi, among others.

UGANDA AS A POLICY MODEL

Uganda is particularly well positioned to be a success story when it comes to policy and strategies that facilitate the inclusion of the displaced. It has a long history with displacement. The story dates back to the aftermath of World War II, when thousands of Europeans displaced by the war found a new home in the Ugandan Protectorate during British colonial rule. The settlement of Polish refugees marked the beginning of Uganda's longstanding commitment to addressing the refugee issue. In 1955, the country welcomed approximately seventy-eight thousand Sudanese refugees fleeing civil conflict.

Over the years, waves of refugees from Congo and Rwanda sought sanctuary in Uganda, primarily in the western regions (Hovil 2018). The establishment of the Nakivale settlement in the district of Isingiro marked the creation of the country's first government-run refugee settlement. Refugees from neighboring territories who were uprooted by unrest and struggles for independence also sought refuge in Uganda. Sudanese refugees fleeing violence in the 1950s, Mau Mau rebels escaping British persecution in Kenya, and Tutsi refugees seeking safety from political turmoil in Rwanda all found temporary shelter within Uganda's borders (Ahimbisibwe 2018).

During the postindependence era, Uganda's approach to forced displacement was characterized by government-controlled settlements along the northern border regions and in the southwest of the country. A policy aimed at self-reliance for refugees, a concept established during the colonial era, was continued by Uganda's independent government and still exists today. The political landscape shifted dramatically in Uganda with the overthrow of Idi Amin's dictatorship in 1979 and the subsequent years of instability. Civil wars, internal conflicts, and human rights abuses further exacerbated the displacement crisis (IRRI 2018). It wasn't until the early 1990s that Uganda began to embrace a more progressive approach to refugee management. In 1999, the government of Uganda and the United Nations High Commissioner for Refugees (UNHCR) worked together to create an official "self-reliance strategy." Some of the key elements of this policy included the allocation of land to refugee settlements for the purposes of enabling refugees to become self-sufficient in food production, relatively free access to healthcare and education for refugees, and the openness of the local communities (Government of Uganda and UNHCR 2004). The generous and welcoming attitude of the Ugandan people toward refugees is certainly related to the fact that many Ugandans themselves had, at one time or another, experienced displacement, as well as the fact that refugees and Ugandan communities had similar cultural practices. But while this policy may seem easy enough in practice, it unfortunately came up rather short on its goals: The land that was granted to refugees was insufficient for farming needs while simultaneously reducing their food rations. The host communities themselves also received no benefit from creating and maintaining these settlements (Hovil 2018). Ultimately, the policy hurt both groups.

In 2006, Uganda passed the groundbreaking Refugee Act, which gained international attention for its inclusive and forward-thinking policies. The act grants refugees various rights, including the right to own property, engage in economic activities, and seek employment. It emphasizes social welfare and local integration, aiming to empower refugees and enable their active participation in society. It grants relative freedom of movement and the right to seek employment and also provides prima facie asylum for refugees as well as a parcel of land to each refugee family for their own agricultural use (World Bank Group 2016). A brief summary of the act indeed presents a progressive policy:

1. The right to own and dispose of movable property and to lease or sublease immovable property
2. The right to engage in agriculture, industry, and business; to practice one's profession; and to access formal and informal employment opportunities
3. The right to economic, social, and cultural benefits, including access to elementary education, protection of intellectual property rights (e.g., copyright protection for musicians and artists), and the issuance of a United Nations convention travel document for the purpose of travel outside Uganda
4. Entitlement to receive fair and just treatment, without discrimination
5. The right to seek asylum and not be refouled
6. Freedom of movement, subject to "reasonable restrictions" on the grounds of national security or public order
7. The right of freedom of association, although this is limited to nonpolitical associations, nonprofit associations, and trade unions

8. The principle of family unity
9. The entitlement of East African Community (EAC) nationals as asylum seekers to all the rights and privileges normally enjoyed by other EAC citizens as conferred by the EAC treaty of cooperation and its protocols
10. The provision of registration and identification and travel documents to refugees

Uganda's self-reliance model can be traced back to its colonial origins yet has played a consistent and convenient function in both Ugandan politics and international relations, affording legitimacy to Uganda's political leaders for generations (Betts 2021). In one study, a comparative analysis of Uganda and neighboring Kenya, researchers found four major advantages to Uganda's regulatory framework and refugee self-reliance model: Uganda's policy affords refugees greater mobility, lower transaction costs for economic activity, higher incomes, and more sustainable sources of employment than in Kenya (Betts et al. 2019). The same report, however, also shines a light on the practical deficiencies of the act, including the insufficient allocation of land to refugees in Uganda's rural settlements, inadequate access to education, and the plight of Uganda's urban refugees caused by weak assistance programs. Notwithstanding its limits and faults, Uganda's "open-door" policy holds strong promise for RLI as a new strategy that will spur economic growth and socioeconomic integration. Today, Uganda ranks among the top three refugee hosting countries in the world and is the leading refugee hosting country in Africa. Over 1.5 million refugees are spread out in a dozen national settlements, in rural communities and periurban settings in the capital, Kampala, and in smaller cities across the country.

In addition, Uganda has one of the most well-articulated and progressive internal displacement policies in the world. Uganda's

National Policy for Internally Displaced Persons was adopted in 2004 and was primarily driven by a need to address the displacement occurring as a result of the conflict between the Ugandan government and the LRA. This conflict began in 1988 but began driving large-scale displacement in 1996 when the government forced people to move into camps as part of its protective policies. Over 1.8 million people in Uganda were displaced as a result of the violence.

The internally displaced persons (IDP) policy draws heavily on UNHCR's Guiding Principles on Internal Displacement. It also commits the government to protecting citizens against internal displacement for arbitrary reasons; promoting durable solutions; facilitating IDPs' voluntary return, resettlement, and reintegration; and making sure that the population is aware of the policy.

LEVERAGING DISPLACEMENT-FRIENDLY LAWS TO GROW REFUGEE LENS INVESTING OPPORTUNITIES

We and the RIN worked with Uganda-based Open Capital (OCA), one of Africa's top management consulting and financial advisory firms, to conduct extensive research on the refugee lens investing opportunities in Uganda. This effort included teaming up with on-the-ground experts to conduct both primary and secondary data collection that involved a robust review of literature, dozens of background interviews, and focused interviews across key identified groups, field visits, meetings, and workshops. This work was supported by the forward-thinking Japan International Cooperation Agency (JICA).

Systems-of-systems methods were employed to assess Uganda's de jure versus de facto policy environment as well as its market and social conditions. Accordingly, the team completed a thorough "inclusive investing" market assessment to identify both social and economic barriers, as well as an exhaustive analysis of the manifold refugee self-reliance initiatives under way in Uganda. Ultimately, this approach proved to be extremely flexible and well suited to comprehensively address the complex and dynamic subject matter and to overcome the data collection challenges presented by the pandemic.

In leveraging private-sector capital and engagement, Uganda is charting a new course in addressing the complex challenges and opportunities presented by the refugee crisis in sub-Saharan Africa. Its open-door policy and permissive environment have created a unique opportunity to explore innovative financial solutions to promote self-reliance and sustainable development for both refugees and host communities. As a result, a number of organizations that work to both support and employ refugees were launched.

While each of these companies works in a different sector—energy, finance, digital literacy—they are all dedicated to supporting refugees and their host communities. The biggest common denominator, and arguably the most effective part about these organizations, is their innovative and forward-thinking mindset. Not only do they promote self-reliance among refugees by providing employment skills and training opportunities, but they do so in exploding industries and with an intention to provide highly desired professional skills like coding, design, and general tech-savviness.

One such organization is Mandulis Energy. Founded in Uganda, Mandulis develops, owns, and operates renewable energy projects throughout Africa. In 2021, when the UN Food and Agricultural Organization set out to make green energy sources available to refugee-hosting districts within Uganda, it partnered with Mandulis to increase knowledge and availability of alternative sources of energy, increase household income through job opportunities, and establish support services and hubs to facilitate the logistics of providing clean energy. As a result, Mandulis has been able to provide sustainable energy solutions to refugees within Uganda while also offering employment opportunities.

Another organization is Techfugees, established in 2018. Techfugees mobilized hundreds of tech workers to design and innovate solutions for forced displacement and to bring more displaced people into the tech industry. The founder Mike Butcher, then editor-at-large of *TechCrunch* in Europe, was inspired to action by the Syrian refugee crisis and brought three hundred people together in London for a first conference, followed by a hackathon. Today they have supported over 79.5 million displaced people and have a mission of building a sustainable ecosystem of tech solutions that support the inclusion of displaced people with tech innovations designed by, with, and for them. Techfugees creates and delivers free programs to support the inclusion of displaced persons by teaching digital skills such as coding or cybersecurity. More specifically, this innovative organization helps refugees achieve self-reliance by providing valuable professional skills and high-quality education that can be put to use by the displaced to work digitally across borders. In September 2021, Techfugees, in partnership with Google for Startups and Coursera, launched Techfugees Digital Spark, an international pilot training program across their chapters in Uganda, Kenya, Lebanon, and the United Kingdom that helps one hundred unemployed refugees with advanced digital skills to enter the labor market in the tech space (Include Her 2023).

One of the biggest barriers keeping refugees from achieving self-reliance is lack of access to financial services and information. Starting a business is a daunting venture in and of itself. For displaced persons, the difficulty is compounded further when the host community's local bank doesn't offer loans to refugees. Lack of financial literacy is another common problem holding refugee communities back. Opportunity International seeks to change this situation. Driven by its goal to break the cycle of poverty via financial literacy initiatives, Opportunity International launched the Refugees, Innovations, Self-reliance and Empowerment (RISE) project in Uganda. This transformative initiative aimed to empower over 1 million refugees by providing them with financial skills, knowledge, and integration into host communities. By May 2020, the project had already trained 950 refugees in financial literacy, with 90 percent actively saving money. Opportunity International's unwavering dedication created a beacon of hope, fostering self-reliance and shaping a brighter future for refugees in Uganda (Opportunity International 2020).

Saving and banking are important, but avenues to make money to save and manage are critical. Since the vast majority of people experiencing displacement are not well resourced and not all are ready to be entrepreneurs, the majority need to find some type of employment. Our team's research found that refugees in Uganda were engaged in a number of sectors, including energy, financial services, agriculture, transport and logistics, education, clothing and textiles, retail and wholesale, housing and hospitality, healthcare, and sanitation services. Ugandan-based companies are incorporating the displaced throughout the entire value chain—sourcing, processing, sales, and distribution.

Many of these companies add value to products by engaging primarily with agroprocessing or energy production and so target communities with large populations to support their work. Because Uganda's refugee policy grants refugees in settlements land to grow crops for their own nutritional needs as well as for commercial sale, this type of business is well suited to supporting displaced persons in Uganda.

Mandulis's SEPARLE project aggregates agricultural waste from thousands of refugee farmers in northern Uganda and transforms it into electricity to support microgrids in rural farming communities. Similarly, Sanivation's waste-to-value project works to improve sanitation services in refugee settlements. Based in Naivasha, Kenya, Sanivation partners with local governments to design, build, and operate fecal matter treatment plants and install sanitation services.

Other Ugandan companies are helping displaced artisans and makers access larger and farther markets through support with marketing, distribution, and sale of refugee-made products to local, regional, and international markets. Essentially, this effort involves businesses that can participate in markets beyond their immediate proximity. Within these types of companies, refugees typically receive training, manufacture products, and finally sell their products via new channels. Support for these efforts can stem from three primary sources: inputs and services, production, and sales and distribution.

Support agencies can also provide equipment and financing to support training sessions and set up projects for refugees and host communities. Girl Up Initiative Uganda trains around one hundred people annually, including refugees, in tailoring skills. The company supports people in starting their own businesses and exporting finished products to Europe and the United States.

A variety of other initiatives are also aimed at promoting self-reliance. Cochaired by Mastercard, the Smart Communities

Coalition (SCC) is a private-public partnership aimed at improving the delivery of essential services to forcibly displaced persons, specifically through the strategic implementation of technology. These efforts are concentrated around energy, connectivity, and digital tools. Coalition members include organizations and corporations alike, including Accenture, World Vision, and the Danish Refugee Council (Mastercard 1994–2025).

The Smart Communities Coalition Innovation Fund is the financing partner to the coalition and works in tandem with its goals. The fund offers financing opportunities to selected projects that serve the coalition's ultimate goal of supporting displaced populations. Each round of funding has focused on a different goal; the first one revolved around improving energy service access to refugee camps and host communities, and the second and most recent round of funding targeted connectivity and digital service access for refugee-hosting areas (USAID 2023).

Continuing in the realm of financing, the Refugee Investment Facility (RIF) was formed as the result of a partnership between the Danish Refugee Council and iGravity, a Swiss firm that specializes in impact investment and innovative finance solutions. RIF offers patient investments to local companies and start-ups that aim to positively impact refugees and host communities in Jordan and Uganda. The organization makes investments to increase employability, financial inclusion, access to relevant products and services, and decent employment for displacement-affected populations (DRC 2025).

Many of these self-reliance initiatives involve partnerships with like-minded agencies and organizations around the globe, and the Re:BUiLD program is no exception. Working in collaboration with IKEA Foundation and the International Rescue Committee, Re:BUiLD is a large-scale initiative focused on providing employment support to refugees and other local community members in Uganda and Kenya. The program specifically promotes economic self-reliance by offering apprenticeships, business grants, mentorships, skills trainings, and more. Initially focusing on Kampala and Nairobi, Re:BUiLD is working to build and share the evidence base for innovative, sustainable livelihoods solutions for urban-based refugees that could be adapted for other cities in East Africa and beyond (Re:BUiLD 2025).

While we've mentioned quite a few different funding and financing organizations, one last such group should be noted: the Displaced Communities Fund (DCF), which primarily provides private equity to microfinance institutions and other inclusive financial institutions that seek to serve forcibly displaced populations. As one of the newest funds to be created, DCF plans to work with organizations that will have large-scale impacts and has a target size of $50 to $75 million, which is considered to be a medium-sized fund in general but in the world of refugee lens investing is a hefty amount of capital (EIB n.d.).

Supporting refugee self-reliance via investments and supporting businesses promotes overall economic independence. But another important aspect is helping refugees develop financial literacy and understand what is and isn't working in how refugee business owners manage their money. Focused in Uganda, the Financial Inclusion for Refugees (FI4R) provides insights into the financial strategies that refugees have used to build their livelihoods and manage their finances. It also includes a groundbreaking twelve-month study to track the financial lives of Ugandan refugees that will inform the development of financial services and products offered to refugees and their host communities (BFA Global, n.d.).

Finally, the Financial Inclusion of Forcibly Displaced Persons and Host Communities Program is a joint program between

UNHCR and the United Nations Capital Development Fund that is designed to benefit refugees and host communities financially by supporting providers of financial products and services. The program also engages at the policy and regulatory level to better understand how different regulations affect the financial well-being of displaced communities (UNHCR 2018a).

All of these initiatives target refugees and displaced persons as their main beneficiaries, and they do so by providing funding to promote refugee businesses, training, and education to support refugees seeking to further their education, as well as funding of businesses that aim to create safer and more sustainable refugee-hosting communities.

But there is always room for improvement. Many of the initiatives that work with refugee settlements focus on the northern Uganda region, often neglecting those in western and southwestern Uganda. Moreover, there are not enough private-sector initiatives to give refugees the same rights as citizens living in host communities, such as legal assistance, identification, and access to housing. Uganda's status as one of the top refugee-hosting countries in the world and its progressive policies toward the refugee population make it an ideal environment for investors looking to participate in refugee lens investing.

UGANDA'S BUSINESS AND INVESTMENT ENVIRONMENT

In 2020, Uganda ranked 116th out of 190 economies in the World Bank's Doing Business index, indicating that there are still some significant challenges to doing business in the country. A closer look at the data shows that Uganda ranked 169th for ease of starting a business, 168th for getting electricity, 80th for getting credit, and 77th for enforcing contracts. These factors can pose obstacles for entrepreneurs, both local and refugee-led, who are the backbone of small and medium-sized enterprises (SMEs) in Uganda today.

Research conducted by Struwig, Krüger, and Nuwagaba in 2019 explored the influence of the business environment on the growth of informal businesses in Uganda, where many SMEs operate. The study found a negative and significant relationship between a challenging external environment and the growth of these businesses. In other words, unfavorable business environments inhibit the growth of SMEs and the formalization of the economy in Uganda.

In a report released in 2020, the World Bank shed light on the pressing need for Uganda to create a better environment for businesses. It stressed the importance of attracting more foreign direct investment (FDI) to the country. But promoting a better environment is not just about wooing international investors; it's also about supporting local businesses. The World Bank emphasized that providing local businesses with access to finance, modern technology, skills, and market information is absolutely crucial for improving the overall business climate.

As a result, the World Bank encouraged Uganda to create a business-friendly environment that will both attract investment and support local businesses with the tools they need to thrive. In doing so, it can transform its economy, create more jobs, and ensure that everyone, including refugees, has the opportunity to participate in and benefit from Uganda's growth.

In their research on financial inclusion and small businesses based on data on 762 firms in Uganda, Lakuma, Marty, and Muhumuza (2019) discovered something interesting. They found that when it comes to accessing finance, small and medium-sized enterprises (SMEs) actually benefit more than large firms because they face more credit constraints than their bigger counterparts. The study also highlighted how vulnerable these small businesses are to corruption, which can seriously impede their growth and viability.

Uganda isn't the only country facing these challenges. A comparative study by Habtamu Legas (2015) zoomed in on entrepreneurial ecosystems in sub-Saharan Africa and found that entrepreneurs across the region regularly come up against tight laws, clunky regulations, poor infrastructure, and limited access to financial services. In addition, they often lack the necessary entrepreneurial training and find themselves grappling with small market sizes, making it tough for their businesses to thrive and expand.

One major hurdle that holds back SME growth, not just in Uganda but also across Africa, is lack of access to finance. Atirado and colleagues (2009) conducted a study that analyzed data from fifty-six thousand enterprises in ninety countries. They discovered that small firms benefit the most when they have access to finance, especially when it comes to investments and fueling growth. This finding aligns with what Mawejje and Sebudde uncovered in their 2019 research, which highlighted how macroeconomic instability, limited access to finance, corruption, and unpredictable weather patterns affecting agriculture act as significant roadblocks to economic growth in Uganda.

The good news is that numerous reports provide valuable policy recommendations to create a more favorable business environment in Uganda and Africa as a whole. The World Bank suggests that city governments have a crucial role to play in this transformation. They can go from being mere regulators to becoming enablers of economic development by investing in transportation, improving land use management, and providing essential training, skills, and business services in urban areas.

There are other important policy actions to consider. Maintaining macroeconomic stability is key. Offering innovative financing solutions, cracking down on corruption, and supporting market access for businesses are all essential steps. Addressing high tax rates, finding ways to improve access to productive resources, and enhancing market access are also critical factors.

In 2020, Uganda's business environment took a massive hit due to the pandemic. The government's containment measures hit SMEs particularly hard. Many businesses faced increased operating expenses due to preventive measures, while agriculture enterprises struggled to get the necessary inputs and participate in weekly markets. Informal and woman-owned businesses were especially affected, leading to job cuts and the possibility of businesses shutting down. Despite these challenges, Uganda still holds immense potential for refugee lens investing.

Like Uganda's business climate, the investment climate has also been the subject of significant analysis and proposed reform. The state of business affairs is heavily linked to investment in Uganda: A study from the World Bank found that sub-Saharan African countries that embrace business reform also attract domestic and foreign investment (Bridgman and Aref 2015). This finding makes a rather strong case for improving the overall Ugandan business climate, for the sake of not only its refugee but also its general population.

While that perk alone should be reason enough to encourage business reform and promote a safer investment climate within Uganda, the same World Bank report also finds that neighboring countries will also be positively influenced to do the same. The country's liberal trade policies and foreign exchange regimes have attracted foreign direct investment, which surged by a remarkable 80 percent to reach $1.75 billion in fiscal year 2018/2019, suggesting strong underlying opportunity before the financial hit of the COVID-19 pandemic in 2020. Uganda has also experienced strong GDP growth, reaching 6.5 percent in fiscal year 2018/2019, which the US Department of State (2020) had projected to grow an additional 6 percent in the following fiscal year if the pandemic had not hit.

President Yoweri Museveni and government officials in Uganda may seem to be courting investors when speaking to the press, but their actions don't always align with their rhetoric. The US Department of State report sheds light on some concerning factors that pose risks for investors. Uganda's economic management leaves much to be desired, and corruption runs rampant. The country's growing sovereign debt, weak rule of law, and inadequate investment in the health and education sectors further compound the challenges. Moreover, competition from local firms can be difficult because some may disregard environmental regulations, labor rights, and taxes and even engage in bribery. Shortages of skilled labor and a complicated land tenure system also hinder investment opportunities. These risks mean careful consideration for future investors, call for proactive strategies to mitigate risk, and present a barrier to the success of RLI.

When it comes to impact investing in Uganda, development finance institutions (DFIs) play a pivotal role. They have been and will continue to be a significant source of impact-oriented funds, channeling investments into infrastructure projects, various funds, and directly to companies. They are a powerful force driving positive change in the country's economic landscape. But DFIs aren't the only players in the game. Crowdfunding platforms are gaining traction and emerging as influential sources of impact capital across the continent. Platforms like Chuffed, Kiva, Seedrs, and bettervest are making their mark in supporting Ugandan entrepreneurs and businesses. This growing trend reflects a democratization of investment, empowering individuals to contribute to meaningful causes. And of course, impact-focused venture capital and private funds remain crucial sources of early and midstage financing, complementing the efforts of non-DFIs such as commercial banks. Impact funding takes various forms, including equity, debt, quasi equity/debt, convertibles, and grants. In Uganda, non-DFI impact investors typically seek out early-stage businesses that demonstrate some level of organization and traction but struggle to secure financing from traditional institutions due to stringent requirements or high costs. Agriculture and financial services have been the primary focus of non-DFI investments, catering to both urban and rural settings. On the other hand, DFIs have directed their investments toward the energy and financial services sectors (Balikuddembe and Kaleebi 2019).

Impact investing in Uganda serves diverse purposes, covering working capital costs and inventory, scaling up from pilot projects to full-scale operations, and expanding product lines and overall business operations. DFIs often provide technical assistance to prepare businesses for investment and thus ensure a higher chance of success.

According to a 2015 report by the Global Impact Investing Network (GIIN), excluding DFI activity, Uganda saw an impressive 139 impact deals that resulted in over $300 million disbursed. This amount accounts for more than 20 percent of all investment activity in East Africa. Furthermore, approximately 119 impact capital vehicles were managed by eighty-two non-DFI impact investors in Uganda, with commitments of at least $54 million to drive positive change, and 50 percent of capital disbursed by non-DFI impact investors exceeded $1 million. These figures tell a compelling story of the impact investing landscape in Uganda. It's a realm where the power of investing is harnessed to empower businesses, foster economic growth, and make a tangible difference in communities across the country.

Within Uganda's long, complex, and tragic history of forced displacement lies a paradox: The government of Uganda and its international partners and Ugandan hosts and refugees are faced with a daunting set of challenges to promote self-reliance and inclusive development for the nation's 1.5 million refugees. At the same time, Uganda's deep experience and familiarity with displacement, its culture of accepting refugees with an "open-door policy," and the strong patronage systems that have supported the creation and stability of the current legal regime make Uganda a relative fortress of prorefugee policy, as well as a stable and high-potential market for innovative financiers and RLI.

Diving deeper into an assessment of the policy and market barriers will help identify existing shortcomings in the respective systems that present barriers to the successful establishment of RLI in Uganda. This next section's purpose will be twofold: to shine a light on the advantages present in the Ugandan market and to identify shortcomings within the systems that are preventing successful implementation of RLI and that could be revised. For readers interested in advancing RLI in their country, this next section can serve as a road map of the types of policies and market factors on which investors should gather information so that they might overcome these barriers or mitigate the risks that they pose.

ASSESSMENT OF MARKET AND POLICY BARRIERS

Refugee investing continues to remain a large segment of untapped potential investment. However, a gradual shift is taking place. Investors are beginning to recognize the economic potential that lies within refugee populations. Initiatives like the groundbreaking Re:BUiLD program, a $30 million partnership between the International Rescue Committee (IRC) and the IKEA Foundation, the PROSPECTS project led by the International Finance Corporation (IFC) in collaboration with other partners, and various efforts under the SCC have emerged to challenge the prevailing narrative. These endeavors aim to redirect targeted investments into refugee communities, challenging the status quo and fostering their self-reliance.

To accomplish this goal, a deep understanding of the refugee market and policy environment is essential. In Uganda, the refugee population is vast and diverse, and the related policies are relatively favorable. However, investors must grapple with a range of barriers as they strive to design responsive solutions. At the market level, the commercial landscape may appear unfavorable and be characterized by high unemployment rates, low-income levels, limited access to education and skills training, inadequate public services such as healthcare and connectivity, and a lack of social integration between refugees and host communities. Similarly, at the policy level, investors often encounter discrepancies between progressive policies on paper and the on-the-ground practices that restrict refugees' ability to participate fully in the local economy.

Investors and supporting actors must implement targeted interventions and advocacy efforts to address these challenges while collaborating with relevant stakeholders. Overcoming market barriers requires increased private-sector engagement to unlock business opportunities within refugee settlements. This approach can foster a free and competitive market, improve service access and quality, generate employment opportunities, develop skills, and ultimately enhance the overall economic value of these communities. On the policy front, active discourse with government offices and influential sector practitioners is crucial to drive needed changes in regulatory frameworks, language, and practices, ultimately relieving refugee groups of the economic constraints they currently face.

MARKET BARRIERS

When it comes to investing in refugee communities, numerous market barriers hinder their access to financing, employment opportunities, and the essential services necessary for a better quality of life. These barriers not only pose challenges for potential investors and support actors but also limit the aspirations of refugees who seek economic empowerment. Although refugees in Uganda are granted civil freedoms that enable them to fully participate in the local economy as employees and entrepreneurs, they face formidable obstacles on the ground. These challenges range from struggles in socially integrating into local workspaces and marketplaces to limitations in accessing opportunities that could contribute positively to the socioeconomic development of their communities.

Refugee communities face significant challenges when accessing employment, training, and business opportunities. The unemployment rates among refugees, especially youth, are alarmingly high, reaching 70 percent. In settlements like Kyaka II, Nakivale, and Kyangwali, youth unemployment rates hover around 74 percent, 65 percent, and 50 percent, respectively, which is at least four times the national average for Ugandan youth (Kempner 2020). This limited employment landscape forces many refugees into low-wage, informal jobs. They often find work in small-scale farming, predominantly in rural areas, or engage in various microenterprises. However, the competition for employment opportunities with the host community puts refugees at a significant disadvantage. Assimilation challenges, limited access to documentation, and language barriers further exacerbate their difficulties.

These unemployment rates are largely linked to the fact that refugees are most likely to be hosted in chronically poor and underdeveloped host communities with limited economic opportunities or access to services. In addition, settlements are often located near remote and underdeveloped villages that happen to be in proximity to reception points along the border where refugees first arrive and request refuge. In Kampala, the fast pace of urbanization is pushing the urban poor into informal settlements and slums such as Katwe, Kinawataka, Namuwongo, Katanga, and Wabigalo, where urban-based refugees are also likely to reside. These informal settlements are characterized by low-quality housing, a shortage or complete absence of public infrastructure such as piped water, and environmental hazards like flooding, as most of them are located in valleys and lack proper drainage systems. These factors mean that jobs taken up by refugee workers are often informal roles in factories or small-scale retail shops (AGORA 2018).

Even where opportunities are available—whether for employment, business, or training—refugees struggle to access the required documentation. As in most other nations, all formal work and most informal jobs in Uganda require government-issued documentation to verify identity. If a person wants to start a business, that also requires registration and licensing that must be verified by local regulators. Similarly, schools and training institutions, especially at higher levels, often require evidence of past accreditation before admission. That kind of documentation is probably not at the forefront of someone's mind when they are fleeing violence and armed conflict in their home country.

Education becomes a casualty of forced displacement, leaving many refugees with disrupted or halted educational trajectories and limiting their ability to acquire competitive and marketable skills. Children and youth constitute approximately 40 percent of the refugee population in any given settlement. The educational disruption they experience sets them back academically and professionally. To gain meaningful employment or become self-employed, refugees often require substantial investment in training. Some refugees are able to leverage their existing skills, such as foreign language proficiency, tailoring, and hair styling, to create self-employment opportunities. Over time, certain trades have seen the emergence of a strong ethnic presence; examples are Congolese refugees excelling in tailoring and hair styling, Burundian refugees specializing in French-language training, and Somali refugees dominating the fast-moving consumer goods (FMCG) distribution. However, these entrepreneurs still face significant barriers to entry, including accreditation requirements for language teaching and fierce competition in saturated markets like salons, which are predominantly controlled by Ugandans and challenging to scale.

Women refugees often bear the burden of household provision, home management, and childcare, but they lack the necessary resources to effectively juggle these responsibilities. A significant proportion of refugee households are led by women—62 percent of refugee households in the West Nile region, compared to 33.3 percent of female-led host community households in Uganda (World Bank Group 2019a). This disparity arises from the fact that women and children make up the majority of survivors in armed conflicts, and during resettlement, refugee men often seek employment outside the settlement to support their families. However, due to limited job opportunities, female refugees find themselves compelled to combine domestic and childcare duties with work. Many women opt to start home-based businesses like tailoring, hair braiding, and cooking, relying on the immediate host community as their customer base. Nevertheless, refugee women encounter challenges in accessing capital to start or sustain their businesses, as well as in accessing markets for customers and suppliers; all of these problems result in meager returns on their investments.

To better understand the lending needs and opportunities for refugees, it is crucial to enhance market knowledge on both the supply and demand sides. Engaging financial service providers in capacity-building efforts is essential to demystifying the perception of "refugee borrowers" and dispelling misconceptions about their creditworthiness. It is important to leverage evidence that demonstrates minimal differences in repayment rates between refugees and nonrefugees and thus highlights their reliability as borrowers. For instance, data from the World Refugee Fund managed by Kiva reveal a repayment rate of 96.6 percent for refugees and IDPs borrowing from partner institutions, which is comparable to the 96.8 percent repayment rate for nonrefugee borrowers across six refugee-hosting countries. Additionally, financial literacy initiatives can play a significant role in preparing refugees for financing opportunities, especially for those who may lack familiarity or experience with borrowing and repayment. By equipping refugees with the necessary knowledge and skills, we can empower them to navigate the financial landscape with confidence.

ADVANCING MARKET SOLUTIONS

A great first step is to engage financial providers in designing tailored financial products and processes for refugee borrowers: for example, by adapting credit assessment processes to factor in refugee challenges around documentation or meeting eligibility criteria like collateral. Financial products can be customized to leverage the unique advantage of refugees as borrowers. For instance, one approach is linking principal repayments to refugees' monthly stipends or allowances. Another option is connecting repayments to remittance accounts in which refugees receive regular deposits. To establish consistent, know-your-customer practices for refugee borrowers, it is important for the government to collaborate with financial institutions in developing a refugee information system. This engagement will help ensure that there are standardized procedures in place to verify the identities and backgrounds of refugee borrowers.

Investment mechanisms that align with one or more of the six refugee investing lenses (see chapter 3) have a vital role in improving financial access for both Uganda's refugee population and the host community. These mechanisms not only facilitate access to finance but also encourage businesses to actively engage with refugee and host communities. In fact, industry insiders, including Wilfred Kamulegeya, a senior agronomist at the Gulu Agricultural Development Corporation (GADC), emphasize how embracing RLI can amplify impact and attract new capital partners who are interested in supporting such initiatives. Refugees in Uganda primarily access finance through direct lending or derisking facilities. However, there is room for innovative approaches that build on these structures and incorporate different elements. A brief review of these financing instruments helps to contextualize potential innovations that can be tailored to refugee lens investing:

- *Commercial direct lending*: This is the traditional approach to lending in which commercial lenders provide already existing lending products to refugees and refugee businesses at market rates. Risk is primarily assumed by the commercial lender in the case of defaults.
- *Concessional intermediated or direct lending*: This is capital, usually provided through public or philanthropic funds, that is characterized by below-market interest rates, payment-free grace periods, or a combination of both. Direct lending is a common component of blended capital (which typically also incorporates impact or private capital), so it can also include steps taken to reduce the level of risk associated with lending, such as technical assistance to entrepreneurs to help ensure their success. These funds are disbursed either via direct lending from development partners or through intermediary private-sector channels such as banks and microfinance institutions.
- *Derisking facilities*: These structures involve multiple partners entering into agreements to provide financing to beneficiaries. Also known as "blended finance," they are designed to engage the private sector and reduce the risks faced by financial service providers. This goal encourages them to develop tailored products and lend to vulnerable communities, including displaced persons and host residents, without compromising their risk management standards. The main types of derisking facilities in the refugee-lending landscape include guarantees, first-loss coverage, and insurance.
- *Other innovative financing methods*: Crowdfunding is a method used to gather investments from various sources that are then

> distributed to specific target groups through partnerships with loan providers like banks. This approach uses derisking models to support lending programs and mitigate potential financial risks. In crowdfunding, individuals or organizations contribute funds toward a common goal or project, often through online platforms; this approach enables collective financial support and engagement from a wide range of contributors.

Obtaining formal financing for refugees has been a long-standing hurdle for commercial and traditional lenders. The high administrative costs associated with small-scale lending, where loan amounts are relatively low, often pose a difficult business model for commercial lenders. Additionally, there exists a perception of high risk associated with lending to refugees, with concerns about their ability to repay loans or the potential that they will relocate, that has dampened lenders' interest in this market. The absence of collateral and essential registration and identification information further restricts commercial lenders' ability to monitor and recover loans.

Loan guarantee facilities (LGFs) offer a solution to address the challenges faced by commercial lenders when financing refugees. These guarantees are often provided by development financial institutions, development agencies, or private foundations. They ensure that defaults will be covered up to a certain amount, thus sharing the risk with lenders and encouraging them to provide financial support to refugee beneficiaries that their normal underwriting requirements would not allow. USAID successfully offered loan guarantees in other parts of Africa, enticing traditional banks to begin lending to vulnerable populations; this would not have happened without the offer of a loan guarantee. By offering guarantees that cover around 50 to 80 percent of the loans disbursed, LGFs promote responsible lending and alleviate the burden of risk borne solely by commercial lenders. When LGFs are integrated into the RLI structure, commercial lenders can offer more affordable financing options to private actors operating in or seeking to engage with the refugee sector. This arrangement enables these actors to expand their economic activities, thus improving livelihoods for both refugee and host communities. When designing guarantee facilities, it is important to consider provisions for technical assistance, guarantee pricing, and monitoring and evaluation.

Several initiatives have employed LGFs to establish sustainable markets. For example, the SIDA/UNHCR Partial Credit Guarantee Facility, piloted in the Palorinya refugee settlement in northern Uganda and Kampala, aimed to encourage financial service providers to offer their services to both refugees and host populations. The project facilitated access to financial services for approximately 100,000 individuals, with 70 percent of the beneficiaries being women. It sought to help create small businesses in sectors such as farming, handicrafts, and trade (UNHCR 2019).

Guarantees and insurance models provide lenders with protection against defaults or nonperformance of the portfolio by compensating the lender through a third party if investment losses occur. In this derisking model, funds from third parties are pooled separately from the investment structure, usually in a blended fund or direct lending model. Lenders offer financing to borrowers, and if there are defaults or nonpayment, the pooled funds cover the losses incurred by the lender. While these insurance models are not commonly used in refugee financing, they offer an additional structure that should be considered.

Another derisking financial structure that can effectively support RLI in Uganda is first-loss coverage. First-loss portfolios are managed so that the lender or manager takes responsibility for absorbing losses up to a predetermined amount, typically around 10 percent of the allocated trading capital. This amount acts as a form of collateral, and investors' capital is only negatively impacted if losses exceed this predefined cap. In certain cases, the first-loss capital contributed by each funder or lender can be combined, creating a collective pool that absorbs losses beyond the cap for a single investment (Akingbehin 2018; Global Impact Investing Network 2013).

Concessional lending typically involves DFIs or other organizations offering debt financing at below-market rates and with long repayment periods to various actors, including the public sector, companies, and individuals (IFC 2021). This type of lending can be channeled through intermediaries like banks and microfinance institutions or provided directly to companies and individuals.

In the context of RLI, concessional lending plays an important role in improving the livelihoods of refugees and host communities. Private actors, who are expected to repay the loans, can utilize the funds for future investments or other purposes and can thus be encouraged to engage in the RLI sector (World Bank Group 2018). For instance, concessional loans can provide refugees with access to affordable borrowing, enabling them to start businesses or participate in economic activities. Another great benefit to concessional loans is that they can incentivize companies to invest in the RLI space. Companies can test new business models, expand operations into new settlements, and offer new products and services to the refugee community. For example, an agroprocessor could establish collection areas or a processing plant that purchases produce from both host and refugee communities while providing employment opportunities.

Results-based financing (RBF) is a form of concessional lending that uses incentives to encourage implementers to achieve specific outcomes and increase utilization. In essence, RBF funders or financiers make payments to intermediaries who commit to achieving predetermined results. While the desired outcomes are agreed upon beforehand, RBF can foster competition among recipients, especially when it targets the same customer base in pursuit of its goals. This competitive aspect makes RBF potentially more effective in generating tangible outputs and outcomes than traditional approaches to development financing.

There are various types of results-based financing, including payments by results (PbR), payment for results (PforR), results-based lending (RBL), performance-driven loans (PDLs), output-based aid (OBA), development impact bonds (DIBs), pay-for-success, and social impact bonds. These funding mechanisms focus on generating specific outputs and outcomes and so are well suited for RLI. By leveraging results-based funding, various targets related to refugees can be achieved, such as boosting employment, increasing product sourcing and volume, and providing training opportunities for both refugee and host businesses. In some countries, pay-for-success models can encourage earlier-stage interventions that have greater social impact and that can save government spending or development spending over the longer term.

The design and structure of RBF are crucial for achieving high-impact results in various settings. In the context of RLI, RBFs can be used in several ways. For instance, they can be employed to enhance gainful employment opportunities for both refugees and host communities by incentivizing private-sector companies to hire refugees through monetary or non-monetary rewards. RBFs can also be designed to stimulate private players to offer goods and services in refugee and host communities by aligning incentives with the number of products sold or customers served, thereby helping to improve livelihoods for refugees and host communities. Additionally, RBFs can incentivize Uganda's agroprocessors to provide training and to source agricultural produce from refugee and host communities engaged in crop farming. In this case, incentives would be linked to outcomes such as yield improvement and outputs like volumes of produce purchased.

And finally, we can leverage technology to expand digital financial services (DFS) into refugee settlements to also support their economic integration. These services mitigate risks for lenders and improve accessibility for refugees by eliminating the need for travel and intermediaries between lenders and refugees. For instance, mobile money has become a popular means of accessing capital. Certain banks operating in Uganda, such as Equity and Kenya Commercial Bank (KCB), offer credit facilities to refugees, especially those with established businesses and a credit history with the bank. However, this practice is not yet widespread. In settlements like Nakivale and Kyaka II, traditional banking methods like village savings and loan associations (VSLAs) and informal lenders still dominate the majority of transactions.

DFS solutions can be effectively combined with remittance channels to serve as a significant source of income for refugees. According to a World Bank survey conducted in Kampala, 74.1 percent of urban refugee households rely on remittances for some or all of their income. In 2019, remittances accounted for 4 percent of the national GDP, with inflows growing at an average rate of 13 percent per year between 2015 and 2017, surpassing the growth rate of neighboring Kenya (7 percent) (Cooper et al. 2018). This makes remittance-based financing particularly attractive for refugees from countries with substantial diaspora populations, such as Ethiopia and Rwanda (VisionFund 2025).

Additionally, DFS solutions enable banks to directly lend to microfinance initiatives run by refugees, which can promote positive repayment habits. A study funded by the Humanitarian Innovation Fund examined existing initiatives in Kampala and found that many urban refugee communities have already established their own financial mechanisms. These refugees are already part of established repayment structures and practices, such as weekly savings meetings, group liability, and strong social cohesion. These factors can enhance individual accountability and create a collective motivation to invest and increase savings (Hakiza and Easton-Calabria 2016). Additionally, market solutions like Questbanker, a banking software developed by Akellobanker, facilitate low-cost connections between institutional lenders and informal savings groups.

POLICY BARRIERS

While the range of solutions to market-based barriers like those just discussed are critical, they cannot make up for policy barriers. Despite a generally progressive and advanced displacement policy in Uganda, various policy barriers are holding refugee lens investing back from its true potential. By policy barriers, we mean relevant government agencies and officials, regulatory frameworks, and the implementation of laws. First, our research team found that many displaced people in Uganda have difficulty with documentation. Refugees often deal with lengthy and overly bureaucratic processes in accessing identification documents. The result is difficulty accessing housing and schooling and limited movement between settlements. There are also unclear and restrictive refugee livelihood policies. The current Employment Act does not lay out a clear framework on the rights of minorities, including refugees, in the workplace. The Trade Licensing Act also lacks guidelines on the establishment and registration of refugee businesses, and the Jobs and Livelihood Response Plan lacks a clear implementation strategy. More work is needed to improve Uganda's implementation of its welcoming refugee policy. International and bilateral donors should work to support Uganda in overcoming these remaining policy barriers; in doing so, they can create a true model for the rest of the world's hosting countries to follow.

Uganda occupies a unique position. It hosts one of the largest refugee populations in the world and also supports an open-door policy environment that provides wide latitude for refugee social and economic integration. Yet barriers continue to prevent Uganda's refugee population from taking advantage of the relatively free environment in which they live. Market barriers to refugee investing are compounded by limited access to finance, employment, training, and business opportunities, frustrating entrepreneurs and job seekers alike. Limited access to basic services like education, healthcare, housing, connectivity, and technology stunts human development and hinders growth and engagement. Policy and administrative failures—such as difficulty accessing documentation—further complicate efforts to promote and achieve self-reliance.

CONCLUSION

Taken together, the market and policy barriers identified here present challenges to impact investing through RLI. However, there are also numerous points of entry for engaged partners. Bilateral and multilateral development agencies can support the integration of the private sector into refugee initiatives by working with both the government and the private sector. By inviting the private sector to participate in the development of refugee programs and initiatives and by contracting with it to help provide services, development partners can help to manage this important cross-sectoral work and integration. Working with the government and private-sector partners can also help strengthen and enforce existing refugee rights and policies and improve the badly needed infrastructure in Ugandan settlements and host communities.

Financial and nonfinancial incentives for the private sector will also help to encourage engagement within the refugee space. So too will the sharing of data, such as data on refugee and host community economic activities, languages spoken, demographic information, refugee qualifications and skill sets, or other potential economic opportunities. These data from well-positioned sources like the US Office of Personnel Management (OPM) would enhance private-sector engagement. All of these actions would help the private sector better understand how it can fit into the refugee and host community space to help achieve economic growth and other common goals.

Indeed, integrating the private sector into refugee programs or initiatives can help boost engagement among key stakeholders. The government can help increase private-sector engagement by improving the enabling environment or by contracting and incentivizing private-sector companies to engage the refugee sector. Increasing access to flexible finance also incentivizes private-sector participation, thereby supporting businesses to test new business models and expand into untapped refugee settlements and urban enclaves.

Innovative finance mechanisms such as guarantee facilities, first-loss vehicles, and results-based financing are examples of how capital can be deployed to increase access to finance and help reduce risk in private-sector investment. Creating coordinated efforts with development partners, NGOs, and DFIs that share similar goals can help to prevent duplication of programs and effort as well as magnify impact. Business development services and technical assistance can further help support and train refugees in the necessary skill sets to effectively work with private-sector companies. Finally, stakeholders can help private-sector companies understand critical training components and provide the necessary training to refugees through various technical assistance programs.

9

EUROPE

A New Paradigm for the Economic Integration of Refugees

On February 21, 2022, the Russian president Vladimir Putin recognized the Ukrainian regions of Donetsk and Luhansk as independent states. To emphasize this point, he also sent troops into these areas to keep the peace. Only a few days later, on February 24, this troop deployment changed to a full-scale invasion, beginning in the Donbas region of eastern Ukraine. In response, the Ukrainian president Volodymyr Zelenskyy declared martial law within his nation and broke diplomatic ties with Russia.

Since the invasion occurred, President Putin's actions have been condemned by most of the world. Over the last several years, the war has continued to drag on, resulting in 6.9 million Ukrainian people fleeing across the border and another 3.7 million internally displaced (USA for UNHCR 2025). The majority of Ukrainian refugees have fled to Germany, Poland, and the Czech Republic, with hundreds of thousands more scattered across the United Kingdom (UK), Spain, Italy, the Netherlands, and beyond (Statista 2025).

This isn't the first time Europe has faced an influx of refugees. Major events in the last thirty years, including the fall of the Berlin Wall, the Kosovo war, and, more recently, the Syrian conflict, have resulted in millions of people seeking refuge. Since 2015, around half the refugees in the European Union (EU) have originated from Afghanistan, Syria, and Iraq. Despite the fact that most European nations are well acquainted with displaced persons, it is not typical for refugees to be granted rights to employment, housing, access to schooling, or other such rights that are naturally given to citizens. In a break from traditional policy responses, and as asylum seekers from Turkey and parts of northern Africa were turned away, the EU pursued a new policy approach.

In March 2022, in an unprecedented move, the EU activated the Temporary Protection Directive (TPD) to support displaced persons fleeing Ukraine as a result of the war. The TPD allows EU member states to provide refugees with the right to housing, medical assistance, education, and work, among other rights. This was the first time that the directive had ever been activated, despite past refugee crises. The directive has currently been extended to March 2027. By October 2022, over 4 million Ukrainians had registered for the EU's protection policies. While they face some of the same language barriers refugees face everywhere, their ability to legally work and launch legal businesses is unprecedented.

While the TPD is limited to Ukrainian refugees, the policy move is an important advancement in the inclusion of refugee entrepreneurs, and it could set a new precedent on how receiving countries could more effectively welcome the displaced and successfully incorporate them into their economies. Ukrainian refugees across Europe are now creating incredible success stories.

This chapter discusses this unprecedented refugee policy development, the impact of that policy on economic integration via employment and entrepreneurship, and the entrepreneurial support and regional start-up ecosystems of the countries hosting the largest populations of Ukrainian refugees. We also discuss the scale and effectiveness of the policies and the social infrastructure in place to support economic integration of the displaced.

THE EUROPEAN UNION'S TEMPORARY PROTECTION DIRECTIVE (TPD) FOR UKRAINIAN REFUGEES: A HUMANITARIAN RESPONSE TO CRISIS

As mentioned, the TPD, a legal framework designed to offer rapid protection to large groups of displaced persons, marked a significant shift in European asylum policy. By temporarily offering refugee status to millions of Ukrainians fleeing war, the EU sought to mitigate the humanitarian crisis while ensuring that host countries could manage the influx of refugees in an organized and sustainable manner.

The TPD was originally adopted in 2001 and was designed to offer a swift and flexible response to mass displacement situations, particularly in the event of war or conflict during which individual asylum procedures might overwhelm national systems. However, it had never been invoked until the 2022 war in Ukraine. The directive enables the EU to provide temporary protection to displaced persons from a non-EU country when their home country is facing widespread conflict or violence, thereby preventing a sudden surge in asylum claims that could strain the systems of individual EU member states.

The activation of the TPD granted Ukrainian nationals—and some non-Ukrainian residents of Ukraine, such as refugees and stateless persons—temporary protection within the EU for an initial period of one year, with the possibility of extension for up to three years, depending on the situation. The activation of the TPD provided Ukrainian refugees with several key rights and protections:

1. *Temporary residency status*: Ukrainian refugees were granted temporary residency status in EU member states that allowed them to live and work legally in any EU country. This

temporary protection is crucial, as it prevents refugees from being subjected to deportation or detention while their claims are being processed, thus offering them a degree of stability.

2. *Access to employment*: One of the most significant aspects of the TPD is its provision for refugees to access the labor market in their host countries. This provision gives Ukrainians the right to work, reducing the financial burdens that might otherwise be placed on host governments and ensuring that refugees can support themselves and their families.
3. *Social rights*: Ukrainian refugees are entitled to social welfare benefits, including healthcare, housing assistance, and education for children. These provisions are designed to ensure that refugees have access to the essential services necessary for their well-being and integration into society.
4. *Family reunification*: The TPD allows for the reunification of family members, ensuring that refugees who have been separated from their loved ones can bring their immediate family members to join them in the EU.
5. *Duration and extension*: The temporary protection status is initially granted for one year but can be extended for up to three years, depending on the evolving situation in Ukraine. This flexibility reflects the EU's commitment to adapting its response to the ongoing conflict and the potential long-term nature of displacement.

Since the activation of the TPD, over 4.3 million Ukrainians have received temporary protection across the EU. The implementation has varied slightly among different member states, reflecting national differences in infrastructure, refugee reception systems, and public attitudes toward refugees. However, the EU's response has been largely regarded as a model of solidarity and rapid action.

Countries like Poland, which hosts the largest number of Ukrainian refugees, have been at the forefront of implementing the TPD, quickly providing accommodation, legal assistance, and financial support. Other countries, such as Germany, the Czech Republic, and Italy, have also put mechanisms in place to support Ukrainian refugees, offering language courses, employment assistance, and integration programs.

In general, the TPD has been highly effective in offering immediate relief to refugees and reducing the strain on national asylum systems. It has allowed Ukrainian refugees to bypass the usual asylum application process, which can be slow and cumbersome, and instead receive immediate legal protection and access to essential services. The flexibility of the TPD, including its provision for extension based on the situation in Ukraine, has enabled the EU to adapt to the evolving nature of the conflict and the needs of the refugees.

However, the scale of the crisis has also posed challenges. Some member states have faced difficulties in providing adequate housing, healthcare, and education due to the sudden influx of refugees. While the EU has provided financial support to member states to assist in these efforts, there have been concerns about the longer-term sustainability of these measures, particularly if the conflict drags on for several years.

BROADER IMPLICATIONS FOR EU ASYLUM POLICY

The activation of the TPD for Ukrainian refugees has had broader implications for EU asylum policy. First, it has demonstrated the potential of a coordinated, collective European response to large-scale refugee movements. The TPD allowed for a more unified approach than the fragmented, often slow, responses that characterized the EU's handling of previous refugee crises, such as the Syrian refugee crisis in 2015. The quick activation of the TPD was seen as a success, demonstrating that the EU is capable of acting swiftly in the face of mass displacement.

Second, the activation of the TPD has sparked discussions about the future of the EU's asylum system. The relative success of the TPD has led some to question whether the EU should expand or formalize the use of temporary protection for other displaced populations, particularly in light of the ongoing crises around the world. The TPD has provided a model for how Europe can respond to humanitarian emergencies in a more flexible, compassionate, and effective way.

However, the implementation of the TPD also highlights some of the ongoing challenges in the EU's asylum system, including disparities in how member states manage refugee integration, public perceptions of refugees, and the need for long-term solutions to displacement. The TPD is a temporary measure, and its continued success depends on ensuring that refugees have access to sustainable employment, education, and housing, while also addressing the political and logistical challenges that arise from such large-scale migration.

UKRAINIAN REFUGEES GETTING JOBS IN EUROPE: PATHWAYS TO INTEGRATION AND ECONOMIC CONTRIBUTION

While the immediate focus for many refugees and the organizations supporting them was on securing safety and meeting basic needs, a significant number have also sought to integrate into their host countries' economies by finding employment. Because of the TPD, this process happened more quickly than it had in the past in other conflict zones.

The TPD has facilitated the integration of refugees into the labor market because it bypasses the lengthy asylum application process, which can often take years to resolve. This right to work has been a critical factor in enabling refugees to support themselves and contribute to their host countries economically. The clear legal framework has also enabled companies to quickly announce their intention to support the massive displacement through proactive hiring. In 2023, at a summit in Paris, around forty companies, including Amazon, pledged to hire tens of thousands of refugees across Europe, particularly those displaced by the war in Ukraine. These commitments from large companies, totaling forty-one, are expected to have a direct impact on 250,000 refugees, generating over 2 billion euros in income annually. Amazon planned to hire at least five thousand refugees in Europe over three years, while other companies, including Hilton, Marriott, and Teleperformance, have made substantial hiring promises. The pledges are seen as the most significant corporate effort to promote the economic integration of refugees (SudOuest 2023).

In Poland, the minister of family and social policy reported that almost 1 million Ukrainian refugees had taken up work, primarily because they were given the same rights as Polish citizens: the right to legal employment, to stay in Poland legally, and to apply for health and other welfare benefits. The addition of these employees to Poland's workforce has not affected the overall unemployment rate within the country, meaning that allowing Ukrainian refugees the right to work has not taken jobs away from Polish citizens.

Moreover, the refugees have been settling into their new careers quite well. According to data from the Social Insurance

Institution (ZUS), over 53 percent of Ukrainians employed in Poland at the end of March 2023 were working in industrial processing, transport and storage, construction, and wholesale and retail trade (Blaszczak 2023). Despite facing language barriers, Ukrainians demonstrate high professional activity and satisfaction with working in Poland. However, many work below their qualifications because of their limited Polish language skills. The desire to return to Ukraine is increasing, but many plan to stay for a few more years because of the ongoing war. There is an increasing demand for specialists and managers with knowledge of the Ukrainian language, driven by the growing number of companies with Ukrainian capital registered in Poland. Ukrainian workers seek stable employment with employment contracts, regular remuneration, and benefits such as paid leave and social security (Blaszczak 2023).

While some have pointed out the lower number of Ukrainian refugees settling in France (only sixty-five thousand) due to large language barriers and smaller Ukrainian communities to welcome newcomers, those who have settled there are finding work, housing, bank accounts, and more stability. A vast network of Facebook groups and refugee support groups has helped Ukrainian refugees navigate paperwork, secure safe housing, and get settled in jobs (Cokelaere and Caulcutt 2024). French companies are seeing the benefits of hiring refugees. For example, Maroquinerie THOMAS's factory has been turning out leather handbags for French luxury brands since the 1970s. In 2022, its CEO, Thierry Thomas, hired twenty-five Ukrainians: "I hired the first five and then more started coming," he says. "Cousins, sisters-in-law. They work hard, they adapt fast. At first I put them all together. That way if one understood, he could teach the others." The CEO offers long-term employment so that the employees can open bank accounts and rent apartments. In

France, Ukrainian refugees have the right to stay and work and receive a small monthly stipend. Thomas says it isn't charity; he can't find enough French workers. The refugees are thankful for the work, as one new hire noted: "It's a wonderful place to work, a very wholesome atmosphere and our French colleagues are welcoming" (Beardsley 2022).

In Vienne, Pôle emploi, the French employment agency, actively encouraged companies to hire Ukrainian refugees and has registered seventy-seven Ukrainians in that city since the start of the war in Ukraine. Because the available job offers were not always suitable for the highly qualified refugees with skills in law, accounting, and communication, language barriers required connecting to lower-skilled jobs. Pôle emploi implemented translation tools to aid communication, collaborated with employment associations, and established a platform to connect willing companies with Ukrainian job seekers (Samit 2022). This level of government support to economically integrate newly arriving refugees is quite unprecedented and a model for other host countries in the future. A government platform called "I am committed to Ukraine" was even launched to facilitate support from local authorities, companies, associations, and individuals. Similar initiatives were launched in German; Deutsche Bahn launched a job and counseling program for Ukrainian refugees with information about the German labor market and specific job opportunities (Uhlenbroich 2022). At the same time, the tech entrepreneur Ivan Kychatyi and his colleagues launched the job exchange platform "UAtalents" in Germany to connect Ukrainian refugees, particularly those with tech skills, with employers who need information technology (IT) specialists. The initiative aims to provide employment opportunities for Ukrainian refugees and support their livelihoods, as well as contribute to the financial aid for those affected by the conflict in

Ukraine. The platform has gained support from various partners, including Google, Meta, and Stepstone. All proceeds generated through the platform will be directly donated to affected families in Ukraine (Seibel 2022).

Nongovernmental agencies also mobilized to advance economic integration. Adecco, a Swiss group, launched a website called adeccojobsforukraine.com that lists job offers in various countries, including France, to help refugees find work. The platform also provides resources for curriculum vitae writing, job searching, and accommodation assistance. Adecco has previously aided refugees in countries such as Iraq, Syria, and Afghanistan (Mahe 2022).

Ukrainian refugees seeking employment in Europe generally follow one of three pathways: They enter low-wage, low-skilled jobs, secure employment in specialized sectors, or become entrepreneurs. The type of job available to refugees often depends on their qualifications, prior experience, and the availability of jobs in their host countries.

1. *Low-wage, low-skilled jobs*: Many Ukrainian refugees, especially those who arrived without sufficient knowledge of the local language or without recognized qualifications, initially find work in low-wage, low-skilled sectors. These jobs include positions in retail, hospitality, agriculture, cleaning, and construction. For example, refugees in Poland have filled numerous vacancies in agriculture, with many working in farms and factories to help meet the demand for labor. While these jobs are essential to the functioning of local economies, they are often characterized by poor working conditions and low wages. In some cases, local governments and organizations are organizing training programs for refugees so that they can enter into a higher skill level. In Saint-Vaury, France, Ukrainian

women living there had the opportunity to complete French-language and professional training with GRETA—the Group of Experts on Action Against Trafficking in Human Beings. Those refugees then secured internships with local companies as part of their journey toward becoming certified "cleaning and hygiene officers." This qualification is expected to open doors for permanent employment opportunities. The initiative arose from collaboration between the town hall, GRETA, and the Federation Exchanges France-Ukraine (FEFU), reflecting a supportive ecosystem for Ukrainian refugees in the town. The trainers commend the women's hard work and highlight the technical aspects of the profession. The success of this collective training approach showcases the strength of solidarity and integration efforts in the region (Bressy 2023).

2. *Skilled employment*: Ukrainians with higher education or specialized skills are often able to find work in professional sectors, particularly in industries where there is high demand for labor. Fields like IT, healthcare, engineering, and teaching have seen a notable influx of Ukrainian refugees. Ukrainian IT specialists, engineers, and healthcare workers have been able to integrate quickly into the European labor market, filling gaps in the workforce and contributing to sectors experiencing labor shortages. For instance, many Ukrainian doctors and nurses have been able to practice in countries like Germany, Poland, and the Czech Republic, thanks to the mutual recognition of their qualifications and fast-track procedures for integration into the health system. In the Netherlands, employers have been eager to hire refugee women in various sectors because Ukrainians are often well educated, particularly in technical fields, and thus align with the country's need for workers in the energy transition. The agrifood sector is particularly interested in hiring refugees when it anticipates labor shortages during the harvest season

(Vries 2022). In Germany, companies showed leadership in this regard as well. The prosthesis manufacturer Ottobock trained Ukrainian orthopedic technicians in Duderstadt, Germany, to help war victims regain mobility. The technicians learned how to attach artificial knee joints, with the goal of providing prosthetic limbs to the numerous war invalids in Ukraine. Ottobock has been active in the Ukrainian market and has delivered a workshop container to Lviv to facilitate quick assistance after amputations. However, the training of technicians remains a bottleneck, and increasing their numbers would enable more war victims to receive prostheses (Weidmann 2023).

3. *Entrepreneurship*: A growing number of Ukrainian refugees have chosen to start their own businesses in their host countries. The entrepreneurial spirit among Ukrainians has been particularly strong in countries like Poland with established Ukrainian communities. Ukrainian refugees have opened restaurants, grocery stores, language schools, and tech start-ups, introducing local markets to Ukrainian products and services. These small businesses not only provide a source of income for refugees but also contribute to the local economy by creating jobs for other refugees and local people. Some refugees with backgrounds in e-commerce and digital marketing have also tapped into online business opportunities and established businesses that can be run remotely. We discuss this pathway to economic integration in more detail later.

CHALLENGES FACED BY UKRAINIAN REFUGEES IN THE JOB MARKET

While many Ukrainian refugees have found employment, their integration into the European labor market has not been without challenges. The main obstacles include language barriers, recognition of qualifications, legal and bureaucratic hurdles, and discrimination and prejudice.

1. *Language barriers*: One of the most significant challenges faced by Ukrainian refugees is the language barrier. While many Ukrainians speak Russian or some English, the official languages of their host countries—such as Polish, German, or Czech—can pose a substantial hurdle in securing skilled employment. Even for refugees with technical or professional qualifications, a lack of fluency in the local language often limits their ability to work in their chosen field. In some countries, language courses have been offered to refugees to help them improve their language skills, but the speed at which refugees can learn and integrate varies widely. In countries like Poland, where many Ukrainians already speak a Slavic language, integration has been smoother, but in others, refugees face more significant challenges. Many employers found this to be the case at a job fair that was organized in Hamburg, Germany. The Horst Busch Group, specializing in electrical and safety engineering, attended a job fair to recruit new employees, including welders and electrical engineers, but language barriers became apparent during interviews because many applicants only spoke English. Around twenty thousand Ukrainian refugees were registered in Hamburg in 2022, and the focus is shifting toward their integration into the labor market. An evaluation revealed that the majority of refugees have academic degrees or have completed apprenticeships, with knowledge of German at a beginner level and English being more prevalent, but the language barrier remains a significant hurdle, and proficiency in German is seen as crucial for successful integration into the workforce. The German

Chamber of Skilled Crafts offered advice and assistance for Ukrainian craftsmen and companies interested in hiring or training refugees (Klesse et al. 2022).

2. *Recognition of qualifications*: While the EU has made strides in facilitating the recognition of foreign qualifications, Ukrainian refugees sometimes encounter difficulties in getting their educational credentials recognized in their host countries. Healthcare professionals, teachers, and engineers, for instance, may need to undergo additional certification or training to practice their profession in the EU. This process can be time-consuming and costly, particularly for those who have already fled a war zone and may have limited resources. In some cases, refugees may have to accept lower-skilled jobs than their qualifications would suggest, which creates a mismatch between their experience and their job.
3. *Legal and bureaucratic barriers*: Even though Ukrainian refugees have been granted temporary protection and the right to work in the EU, navigating the legal and bureaucratic systems of their host countries can be complex. Refugees may face challenges in securing work permits or understanding the tax and social security systems in their new countries. This challenge can create a sense of uncertainty and frustration, particularly for those wishing to work in regulated professions.
4. *Discrimination and prejudice*: Although Ukrainians have generally been welcomed in many European countries due to the shared cultural ties and solidarity in the face of Russia's aggression, some refugees face discrimination and prejudice in the job market. Refugees with darker skin tones or non-Ukrainian backgrounds may experience more overt discrimination, which limits their opportunities. In some cases, Ukrainian refugees may also face resentment from local populations, particularly in areas where economic pressures are already high or where anti-immigrant sentiment is prevalent.

Despite these challenges, Ukrainian refugees have made significant contributions to their host countries' economies. Their labor fills critical gaps in sectors such as agriculture, healthcare, construction, and IT, all of which are vital to the functioning of the economy. Ukrainian refugees are particularly valuable in countries like Poland, where labor shortages in the manufacturing and service sectors have created high demand for workers. Many refugees also contribute to the social and cultural fabric of their host countries by sharing their language, traditions, and cuisine. Ukrainian-run businesses such as restaurants and grocery stores offer local populations a taste of Ukrainian culture while providing jobs for both refugees and local people.

In the long term, as refugees gain better language skills and access to further education and training, they will likely become an increasingly important part of the workforce in their host countries. Many refugees have expressed a desire to build a future in Europe, and their integration into the labor market represents an opportunity not only for personal advancement but also for the economic growth of their new communities.

The influx of Ukrainian refugees into Europe has presented both challenges and opportunities for the continent. While many refugees have faced significant obstacles in securing employment—such as language barriers, recognition of qualifications, and bureaucratic hurdles—they have nonetheless contributed to the European labor market, filling crucial gaps in industries ranging from agriculture to healthcare to technology. The right to work granted under the EU's Temporary Protection Directive has enabled Ukrainian refugees to rebuild their lives while also benefiting the economies of their host countries. As refugees continue to integrate and access better opportunities, the impact of their contributions will only increase, making them an integral part of the European workforce in the years to come.

The EU has been critiqued by journalists, academics, and activists for being too little too late for too many other displaced communities. Specifically, critics have highlighted that the EU will invoke a generous and welcoming refugee policy to white, Christian refugees but fail to be as open to Muslim Syrian and Afghan refugees as well as those fleeing wars in sub-Saharan Africa. While the critiques from the left are strong, so too are the critiques from the far right. Right-wing nationalistic parties have been gaining strength and vote share in European countries for the past twenty years. When EU member states have welcomed new waves of refugees, as Germany did during the height of the Syrian crisis, the right-wing backlash was extreme. Similarly, the UK's Brexit movement was motivated by an anti-EU sentiment largely driven by the perception that the EU was allowing too many migrants into continental Europe who then made their way to the British Isles. As Armstrong (2023) notes:

> In the EU, several countries have become particularly effective breeding grounds for right-wing extremism. In Poland, the Law and Justice party (PiS) came to power in 2015. In the 2019 parliamentary elections, the PiS-led United Right coalition managed to retain a majority of seats in the Polish Sejm, however the coalition lost its majority in the October 2023 parliamentary elections. Nevertheless, it remains in front, and the PiS currently holds 35 percent of seats (42 percent when including its coalition partners).
>
> In Hungary, Viktor Orbán's Fidesz has already been in power for over ten years and won a landslide victory in the 2022 parliamentary elections. It currently holds 59 percent of parliamentary seats and forms a governing coalition with the Christian Democrat NKDP. In Austria, the FPÖ came to power in 2017, but after a sharp decline in the 2019 elections, the party now accounts for just 16 percent (down from 28 percent in 2017), a share similar to that achieved by

> the Rassemblement National after its historic 2022 legislative result in France. In Belgium, the Flemish nationalist party, Vlaams Belang, currently weighs in at 12 percent, while in Germany, the AfD is down to 11 percent after losing 11 seats in the 2021 federal elections.

It is important to understand that welcoming refugee policies can have a backlash effect as right-wing parties, hungry for a scapegoat and rallying call, exploit the presence of the displaced for their political gain.

ENTREPRENEURSHIP AND SEEING THE ECONOMIC VALUE OF DISPLACED UKRAINIANS

Many of the 8 million Ukrainians that fled the Russian invasion, particularly those with professional skills and entrepreneurial aspirations, are not merely looking for safety; they are also seizing opportunities to start businesses and contribute to their host countries' economies. This trend highlights a remarkable narrative of resilience, adaptability, and the transformative power of entrepreneurship in times of crisis. We conducted a media analysis of "Ukrainian refugee" and "Ukrainian entrepreneur" across European language media search engines to develop an understanding of the experience of Ukrainian refugees and their economic integration. We found coverage from papers in Poland, France, the Netherlands, Germany, Romania, Moldova, and Hungary highlighting the successes (and challenges) of entrepreneurship, employment, benefits to local economies, strategies for matching displaced job seekers, and firms that are hiring, as well as the need to support arriving refugees so that they can take advantage of the TPD.

Ukrainian refugees in Europe face numerous challenges—language barriers, legal hurdles, and the trauma of war. However, many are choosing to view their displacement not as a setback but as an opportunity to start afresh. Entrepreneurs are leveraging their skills, experience, and creativity to establish new businesses across various industries, from technology start-ups to restaurants and clothing brands. This entrepreneurial spirit is not only a survival mechanism but also a way to integrate into their new communities and contribute to local economies.

Several factors have facilitated the growth of Ukrainian businesses in Europe. First, many refugees possess valuable skills and experience in fields such as IT, engineering, design, and healthcare. Ukraine has a well-established reputation for its technical and scientific talent, and many refugees are able to transfer their expertise to the European job market. This technical proficiency has been particularly advantageous in countries like Poland, Germany, and the Czech Republic, where there is high demand for skilled labor in sectors such as technology and manufacturing.

Second, European governments and organizations have provided a range of support mechanisms to help refugees start businesses. In response to the influx of Ukrainians, several EU countries have introduced policies that offer refugees easier access to business permits, financial support, and integration programs. For example, Poland, which hosts one of the largest populations of Ukrainian refugees, has seen a surge in the number of Ukrainian-owned small businesses. Local governments and NGOs have facilitated entrepreneurship workshops, mentorship programs, and funding opportunities specifically for refugees, helping them navigate the challenges of starting a business in a foreign country.

Third, impact investors have mobilized as well. For example, Ukrainian Tech Ventures, a nonprofit venture fund, worked to raise $50 million to support Ukrainian entrepreneurs who have been forced to relocate their businesses to the West due to the Russian invasion. The fund planned to back two hundred startups and help Ukrainians gain a foothold and grow successfully in their new locations. The founders of the fund, which launched on May 1, 2022, personally invested in it and did not take salaries, emphasizing the humanitarian and commercial nature of the initiative. The fund's nonprofit status and profit-sharing approach aimed to attract investors and mitigate the negative impacts of the conflict on Ukraine's tech industry (Jamal 2022).

Additionally, European cities with large refugee populations have become hubs of multicultural innovation, merging different cultural perspectives and ideas to create new business ventures. Cities like Warsaw, Berlin, and Prague have seen an influx of Ukrainian-run cafés, restaurants, and retail outlets that blend Ukrainian traditions with local tastes. These businesses not only provide employment opportunities for Ukrainians but also introduce local populations to the rich cultural heritage of Ukraine.

Numerous success stories have emerged from the refugee business community in Europe. For instance, in Poland, a country that has welcomed over 1.5 million Ukrainians, many refugees have started small-scale enterprises that have quickly gained traction. In Warsaw, several Ukrainian entrepreneurs have opened tech companies that offer software development, app creation, and IT consulting services to European clients. These companies have flourished due to the high level of technical expertise among the founders and the region's growing demand for digital services.

Another noteworthy example comes from the food industry. Ukrainian refugees have opened restaurants and food trucks in cities like Berlin and Krakow that offer traditional Ukrainian cuisine. These establishments not only cater to the local demand for authentic international food but also provide a sense of comfort and connection to fellow Ukrainians who are far from home. Some restaurants have even gained recognition in the local media, contributing to the broader awareness of Ukrainian culture and cuisine.

The impact of Ukrainian entrepreneurship extends beyond the businesses themselves. The success of these enterprises has a ripple effect on the local economy, creating jobs, stimulating local markets, and encouraging cross-cultural exchange. For example, many Ukrainian refugees have fostered integration and mutual understanding by hiring local people to work in their businesses. Ukrainian businesses have also contributed to the local economy by paying taxes, purchasing goods and services, and engaging in the broader business ecosystem.

CHALLENGES AND BARRIERS TO ENTREPRENEURIAL SUCCESS

Despite the opportunities and support, Ukrainian entrepreneurs face several challenges in Europe. One of the most significant hurdles is the language barrier. While many Ukrainians speak some level of English, fluency in the local language is often crucial for navigating bureaucratic systems, negotiating contracts, and effectively marketing products and services. This hurdle can be particularly challenging in countries where language differences are more pronounced, such as in Germany or Hungary.

Another challenge is the uncertainty surrounding refugee status and the associated legal and bureaucratic processes. While the EU has implemented temporary protection measures for Ukrainian refugees that grant them residence and work rights, the long-term stability of these protections remains uncertain. This situation can create anxiety among entrepreneurs who fear that changes in legal status may affect their ability to operate businesses or access funding. Access to capital is also a common issue. While there are various funding programs available for refugees, securing investment can be difficult for newcomers, especially those without a strong credit history in their host country or established networks. Furthermore, many refugees lack the collateral or financial resources required to take out loans and so have limited ability to scale their businesses.

The entrepreneurial ventures launched by Ukrainian refugees in Europe represent a powerful testament to human resilience and ingenuity. Despite facing numerous challenges, these individuals are transforming adversity into opportunity, not only rebuilding their own lives but also contributing to the economies of their host countries. The success of Ukrainian-run businesses in Europe serves as a reminder of the importance of support systems—whether in the form of government policies, community networks, or access to capital—in empowering refugees to thrive.

As Ukraine continues to endure the hardships of war, the stories of entrepreneurial refugees provide hope and inspiration, showcasing the potential for refugees to become key drivers of economic growth and social integration. By harnessing their skills and creativity, Ukrainian refugees are proving that even in the darkest times, entrepreneurship can be a beacon of light, offering new possibilities and pathways to a better future.

In Poland in 2022, Ukrainians established an incredible 17,457 businesses. The most common types of businesses were cosmetology, computer programming, and building- or construction-related activities. Since the beginning of 2023, these types of businesses are still the most common. As of early 2022, Ukrainians were most likely to establish businesses in Warsaw, Krakow, or Wroclaw (ZPP 2023).

This high level of entrepreneurial activity also made it to European-wide news; Euronews reported that as of 2023 the influx of Ukrainian refugees into Poland had led to the creation of roughly twenty-five thousand businesses within the country. This success was primarily due to Poland's policy of supporting the entry of Ukrainians into the business sector and allowing them to operate on the same terms as Polish citizens. There have been many benefits from this approach, as these new businesses have paid taxes and filled gaps in the labor market. However, some parts of Polish society have expressed concern about limited access to healthcare or social benefits as a result of these changes (Euronews 2023)

In addition to founding new start-ups, Ukrainians have been moving into neighboring countries. As *Rzeczpospolita* reported, Ukrainian innovators are increasingly establishing themselves in the Polish start-up scene, attracted by geographical and cultural proximity as well as by a relatively small language barrier. The war in Ukraine has led to a significant influx of Ukrainian start-ups to Poland, with the country serving as a hub for innovation and entrepreneurship. Polish start-up ecosystems have offered support programs for Ukrainian entrepreneurs, and venture capital funds are recognizing the potential of Ukrainian start-ups. However, while Poland has become a temporary hub for Ukrainian innovators, it is not expected to be a long-term center of activity, as many teams may return to Ukraine after the conflict ends. The competition for becoming the leading regional start-up hub includes countries like Lithuania, Latvia, and Estonia (Duszczyk 2023).

Not only do these new start-ups provide new ideas and innovative richness to the Polish entrepreneurial ecosystem, but these newly founded refugee businesses can also contribute to the growth of the Polish economy. According to Roman Dryps, the head of the Silesian branch of the Polish-Ukrainian Chamber of Commerce, Ukrainian businesses with capital in Poland can contribute to the country's economic growth and become a "transmission belt" for Polish companies during the reconstruction of Ukraine. Many of these Ukrainian companies operate in trade, construction, and transport and storage sectors. However, starting a business in Poland is not easy or cheap for Ukrainians because they face challenges with regulations, relocation of assets, and lack of specialists. Dryps believes that integrating Ukrainian capital investments with the Polish legal system and labor market is crucial, and he highlights that Ukrainian entrepreneurs must be aware of the differences in business ecosystems between the EU and Ukraine. Nonetheless, Ukrainian businesses can make contributions to the Polish economy through tax payments and consumption, and many of these entrepreneurs intend to remain in Poland even after the war ends (*Gazeta Olsztyńska* 2023).

Through employment, entrepreneurship, and investment, Ukrainian refugees are bringing economic benefits to receiving countries across Europe. The economist Giovanni Peri argues that refugees can significantly contribute to the labor market when the right policies match them to job shortages and minimize competition with native people. He emphasizes that investing in the human capital of refugees can lead to their integration, employment, and economic growth in the long run (Edwards 2022).

The policies the EU put in place in this crisis should be a model for hosting countries around the world. The efforts that European national, state, and local governments have put forward to integrate the displaced should be replicated by countries seeking to not only best support the displaced and the citizens hosting them but to also benefit from their enormous potential, contributions, and assets. Finally, the network of nonprofits and for-profit initiatives across Europe stand out as a powerful model of what expedited economic integration can look like.

10

A BLUEPRINT FOR BELONGING

Scaling Refugee Lens Investing Worldwide

The opening of 2025 felt as if the world was in free fall. A newly instated Trump administration froze the US refugee resettlement program, trapping thousands of Afghans that supported US troops in the Taliban's crosshairs and overnight crushing the dreams of thousands who have rigorously vetted to move to America, begin a new life, and contribute to the American economy. It dismantled the United States Agency for International Development (USAID), which had provided billions of dollars of support to save the lives of those forced to run for their lives and to stabilize their families as they worked to move forward. The Trump administration froze billions of dollars in grants and loans appropriated by Congress and contractually obligated by the previous government, ensuring that there would be no taxpayer dollars to support the nonprofits providing lifesaving shelter, food, and medicine to the displaced. It acted on its campaign promise to round up undocumented refugees and migrants, put them in handcuffs in front of their children, and deport them to dangerous parts of the world. And yet, the arguments of this book are as relevant now as they were a month ago, a year ago, and a decade ago. When governments fail or are unable to act, it falls to the rest of us to help our most vulnerable. When the lives of the displaced are saved and they are provided with the basic building blocks of life, they thrive, lead lives of impact, love their families, support their communities, build companies that transform markets, and create jobs and economic value, ultimately preventing the next conflict and new waves of displacement. Each of us can play a role in kick-starting these virtuous cycles.

Across the world from Europe to Mexico, California to Jordan, host communities are proactively welcoming the displaced and seeing them for the hardworking, resourceful employees and entrepreneurs they are. Dozens of examples and test cases show that the right mix of policies, support, and investments can help bring about economic integration of the displaced and higher levels of human thriving for both refugees and the communities hosting them.

As we have traveled the world and worked with refugee representatives while hosting governments, impact investors, and international donors, we have learned a few things. As chapter 5 has shown us, there is an opportunity for US-based impact investors to use creative financing to help new Americans improve their prospects at home as well as be a force for good in the broader world.

US politics over the past one hundred years has shown the rise and fall and rise again of anti-other politics. Periodically politicians come to power by demonizing the most vulnerable and blaming them for the ills of the country. But no matter how antirefugee the politicians in the White House and Congress are, millions of Americans are welcoming new neighbors, helping their children get enrolled in school, donating old pots and pans to help them set up their new kitchens, and selling cookies at bake sales to raise funds for the needs of new mothers. The United States has dominated the global economy through the decades because it has welcomed waves of innovators with new perspectives and ideas and the grit, will, and determination to build a better life for themselves and their families. Antirefugee and anti-immigrant propaganda by politicians is dangerous and does influence public opinion when it is paired with lies like those propagated by Donald Trump and J. D. Vance about Haitians eating household pets in Ohio. But Americans largely support welcoming the other. A 2022 Gallup poll showed that 78 percent of Americans supported resettling 100,000 Ukrainian refugees (Saad 2022). And people have rallied to support refugees when they've come: Nonprofit volunteers have found rooms to rent out to them, church groups have helped them set up a new life, musicians have offered benefit concerts, and college students have offered language tutoring. We have worked with refugee resettlement nonprofits in the many cities we have lived in, and in each town, there are teachers running afterschool programs for Karen children fleeing Burma, businesses proactively hiring refugees from the Democratic Republic of the Congo, and nonprofits providing microloans to launch a new crop of entrepreneurs.

US impact investors have also used another creative tool of finance to protect the displaced: divestment. Impact investors and philanthropists who were horrified by the family-separation policies of the first Trump administration decided to move their money out of the real estate investment trusts (REITs) that were building detention centers to separate mothers from their children. The Real Money Moves campaign used what it had learned from its campaigns to divest from private prisons and thus ensure that its dollars weren't going to traumatize migrant and refugee children.

A third lesson that emerged from chapter 5 is that when a political regime is in power that believes in an American role in the world, development banks like the US Development Finance Corporation (USDFC) can be important partners to a global network of impact investors. For example, in November 2024, the USDFC signed a first-of-its-kind agreement with Opportunity Bank Uganda Limited that will enable an increase in lending to refugee businesses and Ugandan host communities by up to $9 million over six years. This partnership is intended to help create and grow sixty-thousand small enterprises across Uganda. Roughly 70 percent of these loans will be for refugees, and 30 percent will be allocated to members of Ugandan host communities. USAID planned to support the partnership by providing advisory services to prospective borrowers and Opportunity Bank (US Embassy of Uganda 2024). Since eighteen thousand loans were planned to be specifically for women, USAID was to provide financial training to women borrowers and help Opportunity Bank to design and market the loans to women. With the shuttering of USAID in January 2025 by the Trump administration, it is unclear how this critical piece of the partnership will play out.

This lesson reminds us that politics does matter because it drives policy. While the current Trump administration does not yet seem interested in using the USDFC as an instrument to build peace and prosperity around the world and to secure America at home, there is still hope that a future American administration could return to the power of this approach.

Chapter 6, which focused on the Middle East and specifically the story of refugees in Jordan, showed that refugees are incredibly entrepreneurial and benefit from the same types of support as all entrepreneurs do, including incubators and mentorship. Rates of entrepreneurship vary across countries, as founding companies can be easier or harder, depending on the location. But regardless of the nation, entrepreneuring is a challenging pursuit. Entrepreneurs are often developing a new product or service while simultaneously trying to recruit a team; market their business; build their website; incorporate; establish their books; get up to speed on regulations, bookkeeping, and supply chain management; understand pricing models; and establish their brand, all on a resource-constrained budget. To quickly make these most critical business decisions, entrepreneurs everywhere can benefit from educational models and from mentorship from other businesspeople who have already walked the path. The examples of ShamalStart in Jordan are a model for welcoming communities around the globe.

Chapter 7 took us halfway around the world by focusing on Latin America and the specific experience of the displaced from all over Central and South America as they arrived in Mexico. We learned more lessons here, underscoring what we have seen both in the United States and the Middle East: Refugees are exceptionally hardworking and need the same social infrastructure that all working parents need, including childcare and schools. The United Nations High Commissioner for Refugees (UNHCR) program that resettles refugees in the busy export cities of northern Mexico is a proof point. Proactive policies and programs that provide workers with the basic social infrastructure to keep their children safe and learning have a related outcome of helping those parents be dependable and hardworking employees. Just as ShamalStart provides a model for what communities can do to support refugee entrepreneurs, the local refugee program run by the UNHCR and the Mexican refugee agency, which was supported, historically, by the US government, is a model for what communities around the world can do to quickly integrate families into their economies and help mothers and fathers contribute to the workforce while their children are educated for the next generation of economic evolution.

While our travels through Latin America and the Middle East highlighted the power of supporting entrepreneurs and workers with basic necessities, our work in East Africa, discussed in chapter 8, also highlighted the power of microfinance. Mentorship and education are important, but at the end of the day, most businesses, no matter how small, require some capital to launch and grow. The success stories of refugee lens investments and companies in Kenya, Uganda, and beyond in East Africa show that refugees stay and build new lives if given the chance, with microfinance providing a stabilizing force. The visionary work of Kiva's World Refugee Fund and the early work of Acumen show that a small loan will be repaid and go a very long way in helping the displaced get back on their feet and build a new life for themselves and their families.

While the 2025 political context in the United States demonstrates a worst-case scenario when xenophobic and anti-refugee regimes gain power, a counterpoint can be seen in the European Union (EU) during the Russian invasion of Ukraine. As chapter 9 demonstrated, in an unprecedented, generous, and enlightened move, the EU ushered in a new paradigm for the economic integration of refugees. The Temporary Protection Directive (TPD), which allowed refugees fleeing Russian aggression to participate in the economy, enabled high levels of workforce participation, new business incorporation, and self-sufficiency for Ukrainian refugees. This directive provides a model for nations and communities around that world that want to strengthen their economies while also subscribing to values of generosity and solidarity. With nationwide or region-wide policies like the TPD, we see that refugee investment opportunities are scalable and can offer an incredible return on investment.

This book, we hope, has shown that concerned communities around the world have developed creative solutions to support refugee entrepreneurs and workers. But what the last twenty years working in this space has also taught us is what all MBA students learn: All investment involves risk. And this is even more true when we are discussing investing in people who are in, proximate to, or fleeing active war zones. We should never underestimate the ability of power-hungry people to destroy a peace for their own personal gain. In regions where we thought war was part of the distant past, we have seen an autocrat attack a peaceful neighbor in Ukraine, resulting in hundreds of thousands killed, a half-million to a million maimed, and 11 million displaced internally and across borders.

In places like Gaza, where creative microfinance platforms supported Palestinian refugees with the hope of a better tomorrow, we see all their gains lost, bakeries destroyed, markets in rubble, and people's livelihoods blown apart. According to the United Nations, over sixty-six thousand men, women, and children have been killed and 90 percent of the Gazan population has been forcibly displaced, often multiple times. One in five children were acutely malnourished by September 2025, according to the World Health Organization, and famine was officially confirmed in Gaza City by the Integrated Food Security Phase Classification. In November 2024, a UN special committee found Israel's warfare methods in Gaza consistent with genocide, including the use of starvation as a weapon of war. Amnesty International, the International Association of Genocide Scholars, Physicians for Human Rights Israel, and the Israeli human rights organization B'Tselem, as well as over forty nations around the world, have declared Israel's war on Gaza a genocide.

A PATHWAY FORWARD

When governments are unable or unwilling to support forcibly displaced people, the burden falls on compassionate private citizens. Yet without lasting political solutions, even the most dedicated efforts risk being undone in a matter of months or years. We need a new global initiative, engaging all stakeholders, that will scale up the successful pilots showcased in this book to establish inclusive economies around the world. Our Blueprint for Inclusive Economies involves moving forward, past governments that are inactive or hostile and around governments that are barriers, and instead working with governments that are creative moral leaders. It includes at least eight strategies, outlined briefly here and then more thoroughly discussed in the following paragraphs:

1. Catalyze a G7 challenge for development finance institutions to mobilize $1 billion for refugee lens investing in the next three years.
2. Forge a collaboration across private-sector impact investing networks, including the Global Impact Investing Network (GIIN), Toniic, the Mission Investors Exchange, and other regional impact investing groups, to unlock $1 billion in private refugee lens investing.
3. Mobilize philanthropists and foundations serving the displaced to begin making program-related investments (PRIs) and mission-related investments (MRIs) according to the refugee lens and to use their philanthropic funds as catalytic capital in blended finance deals to help the displaced and their host communities.
4. Facilitate community development financial institutions (CDFIs) and community foundations to provide PRIs that

will bridge the gap between refugee resettlement agency support and thriving economic integration of refugees into their new communities.

5. Encourage executives of large corporations to consider how they could incorporate refugee businesses in their supply chains, target services, and products to benefit the displaced, as well as how they could integrate refugee hiring in their business operations globally.
6. Mobilize a campaign focused on small-business owners to encourage small-business entrepreneurs to incorporate refugee lens businesses into their supply chains, target products and services in service of the displaced, and encourage refugee hiring.
7. Mobilize everyday consumers to consider using their wallets to support the displaced by proactively buying from and supporting refugee lens companies.
8. Looking forward to a new US administration that sees a role for US leadership in the world, begin laying the groundwork for the USDFC to launch a $100 million refugee lens fund.

First, building on the success of the gender lens investing movement, we see an opportunity for leadership by the G7, or possibly the G7 minus the United States. The Group of Seven (G7) is an intergovernmental political and economic forum consisting of Canada, France, Germany, Italy, Japan, the United Kingdom, and the United States; the EU is a "nonenumerated member." It is organized around shared values of pluralism, liberal democracy, and representative government. Japan has already established itself as an innovative leader in the area of refugee lens investing. Japan's development agency, Japan International Cooperation Agency (JICA), provided early catalytic capital to the Refugee Investment Network and explored how it could more creatively and impactfully use its grant dollars to support the displaced in the Middle East and East Africa. The European G7 members of France, Germany, and Italy, as discussed in chapter 9, have ushered in an unprecedented framework for supporting refugees with the right to work through the Temporary Protective Status for all Ukrainian refugees. Canada has had its own creative refugee economic integration programs, including its Refugee Assistance Program (RAP), its Immigration, Refugees, and Citizenship Canada (IRCC) Settlement Program, and IOM O-Canada app which assists refugees with future integration. This group of countries had demonstrated leadership in ushering in a new approach to refugee reception, and through their development financial institutions could commit to investing in a way that would strengthen this new approach. We call for G7 (or G6 without the United States) development finance institutions to mobilize $1 billion for refugee lens investing in the next three years.

Second, geopolitics are uncertain, and with Trump-induced trade wars emerging and a cascade of recessions around the world, we must be realistic that the world's most vulnerable may not rise to the top of the agenda for G7 leaders (though we hope and advocate they do). In the face of government inaction, we believe that private-sector impact investing networks, including the Global Impact Investing Network (GIIN), Toniic, the Mission Investors Exchange, and other regional impact investing groups, could collaborate to unlock $1 billion in refugee lens investing. Every year these powerful networks organize global convenings in which mission-driven investors flock together to learn about strategies, tools, and frames to increase their impact. We believe a series of refugee lens investing actions at each of these global convenings can help educate investors about this powerful vehicle for impact and forge collaborations to mobilize significant new pools of capital for refugee lens investing deals.

Third, we believe that there is a significant opportunity to mobilize philanthropists and foundations serving the displaced to begin making PRIs and MRIs according to the refugee lens and to use their philanthropic funds as catalytic capital in blended finance deals to help displaced and host communities. A major driver of the growth of impact investing over the past fifteen years has been the realization by large private and community foundations that while they might be directing 5 percent of their endowments toward their mission, they have been leaving billions of dollars of potential impact capital on the table by not considering the impact of their corpus (the principal endowment). Increasingly, private and community foundations have gone on a learning journey to become comfortable moving beyond 0 percent return grants and to use some of their philanthropic funding to support social enterprises that allow them to achieve their purported mission while also recovering the grant and then using the funds again for future impact down the road. These are called Program Related Investments, or PRIs, because they draw from the 5 percent of funding traditionally earmarked for *programs*, but they can be paid back with no interest (a recoverable grant) or may have some level of interest (often just enough to keep pace with inflation to ensure capital preservation). Foundations have also dipped into their endowments and, instead of investing only in public equities and through large asset managers, have decided to invest some of their corpus in investments that could have an impact. These are the Mission Related Investments, or MRIs. For the large foundations and private family offices that have historically committed to philanthropically supporting refugees and the displaced, there is a huge opportunity to educate and unlock program- and mission-related investments into refugee lens investing deals.

In addition, private and community foundations have learned that they can have outsized impact by "blending" their philanthropic grants and low-interest PRIs with market rate capital in blended finance deals. Blended finance is the use of catalytic capital from public or philanthropic sources to increase private-sector investment in economic development projects. For example, an affordable housing development in a community hosting a large resettled refugee population would be an opportunity for foundations to catalyze the participation of more risk-averse lenders like private-sector banks or investors. Partnering with global thought leaders in blended finance would provide a platform for connecting, convening, and building deals. Such a thought leader is Convergence, the global network for blended finance that exists to increase private investment in emerging markets and developing economies.

A special emphasis in this area would be on faith-based impact investors. Impact investment's history began with faith-based investors. The Quakers chose to not invest in the slave trade and slave ships. Then the Protestants decided to not invest in "sin-stocks" like gambling, alcohol, and prostitution. Catholic nuns, Lutheran congregations, and Jewish values-aligned impact investing funds have been directing their dollars to investments in line with their values for years. "Welcoming the other" is an important concept in Judeo-Christian traditions. In 2018 the Vatican organized an impact investing conference in which we had the opportunity to learn much from faith-based investors around the world that are aligning their portfolios and retirement funds with their values. The conference focused on four areas of importance to the global community: climate change, health, migrants and refugees, and youth unemployment.

Fourth, there is an opportunity to help CDFIs bridge the gap between refugee resettlement agency support and economic integration of refugees into their new communities. CDFIs expand economic opportunity in low-income communities by providing access to financial products and services for local residents and businesses. They can be structured as banks, credit unions, loan funds, microloan funds, or venture capital providers. CDFIs often help families finance their first homes, support community members starting businesses, and invest in local health centers, schools, or community centers. They strive to foster economic opportunity and revitalize neighborhoods. A little bit of proactive thought and outreach could go a long way in connecting these CDFIs with newly arrived residents and helping them start businesses, buy homes, and begin building assets.

Fifth, all business leaders have a role to play and a positive impact to make by considering how they could incorporate refugee businesses in their supply chains, target services, and products and also how they could hire refugees in their global business operations. Larger businesses can have large impacts. The Business Roundtable and other industry and trade associations of large *Fortune* 500 companies could mobilize commitments to support the displaced through the private sector. The Obama administration began this work in the "Partnership for Refugees," while the Tent Foundation carried on this work during the first Trump presidency and expanded commitments to European companies. Now perhaps is the moment for a renewed set of public commitments by top global CEOs. Private companies can be a powerful force for integrating the displaced and creating a pathway for the private sector to help build peace.

Sixth, the power of the private sector to hire, buy from, and support refugees and the displaced isn't limited to large multinational companies. We believe there is an opportunity to mobilize worldwide campaigns that can encourage small-business entrepreneurs to incorporate refugee lens businesses into their supply chains, to target products and services in service of the displaced, and to hire refugees. This effort could be motivated by organizations like Global Chamber, a network of chambers of commerce in 525 metro areas around the world.

Seventh, the wide-scale adoption of refugee lens ideas could create an opportunity for every individual to be a changemaker. We believe that everyday consumers can be mobilized, in markets around the world, to consider using their wallets to support the displaced by proactively buying from and supporting refugee lens companies. This effort could benefit from partnership with major global platforms like Global Citizen and World Refugee Day, as well as from partnerships with faith-based organizations.

Finally, while not likely a strategy pursued immediately due to the Trump administration's hostility toward refugees, development, and internationalism, we believe there is an opportunity to begin laying the groundwork and building a coalition to support a $100 million refugee lens investing fund through the USDFC under a new, future US administration that sees a role for US leadership in the world. The USDFC is America's development finance institution and partners with the private sector to finance solutions to the most critical challenges facing the developing world. It was created in 2018 by the BUILD Act by merging the Overseas Private Investment Corporation (OPIC) with the Development Credit Authority (DCA) of USAID. As discussed in chapters 3 and 5, the USDFC's 2X Women's Initiative has catalyzed billions of investments in projects that are owned or led by women or that provide a product or service that empowers women. This initiative provides an actionable model for a USDFC refugee initiative that can build on the success and learnings of the 2X initiative but will be targeted at supporting and stabilizing the world's displaced.

During Trump's first presidency, coalitions of impact investors and changemakers, recognizing that little could be accomplished in partnership with the administration, took a longer-term view and collaborated and planned initiatives that could be implemented when there was a change in administration. Similarly, global impact investors, foundations, and family offices could work to develop a proposed new initiative for USDFC, to introduce if and when the winds change again.

CONCLUSION

As with many things in life, the past fifteen years of our work on massive, forced displacement have brought us incredible stories of resilience, hope, and beauty; they have also shown us the most violent and heartbreaking sides of humanity. As President Obama noted: "Progress does not happen in a straight line," nor will it in the realm of refugee lens investing. We must build a movement to support the world's most vulnerable in the face of careless governments. We must mobilize to elect governments that do better. By building economies of belonging, we can transform stories of resilience and hope into sustainable systems of shared prosperity.

ACKNOWLEDGMENTS

First, we would like to thank all the individuals who have so graciously shared their harrowing stories of hardship, struggle, and displacement with us, as well as their incredible stories of resilience and in many cases innovation. We have been honored to work with refugees and internally displaced people around the world who have shown us that an alternative reality is possible, one in which the displaced are welcomed, integrated, and thriving in their new homes.

We would like to thank the Refugee Investment Network (RIN), especially our partners Tim Docking and Joanne Edelman, team members Selen Ucak and Danny Cutherell, and the visionary supporters of RIN's work, including Barry Landry, the Hilton Foundation, the Rockefeller Foundation, the Patrick J. McGovern Foundation, the Dunn Foundation, the Japan International Cooperation Agency, the Swiss Development Corporation, and the IKEA Foundation. We'd like to thank Andrew Stern at the Global Development Incubator for believing in our vision and seeing us through more than a few storms. A special thank you to our "early adopters," including RIN's Advisory Council, our Board of Directors, and supportive champions Cheryl Kiser, Sasha Chanoff, Mary Nazal, Shwan Taha, and the late Michael Levett.

We would like to thank the research assistants and translators who helped us deeply understand conditions on the ground, including Patrick Timmons for our fieldwork in Mexico; Expectation State, Andrew Collingwood, Lucy Hovil, Mary Nazzal, Abier Amarin, Ruby Assad, and Mona Labadi for our fieldwork in Jordan; and Open Capital Partners (OCP) for fieldwork in Uganda and East Africa. We'd also like to thank our friend Ross Perlin, who provided early guidance on framing our proposal, and Raegan Larussa, a Master of Public Policy candidate at the University of Virginia, who provided research assistance on early drafts of the manuscript. We would also like to thank the Frank Batten School of Leadership and Public Policy at the University of Virginia, which supported fieldwork in Mexico through a sabbatical in 2019–2020.

We'd also like to thank Myles C. Thompson and Brian Smith at Columbia University Press for originally believing in this project and for Greg Shaw, who helped us hone the argument and make it connect with a broader audience.

And of course, we'd like to thank our families for supporting us when we traveled to far-off places to better understand one of the biggest challenges of our time and to learn about promising ways to help the world's forcibly displaced people to integrate, thrive, and belong.

Appendix A

TERMINOLOGY

Asylum seeker: an individual who is seeking international protection. In countries with individualized procedures, an asylum seeker is someone whose claim has not yet been finally decided on by the country in which the claim is submitted.

Blended finance: the combination of public, philanthropic, and private capital that is used to fund economic development initiatives. Its goal is to attract private investment to emerging or struggling markets where projects might be considered too risky for commercial investors alone.

Concessionary return: a return on an investment that sacrifices some financial gain to achieve a social benefit, unlike market-rate returns.

Development finance institution: a financial institution that provides risk capital for economic development projects on a noncommercial basis.

Economic migrant: a migrant who crosses an international border motivated not by persecution or possible serious harm or death but for other reasons, such as to improve living conditions by working.

Forcibly displaced persons: all persons whose decision to move is forced in nature, including refugees, internally displaced persons, and asylum seekers. The total number of forcibly displaced persons worldwide was estimated at approximately 120 million people by 2026.

Guarantee: a form of credit enhancement in which a third party agrees to cover (or guarantee) a certain amount of loss for an investor. A standard guarantee is a broad commitment by a third party (the guarantor) to cover losses or fulfill obligations if the primary borrower or obligor defaults. It can cover the full amount of the obligation, and the guarantor assumes full liability for the guaranteed amount. It is commonly used in loans, bonds, and other credit arrangements to reassure lenders or investors. In first-loss guarantees, which are more specific, the guarantor agrees to cover initial losses up to a certain limit, not the entire exposure. These guarantees are limited in scope to a predefined amount or percentage of the total risk. The guarantor absorbs the first layer of losses, making the remaining risk more attractive to other investors or lenders. First-loss guarantees are often used in structured finance, development finance, or impact investing to catalyze private-sector participation by reducing perceived or actual risk.

Impact investing: a strategy of investing with the intention to generate positive, measurable social and environmental benefits alongside financial return.

Internally displaced persons (IDPs): all persons who are forced to flee due to armed conflicts, generalized violence, or human rights violations and who remain within their own countries.

Limited partner: a partner in a company or venture who receives limited profits from the business and whose liability toward its debts is legally limited to the extent of his or her investment.

Microfinance institutions: financial institutions that assist typically poor households and small enterprises in gaining access to financial services.

Private equity funds: closed-end funds that are considered an alternative investment class. Because they are private, their capital is not listed on a public exchange. A typical investment strategy undertaken by private equity funds is to take a controlling interest in an operating company or business—the *portfolio company*—and engage actively in the management and direction of the company or business in order to increase its value. Other private equity funds may specialize in making minority investments in fast-growing companies or start-ups.

Refugee: any person who "owing to a well-founded fear of being persecuted for reasons of race, religion, nationality, membership of particular social group, or political opinion, is outside the country of [their] nationality and is unable or, owing to such fear, is unwilling to avail [themself] of the protection of that country; or who, not having a nationality and being outside the country of [their] former habitual residence . . . is unable or, owing to such fear, is unwilling to return to it."

Refugee lens investments: investments that are made to improve the lives and well-being of refugees and their host communities. The Refugee Investment Network developed the "refugee lens" tool to provide investors with a framework for assessing and qualifying prospective deals as a refugee investment. The framework includes six categories: refugee-owned, refugee-led, refugee-supporting, refugee-supporting and host-weighted, refugee-lending facilities, and refugee funds.

Returnee: a refugee or internally displaced person who has returned to their country or area of origin to remain there permanently.

Venture capital fund: a type of private equity financing that fuels the growth of start-ups and early-stage companies with significant potential. Venture capitalists normally provide not only capital but also expertise, guidance, and network connections to help burgeoning businesses succeed.

Appendix B

REFUGEE LENS INVESTING TECHNICAL ASSISTANCE PLAYBOOK

Forced migration and displacement are the defining social challenges of our time. The Refugee Investment Network (RIN) creates long-term economic solutions to these challenges through refugee lens investing (RLI) and serves as a specialized intermediary between impact investing, blended-finance communities and the growing ecosystem of refugee-led and refugee-supporting enterprises. With support from the Hilton Foundation, RIN and Acumen have collaborated to develop a program entitled "Refugee Lens Investing in the Greater Horn of Africa." The program aims to boost economic opportunities for forcibly displaced people (FDPs) by fostering the growth of businesses that engage the displaced as customers, employees, or suppliers. As part of this program, RIN provided technical assistance to three locally based private-sector enterprises, with the result that an increased number of refugees and internally displaced people were incorporated into their operations. Based on the demonstrated success of these pilot cases, RIN created a playbook outlining a technical assistance (TA) strategy and an implementation process to provide interested refugee lens investors and enterprises with best practices, learnings, and recommendations. The playbook thus documents the process and outcomes of these engagements to create a series of enterprise-engagement models that could be applied elsewhere.

RATIONALE FOR RLI-TA

While RIN's assessments in Ethiopia, Kenya, and Uganda during Phase I of the "Refugee Lens Investing in the Greater Horn of Africa" program identified a full spectrum of RLI opportunities, ranging from micro- and small enterprises to large businesses and local corporations, an important finding was that refugees needed to be economically included at scale. Large companies and financial institutions working in areas that host significant FDP populations present an opportunity for scaling, mostly by functioning as refugee-supporting ("R3") or host community–weighted and refugee-sourcing investments ("R4"). However, large companies face significant barriers to adapting operations for FDP engagement, even if there is buy-in for these efforts from senior management. Building on the insights and opportunities identified in Phase I, RIN introduced a TA model aimed at unlocking private-sector RLI engagement that is designed to spark systems change. Recognizing the unique challenges and opportunities that displacement presents in the economy of the Greater Horn of Africa, there is a pressing need for a more specialized approach to business capacity development and advisory services—specifically, RLI-TA. This type of TA helps to create a pipeline of enterprises that specifically align with RLI and attract new capital, which in turn provides incentives for additional businesses to participate, ultimately growing the RLI ecosystem and sustainably advancing refugee self-reliance.

For the full playbook and report, please visit:

https://refugeeinvestments.org/resources/rli-ta-playbook-enhancing-refugee-lens-investing-through-technical-assistance-report-october-2024/

Appendix C

FURTHER READING AND RESOURCES

IMPACT INVESTING BOOKS

- *The Purpose of Capital: Elements of Impact, Financial Flows, and Natural Being*, by Jed Emerson (2018)
- *Real Impact: The New Economics of Social Change*, by Morgan Simon (2017)
- *Capital and the Common Good: How Innovative Finance Is Tackling the World's Most Urgent Problems*, by Georgia Keohane (2016)
- *The Impact Investor: Lessons in Leadership and Strategy for Collaborative Capitalism*, by Cathy Clark, Jed Emerson, and Ben Thornley (2014)
- *Impact Investing: Transforming How We Make Money While Making a Difference*, by Antony Bugg-Levine and Jed Emerson (2011)
- *Impact Investing Handbook: An Implementation Guide for Practitioners*, by Steven Godeke and Patrick Briaud (2020)

REFUGEE LENS INVESTING RESOURCES

- *Refugee-Related Investment: Myth or Reality?*, by World Bank Group—Private Sector for Refugees (PS4R) Platform Policy and Research Paper (2023)

- "From Displacement to Development: How Ethiopia Can Create Shared Growth by Facilitating Economic Inclusion for Refugees," by Sarah Miller and Jimmy Graham—Refugees International Case Study (2021)
- *The Wealth of Refugees: How Displaced People Can Build Economies*, by Alexander Betts (2021)
- "Humanitarian Investing—Mobilizing Capital to Overcome Fragility"—World Economic Forum White Paper (2019)
- "Kakuma as a Marketplace: A Consumer and Market Study of a Refugee Camp and Town in Northwest Kenya"—International Finance Corporation Case Study (2018)

IMPACT INVESTING ORGANIZATIONS AND NETWORK RESOURCES

- Refugee Investment Network: www.refugeeinvestments.org
- Global Impact Investing Network: www.thegiin.org
- Convergence—The Global Network for Blended Finance: www.convergence.finance
- SoCap Impact Investing Conference—www.socapglobal.com
- ImpactAlpha—https://impactalpha.com
- The US Impact Investing Alliance—https://impinvalliance.org
- Mission Investors Exchange (foundation focus)—https://missioninvestors.org

Appendix D

REFUGEE LENS INVESTMENT VEHICLES AND INSTRUMENTS

RLens[a]	Name	Industry	Country	Description
R4	NeedsList	Tech, humanitarian relief	Canada, USA	Tech platform that matches needs with support offers
R3	EthioChicken	Agriculture, poultry	Ethiopia	Employs 1,600, distributes 20 million birds to farmers
R3	Brothers Flour and Biscuit Factory PLC	Agriculture	Ethiopia	Produces wheat flour and biscuits locally
R1	Aroma Kava	Food and beverages	EU	Ukrainian-led coffee chain expanding in Europe
R1	Chernomorka	Food and beverages	EU	Ukrainian-founded seafood restaurant chain
R3	SINGA	Incubator and accelerator	EU	Refugee-focused incubator and accelerator
R6	Ukrainian Tech Ventures	Finance, tech	EU and USA	Invests in Ukrainian immigrant tech start-ups
R4	Maroquinerie THOMAS	Fashion and apparel	France	Manufactures luxury leather with refugee hires
R3	UAtalents	Workforce development, tech	France	Connects Ukrainian tech refugees to employers
R4	Ottobock	Healthcare, manufacturing	Germany	Trains Ukrainian orthopedists in prosthetics

(continued)

(*continued*)

RLens[a]	Name	Industry	Country	Description
R5	Kiva Refugee Investment Fund (KRIF)	Blended finance, debt	Global	Offers concessional multicountry debt fund
R3	MADE51	E-commerce	Global	E-commerce for refugee-focused companies
R6	Developing World Markets	Equity, microinvestment	Global	Equity-focused microenterprise investment
R2	Senara	Agritech, call center	Jordan	Refugee-led hydroponics and job training
R3	Teenah	Fashion and apparel	Jordan	Makes accessories with displaced employees
R4	Classic Fashion	Fashion and apparel	Jordan	Prototypes large-scale refugee apparel jobs
R3	SOLVillion	Wastewater management tech	Jordan	WASH[b] provider that hires refugees and serves communities
R3	Mrayti	E-commerce, beauty	Jordan	Gig platform that links beauty workers to customers
R4	Ghoorcom	Marketplace, e-commerce, agritech	Jordan	Online marketplace that connects farmers to buyers
R3	360 Moms	Online services (e-parenting)	Jordan	Parenting platform that offers Arabic and English content
R3	Batrina	Services, retail	Jordan	Sells culturally infused consumer-packaged and home goods
R4	Visit North Jordan	Sustainable tourism	Jordan	Inclusive ecotourism company
R3	Rosmeh W Nabteh	Manufacturing, packaging, and recycling	Jordan	Makes biodegradable recycled paper packaging
R3	Alchemist Lab	Education	Jordan	Provides STEAM[c] e-learning platform
R3	Keprita	Packaging and recycling	Jordan	Designs ecopackaging from upcycled materials

RLens[a]	Name	Industry	Country	Description
R3	B12	Communication	Jordan	Offers learning management systems for school-family engagement
R4	Bilforon	Marketplace, catering	Jordan	Empowers women in home-food business
R3	Dar Ali	Online platform, construction bids	Jordan	Tracks Jordanian construction projects online
R3	DARB Solar Cleaning Solutions	Services, cleaning technologies	Jordan	Robotics solar cleaning with refugee hires
R3	IBTECAR	Consulting services	Jordan	Consults for social enterprises and displaced people
R3	Mind Rockets	Education	Jordan	Develops assistive tech for the Deaf
R3	Salalem	E-learning, financial sector	Jordan	Provides AI-based learning management system
R4	Sitat Byoot	Marketplace	Jordan	Platform for housewives to sell handmade goods
R3	Code Circle	Education	Jordan	Teaches coding, robotics, and AI education
R1	Al-Haramain Factory	Manufacturing, paper	Jordan	Specialty cardboard cups factory
R1	Al-Shaffaf	Manufacturing, plastic	Jordan	Makes transparent acrylic retail products
R1	Al Nasser Joinery	Manufacturing, wood	Jordan	Crafts fire-rated and wood doors locally
R3	Jordan Omani Plastic Industries	Manufacturing, plastic	Jordan	Exports plastic films for various uses
R1	Orbit Aluminum Industries	Manufacturing, aluminum	Jordan	Manufactures aluminum with refugee-local mix
R3	SEP Jordan	Fashion	Jordan	Apparel company that employs refugee women
R1	Martha EDU	Education	Jordan	Develops educational tools for hearing-disabled
R2	Sitti Soap	Artisan	Jordan	Beauty company that hires refugee women

(*continued*)

(*continued*)

RLens[a]	Name	Industry	Country	Description
R4	Cewas	Water and sanitation	Sri Lanka	Develops regional water and sanitation ecosystems
R3	Luminus ShamalStart	Manufacturing incubator	Jordan	Incubator for social cohesion manufacturing
R4	GroFin Nomou Jordan Fund	Mezzanine quasi equity	Jordan	Funds small and medium-sized enterprises with refugee- and women-owned focus
R5	Tamweelcom	Risk-sharing facility	Jordan	Provides microfinance services in Jordan
R6	KOIS Refugee Development Impact Bond	Blended finance	Jordan, Lebanon	Funds programs for Syrian refugees
R3	AlFanar	Blended finance	Jordan, Lebanon, Egypt	Flexible capital fund for MENA[d] enterprises
R6	Refugee Investment Facility (RIF)	Blended finance	Jordan, Uganda	Blended finance fund for RLIs
R3	Sanivation	Waste, energy	Kenya	Offers urban sanitation and waste-to-energy services
R3	Five One Labs	Incubator and accelerator	Kurdistan, Colombia	Refugee-focused incubator
R5	PROSPECTS Partnership	Debt and technical assistance	MENA[d], East Africa	Supports livelihoods and workforce readiness
R4	Pixza	Food and beverages	Mexico	Restaurant that employs migrants and refugees
R4	Hola<Code/>	Tech, coding	Mexico	Trains displaced as software developers
R1	Mabe	Manufacturing, appliances	Mexico	Refugee-founded appliance manufacturer
R1	EZ Call Center	Call center	Mexico	Deportee-founded call center for migrants
R3	Ejido Verde	Agroforestry	Mexico	Regenerative agroforestry for pine resin

RLens[a]	Name	Industry	Country	Description
R4	Échale	Housing	Mexico	Develops postearthquake affordable housing
R4	Wizeline	Tech, software	Mexico	Software company with 5,000+ global developers
R5	VIWALA	Finance	Mexico	Offers fair debt for inclusive businesses
R3	Rendichicas	Transportation	Mexico	Gas stations that employ 98% women staff
R3	Palliser	Manufacturing, wood, furniture	Mexico, Canada	Furniture maker with inclusive refugee jobs
R3	INTRARE	Workforce development, tech	Mexico, Colombia	Tech platform for refugee economic integration
R3	Manpower Group	Staffing agency and workforce	Mexico, France, Global	Staffing with refugee hiring focus
R1, R3	Makers Unite	Consumer, retail	Netherlands	Employs refugee and local designers together
R1	Gomex	Retail, groceries	Serbia	Refugee-founded and Serbia's largest grocery chain
R1	Mandulis	Energy, renewables	Uganda	Develops and operates renewable energy
R3	Portico	Energy, renewables	Uganda	Produces affordable eco-friendly biofuels
R3	Asili Agriculture	Agriculture	Uganda	Integrated food security platform in East Africa
R3	GADC	Agriculture	Uganda	Employs local and displaced in agriculture
R4	KadAfrica	Agriculture	Uganda	Passion fruit farming that targets youth and women
R5	FI4R	Finance, technical assistance	Uganda	Technical assistance for financial service providers
R3	WimRob Bees	Agriculture	Uganda	Large honey cooperative with displaced beekeepers
R3	Livara	Beauty	Uganda	Cosmetics company with refugee staff

(*continued*)

(*continued*)

RLens[a]	Name	Industry	Country	Description
R5	Vision Fund Uganda	Finance, debt	Uganda	Microfinance provider in Uganda
R3	Kechi Bee Source Farm	Agriculture	Uganda	Sustainable apiary with refugee beekeepers
R5	Re:BUiLD	Finance, technical assistance	Uganda, Kenya	Finances technical assistance for urban refugee integration
R1, R3, R5	Equity Bank	Finance, banking	Uganda, Kenya	Commercial bank
R3	TERN	Incubator and accelerator	UK	Refugee-focused incubator
R5	IRC-CEO	Finance	USA	Offers loans for refugees and locals
R1	Al Najad Bakery	Food and beverages	USA	Refugee-led bakery with multistate reach
R1	Webflow	Tech	USA	Website platform founded by refugee, acquired by Discord
R3	Eat Offbeat	Food and beverages	USA	Refugee-run catering with global food menu
R1	Avant, LLC	Finance	USA	Financial services cofounded by refugees
R6	Unshackled Ventures	Venture capital	USA	Targets immigrant and refugee founders
R6	One Way Ventures	Venture capital	USA	Focuses on immigrant and refugee founders
R1	Affirm	Fintech	USA	Ukrainian-founded, offers point-of-sale loans
R1	Huy Fong Foods	Food and beverages	USA	Vietnamese refugee-founded sriracha maker
R3	Launch Capital Partners	Housing and real estate	USA	Housing developer for displaced clients
R3	Courage Housing	Housing and real estate	USA	Housing developer for displaced clients

RLens[a]	Name	Industry	Country	Description
R5	Massachusetts Pathways to Economic Advancement	Blended finance, pay-for-success financing	USA	Workforce pay-for-success development model
R3	Leaf Global Fintech	Fintech	USA	Blockchain finance for refugees, acquired by IDT
R1	734 Coffee	Food and beverages, agriculture	USA, East Africa	Coffee enterprise that supports education for the displaced

[a]The refugee lens designates six different types of investments, each with specific baseline criteria for qualifying as a refugee lens investment: R1: refugee-owned; R2: refugee-led; R3: refugee-supporting; R4: refugee-supporting and host-weighted; R5: lending facilities; and R6: refugee funds.

[b]WASH: water, sanitation, and hygiene.

[c]STEAM: science, technology, engineering, the arts, and mathematics.

[d]MENA: Middle East and North Africa.

NOTES

1. ENDLESS CRISES

1. This is not to be confused with the American Refugee Committee (ARC), which coincidentally rebranded in 2020 as Alight.
2. World Refugee Day is an annual day of celebration created by the United Nations in 2001 in recognition of the fiftieth anniversary of the 1951 Convention Relating to the Status of Refugees, which was designed to celebrate and honor refugees around the world.

2. DURABLE SOLUTIONS

1. GDI defines MSIs as "organizations (1) focused on bringing about collective action solutions for global public benefit, (2) comprised of actors across the public and private sectors (both for-profit and philanthropic), and (3) whose governance bodies and capabilities are wholly new, rather than simply reliant on those of the constituent actors." https://globaldevincubator.org/wp-content/uploads/2023/10/Making-MSIs-Work.pdf.

3. REFUGEE LENS INVESTING

1. In our interviews with Mark Manley, director of UNHCR Mexico, Manley shared results of the Programa de Integración (School Integration Program). A UNHCR assessment of nearly five thousand refugees

participating in this economic integration program found that 86 percent of refugees permanently resettled into their new communities, with another 10 percent relocating to another Mexican city, and after twelve months, over 60 percent escaped poverty.

BIBLIOGRAPHY

Aaron, Daniel, and David A. Long. 2001. *Take the Measure of the Man: An American Success Story*. Veritas.

Abramitzky, Ran, and Leah Boustan. 2022. *Streets of Gold: America's Untold Story of Immigrant Success*. Public Affairs.

Acumen Academy. 2022. "Meet 3 Grantees Empowering Forcibly Displaced People in East Africa." *Acumen Academy* (blog), September 28. https://blog.acumenacademy.org/forcibly-displaced-accelerator-awardees.

Agenda for Humanity. 2016. "World Humanitarian Summit 2016." https://agendaforhumanity.org/summit.html.

AGORA. 2018. *Understanding the Needs of Urban Refugees and Host Communities Residing in Vulnerable Neighborhoods of Kampala*. https://www.kcca.go.ug/media/docs/Kampala%20Urban%20Refugees%20And%20Host%20Community%20Needs%20Report.pdf.

Ahimbisibwe, Frank. 2018. "Uganda and the Refugee Problem: Challenges and Opportunities." Working Paper No. 2018.05. Institute of Development, University of Antwerp, May.

AIC. 2023. *Starting Anew: The Economic Impact of Refugees in America*. American Immigration Council, June. https://www.americanimmigrationcouncil.org/sites/default/files/research/05.23_refugee_report_v3_0.pdf.

AIC. 2024. "'The Migrant Protection Protocols': An Explanation of the Remain in Mexico Program." American Immigration Council, January 22. https://www.americanimmigrationcouncil.org/research/migrant-protection-protocols.

Akingbehin, Charles. 2018. "A Second Look at First Loss Platforms." Aurum, November. https://www.aurum.com/insight/thought-piece/a-second-look-at-first-loss-platforms/.

Almaguer, Fernando, and Abigayle Davidson. 2023. *Impact Investing in Latin America: Trends 2020–2021*. Aspen Network of Development Entrepreneurs. https://andeglobal.org/wp-content/uploads/2023/06/latam-report-2023-v8.pdf.

Al Monitor Feb 10, 2025. "Norwegian Refugee Council halts aid in over 20 countries after USAID cuts." https://www.al-monitor.com/originals/2025/02/norwegian-refugee-council-halts-aid-over-20-countries-after-usaid-cuts

Altindag, Onur, Ozan Bakis, and Sandra V. Rozo. 2020. "Blessing or Burden? Impact of Refugees on Businesses and the Informal Economy." *Journal of Development Economics* 148 (September): 102490.

Amnesty International. 2024. "Israel/Occupied Palestinian Territory: 'You Feel Like You Are Subhuman': Israel's Genocide Against Palestinians in Gaza." Amnesty International, December 5. https://www.amnesty.org/en/documents/mde15/8668/2024/en/.

Androwich, Rose. 2025. "Catholic Relief Services Hit by USAID Budget Cuts." *The Observer*, March 31. https://www.ndsmcobserver.com/article/2025/03/catholic-relief-services-hit-by-usaid-budget-cuts.

Armstrong, Martin. 2023. "Where Europe's Far-Right Has Gained Ground" Statista. November, 23, 2023. https://www.statista.com/chart/6852/seats-held-by-far-right-parties-in-europe/

Arnold, Tyler. 2025. "Catholic Relief Services Loses Federal Funds for 11 of 13 International Food Aid Programs." Catholic News Agency, May 22. https://www.catholicnewsagency.com/news/264301/catholic-relief-services-loses-federal-funds-for-11-of-13-international-food-aid-programs.

Ashden. 2022. "Energising Refugee Livelihoods: Kakuma Ventures." Ashden Climate Solutions in Action. https://ashden.org/awards/winners/kakuma-ventures/.

Aterido, Reyes, Mary Hallward-Driemeier, and Carmen Pages. 2009. "Big Constraints to Small Firms' Growth? Business Environment and Employment Growth Across Firms." *Economic Development and Cultural Change* 59, no. 3 (April): 609–647.

Australian Government, Department of Foreign Affairs and Trade. 2025. "Australia's Official Development Assistance Budget Summary 2025-26." August 30. https://www.dfat.gov.au/about-us/corporate/portfolio-budget-statements/australias-official-development-assistance-budget-summary-2025-26.

Bahar, Dany, Bo Cowgill and Jorge Guzman. 2023. "Refugee Entrepreneurship: The Case of Venezuelans in Colombia" AEA Papers and Proceedings. Vol. 113, May 2023 (pp,352–56)

Balikuddembe, Joseph Kibombo, and Josephine Kaleebi. 2019. *Mapping Uganda's Social Impact Investment Landscape, PLUG series (Kampala: KONRAD and ACTADE).*

Bandyopadhyay, Subhayu, and Asha Bharadwaj. 2018. "Immigration's Effect on Future Workforces." Federal Reserve Bank of St. Louis, December 4. https://www.stlouisfed.org/on-the-economy/2018/december/immigrations-effect-future-workforces.

Beard, Allison. 2022. "The Case for Welcoming Immigrants." *Harvard Business Review*, May–June. https://hbr.org/2022/05/the-case-for-welcoming-immigrants.

Beardsley, E. 2022. "At a French Factory, the Newest Employees Come from Ukraine." *NPR*, December 29. https://www.npr.org/2022/12/29/1145082842/france-ukraine-kharkiv-migrants-employment.

Betts, Alexander. 2021. "Refugees and Patronage: A Political History of Uganda's 'Progressive' Refugee Policies." *African Affairs* 120, no. 479 (April): 243–276. https://doi.org/10.1093/afraf/adab012.

Betts, Alexander, Imane Chaara, Naohiko Omata, and Olivier Sterck. 2019. "Research in Brief: Uganda's Self-Reliance Model: Does it Work?" Research in Brief 11, Refugee Studies Centre. https://www.rsc.ox.ac.uk/publications/research-in-brief-ugandas-self-reliance-model-does-it-work.

BFA Global. n.d. "The Financial Inclusion for Refugees Project in Uganda," Accessed July 13, 2023. https://bfaglobal.com/our-work/the-financial-inclusion-for-refugees-project-in-uganda-fi4r/.

Blaszczak, A. 2023. "Ukrainians Are Professionally Active and Satisfied with Their Work." *Rzeczpospolita*, April 13. https://rp.pl/rynek-pracy/art38304311-ukraincy-aktywni-zawodowo-zadowoleni-z-pracy.

Bond, Shannon, Jenna McLaughlin, Fatma Tanis. Feb 6, 2025. "USAID unions sue Trump administration to halt 'unconstitutional and illegal' cuts." NPR https://www.npr.org/2025/02/06/g-s1-46885/usaid-cuts-state-department-trump-rubio

Bressy, Floris. 2023. "Comment la Creuse aide cinq Ukrainiennes à s'intégrer par l'emploi" [How the Creuse region is helping five Ukrainian women integrate through employment]. *La Montagne*, May 15. https://www.lamontagne.fr/saint-vaury-23320/actualites/comment-la-creuse-aide-cinq-ukrainiennes-a-s-integrer-par-l-emploi_14310004/.

Bridgman, David, and Aref Adamali. 2015. *Investment Climate in Africa.* Viewpoint Note 346, World Bank. https://doi.org/10.1596/23484.

Buchanan, Maggie Jo, Philip E. Wolgin, and Claudia Flores. 2021. "The Trump Administration's Family Separation Policy Is Over: What Comes Next?" Center for American Progress, April 12. https://www.americanprogress.org/issues/immigration/reports/2021/04/12/497999/trump-administrations-family-separation-policy/.

Capps, Randy, Kathleen Newland, Susan Fratzke, Susanna Groves, Michael Fix, Margie McHugh, and Gregory Auclair. 2015. "The Integration Outcomes of U.S. Refugees: Successes and Challenges." Migration Policy Institute, June. https://www.migrationpolicy.org/research/integration-outcomes-us-refugees-successes-and-challenges.

Chestnutt, Cordelia. 2024. *Refugee Employment: Perspectives for Businesses, Policymakers, and Intermediaries.* World Bank Group, June 14. https://thedocs.worldbank.org/en/doc/51e229cb3b4abfa22db1d93b5354c496-0570062024/original/Refugee-Employment-PS4R-Study.pdf.

Cokelaere, Hanne, and Clea Caulcutt. 2024. "Why Ukraine's Refugees Aren't Going to France." *Politico*, March 25. https://www.politico.eu/article/why-ukraines-refugees-arent-going-to-france/#:~:text=France%20is%20.

Cooper, Barry, Antonia Esser, Rose Tuyeni Peter, and Shazeaa Lal Mohamod. 2018. *Where Are the Flows? Exploring Barriers to Remittances in Sub-Saharan Africa, Volume 3: Remittances in Uganda.* Cenfri, October. https://cenfri.org/wp-content/uploads/2018/04/Volume-3_Barriers-to-remittances-in-Uganda_FSDA_October-2018.pdf.

CSIS. 2018. "Confronting the Global Forced Migration Crisis." Center for Strategic and International Studies https://www.csis.org/analysis/confronting-global-forced-migration-crisis

Data for Progress. 2022. U.S. Refugee Program survey, October. https://www.filesforprogress.org/datasets/2023/1/dfp_refugees_advocacy_program_tabs.pdf.

Diaz, Lizbeth, and Delphine Schrank. 2019. "Mexico's Refugee Agency Turns to U.N. amid Asylum Surge, Funding Cuts." Reuters, May 22. https://www.reuters.com/article/us-usa-immigration-mexico/mexicos-refugee-agency-turns-to-u-n-amid-asylum-surge-funding-cuts-idUSKCN1SS06N.

DRC. 2025. "The Refugee Investment Facility." Danish Refugee Council. https://drc.ngo/what-we-do/innovation/innovative-finance/the-refugee-investment-facility/.

Duszczyk, M. 2023. "Innovative Firms Are Attracted to Poland." *Rzeczpospolita*, November 4. https://www.rp.pl/orzel-innowacji/art38299181-nowatorskie-firmy-ciagnie-do-polski.

Economist Impact. 2023. *Refugee Opportunity Index: Latin America and the Caribbean Regional Report*. https://web.archive.org/web/20241005071900/https://impact.economist.com/perspectives/sites/default/files/refugee_opportunity_index_-_latin_america_and_the_caribbean_regional_report.pdf

Edwards, B. 2022. "Refugees as Assets to Their New Countries." International Monetary Fund, June. https://www.imf.org/en/Publications/fandd/issues/2022/06/investing-in-refugees-cafe-economics.

Egusa, Conrad. 2018. "An entrepreneur's guide to Mexico City's tech scene." *The Next Web*, October 19, 2018. https://thenextweb.com/news/an-entrepreneurs-guide-to-mexico-citys-tech-scene?ref=interconnected.blog

EIB. n.d. "DWM Displaced Communities Fund (EIB-20220378)." European Investment Bank. https://ewsdata.rightsindevelopment.org/projects/20220378-dwm-displaced-communities-fund/.

Elias, Jennifer. 2026. "Alphabet hits $4 trillion market capitalization" CNBC News. January 12, 2026. https://www.cnbc.com/2026/01/12/alphabet-4-trillion-market-cap.html

Euronews. 2023. "Inside the Ukrainian Businesses Refugees Have Opened in Poland." Euronews.com, May 5. https://www.euronews.com/2023/05/05/inside-the-ukrainian-businesses-refugees-have-opened-in-poland.

Evans, William, and Daniel Fitzgerald. 2017. "The Economic and Social Outcomes of Refugees in the United States: Evidence from the ACS." NBER Working Paper No. 23498. National Bureau of Economic Research, June. https://www.nber.org/system/files/working_papers/w23498/w23498.pdf.

Ferguson, Jane. 2018. "Why the Human Toll of the Battle for Mosul May Never Be Known." *PBS News Hour*, December 19. https://www.pbs.org/newshour/show/why-the-human-toll-of-the-battle-for-mosul-may-never-be-known#:~:text=But%20investigations%20by%20the%20Associated,buried%20deep%20under%20this%20rubble.

Foner, Nancy. 2022. *One Quarter of the Nation: Immigration and the Transformation of America*. Princeton University Press.

Garduno, Silvia. 2020. "As COVID-19 Rages, Mexican Firm Steps Up to Save Lives." UNHCR, October 16. https://www.unhcr.org/en-us/news/stories/2020/10/5f88b30e4/covid-19-rages-mexican-firm-steps-save-lives.html?query=mexico%20relocation%20program.

Gaynor, Tim. 2021. "Refugees find safety and a new life in Mexico." UNHCR June 8, 2021. https://www.unhcr.org/au/news/stories/refugees-find-safety-and-new-life-mexico

Gazeta Olsztyńska. 2023. "Ukrainian Businesses Can Contribute to the Growth of Polish GDP." *Gazeta Olsztyńska*, February 24, 2023. https://gazetaolsztynska.pl/911057,Ukrainski-biznes-moze-przyczynic-sie-do-wzrostu-polskiego-PKB.html.

Ghertner, Robin, Suzanne Macartney, and Meredith Dost. 2024. "The Fiscal Impact of Refugees and Asylees at the Federal, State and Local Levels from 2005–2019." Office of the Assistant Secretary for Planning and Evaluation, U.S. Department of Health and Human Services, February 15. https://aspe.hhs.gov/reports/fiscal-impact-refugees-asylees.

Global Impact Investing Network. 2013. "Catalytic First-Loss Capital." GIIN, October 10. https://thegiin.org/research/publication/catalytic-first-loss-capital/.

Global Impact Investing Network. 2015. *The Landscape for Impact Investing in East Africa*. GIIN, August. https://thegiin.org/assets/161025_GIIN_EastAfrica_FULL_REPORT%20(002).pdf.

Global Refuge. 2024. "U.S. Resettles Most Refugees in Three Decades, Maintains FY 2025 Refugee Cap at 125,000." Press release, September 30. https://www.globalrefuge.org/news/refugees-resettlement-three-decades/.

Government of Uganda and UNHCR. 2004. *Self-Reliance Strategy (1999–2003) for Refugee Hosting Areas in Moyo, Arua and Adjumani Districts, Uganda: Report of the Mid-Term Review, April 2004*. https://www.unhcr.org/sites/default/files/legacy-pdf/41c6a4fc4.pdf.

Government of Mexico. 1917. *Political Constitution of the United Mexican States: Reorganized and Consolidated Version*. Comparative Constitutions Project, February. https://comparativeconstitutionsproject.org/wp-content/uploads/UNAM-Mexican-Constitution_vf.pdf.

Gramm, Phil. 2025. "The Immigrants America Needs: Limit asylum claims, reduce welfare and open the door to highly skilled foreign nationals." *The Wall Street Journal*, January 13

Gratton, Peter. 2024. "How WhatsApp Makes Money." *Investopedia*, December 11. https://www.investopedia.com/articles/personal-finance/040915/how-whatsapp-makes-money.asp.

Green, Jeff. 2025. "Trump's DEI Purge Drives 34% Drop in Pro-ESG Investor Proposals." *Bloomberg*, April 3. https://www.bloomberg.com/news/articles/2025-04-03/trump-s-dei-purge-drives-34-drop-in-pro-esg-investor-proposals.

GroFin. 2020. *Nomou Jordan Fund: Q3 2019 Report.* https://grofin.com/wp-content/uploads/2020/08/Nomou-Jordan-Fund-Report-Q3-2019.pdf.

Habeshian, Sareen, and Rebecca Falconer. 2025. "Trump Administration to Cut 92% of USAID Foreign Aid Contracts." *Axios*, February 26. https://www.axios.com/2025/02/27/trump-administration-to-cut-92-of-usaid-foreign-aid-contracts.

Haines, David W. 2015. *Learning from Our Past: The Refugee Experience in the United States.* American Immigration Council.

Hakiza, Robert, and Evan Easton-Calabria. 2016. "(Loan) Cycles of Innovation: Researching Refugee-Run Micro-Finance." *Humanitarian Exchange Magazine*, issue 66, article 12. Humanitarian Practice Network, April 20. https://odihpn.org/publication/loan-cycles-of-innovation-researching-refugee-run-micro-finance/.

Hand, Dean, Maddie Ulanow, Hongyu Pan, and Kelly Xiao. 2024. "Sizing the Impact Investing Market 2024." *GIIN*, October 23. https://thegiin.org/publication/research/sizing-the-impact-investing-market-2024/.

Hathaway, Ian. 2017. "Almost half of Fortune 500 companies were founded by American immigrants or their children." *Brookings Institute*, December 2017. *https://www.brookings.edu/articles/almost-half-of-fortune-500-companies-were-founded-by-american-immigrants-or-their-children/*

Hesson, Ted, and Steve Holland. 2021. "Biden Moves to Reverse Trump Immigration Policies, Too Slowly for Some." Reuters, February 2. https://www.reuters.com/article/us-usa-biden-immigration-actions/biden-moves-to-reverse-trump-immigration-policies-too-slowly-for-some-idUSKBN2A212D.

Ibrahim, H., V. Ertl, C. Catani, A. A. Ismail, and F. Neuner. 2018. "Trauma and Perceived Social Rejection Among Yazidi Women and Girls Who Survived Enslavement and Genocide." *BMC Medicine* 16, no. 1: 154. https://doi.org/10.1186/s12916-018-1140-5.

ICG. 2018. "Mexico's Southern Border: Security, Violence and Migration in the Trump Era." International Crisis Group, Report No. 66, May 9. https://www.crisisgroup.org/latin-america-caribbean/mexico/066-mexicos-southern-border-security-violence-and-migration-trump-era.

IFC. 2021. "Using Blended Concessional Finance to Invest in Challenging Markets." International Finance Corporation, February. https://www.ifc.org/content/dam/ifc/doc/mgrt/ifc-blendedfinance-fin-092021.pdf.

IFC. 2024. "IFC and Equity Bank of Kenya Partner in Landmark Facility to Support Financial Inclusion for Refugees." International Finance Corporation, October 23. https://www.ifc.org/en/pressroom/2024/ifc-and-equity-bank-of-kenya-partner-in-landmark-facility-to-support-financial-inclusion-for-refugees.

IMF. 2019. "Mexico: 2019 Article IV Consultation: Press Release and Staff Report." International Monetary Fund, November 5. https://www.imf.org/en/Publications/CR/Issues/2019/11/05/Mexico-2019-Article-IV-Consultation-Press-Release-and-Staff-Report-48788.

Include Her. 2023. "Techfugees Digital Spark." Include Her: Empowering Female Migrants for Digital Competencies. https://www.includeher.eu/techfugees-digital-spark/#:~:text=In%20September%202021%2C%20Techfugees%2C%20in,market%20in%20the%20tech%20space.

Incofin. 2019. "Crystal Raises Equity Investment of $10 Million GEL from GWM and agRIF." Incofin, April 2. http://www.incofin.com/crystal-raises-equity-investment-of-10-million-gel-from-dwm-and-agrif/.

Ingram, Mrill. 2018. "The Refugees of North Dakota." *Progressive Magazine*, April 1. https://progressive.org/magazine/the-refugees-of-north-dakota/.

IRRI. 2018. "Uganda's Refugee Policies: The History, the Politics, the Way Forward." Rights in Exile Policy Paper, International Refugee Rights Initiative, October. https://reliefweb.int/report/uganda/rights-exile-policy-paper-ugandas-refugee-policies-history-politics-way-forward#main-content.

Jamal, U. 2022. "A Non-Profit Venture Fund Aims to Back 200 Startups Established by Refugee Ukrainian Entrepreneurs." *Business Insider*, April 22. https://www.businessinsider.com/ukrainian-venture-fund-to-back-200-ukrainian-refugee-startups-2022-4.

Jones, James, and Olivier Sarbil, dirs. 2017. "Mosul." *PBS News Hour*. https://www.pbs.org/wgbh/frontline/documentary/mosul/.

Kallick, David Dyssegaard and Cyierra Roldan. May 2018. "Refugees as Employees: Good Retention: Strong Recruitment." Fiscal Policy Institute & Tent. chrome-extension://efaidnbmnnnibpcajpcglclefindmkaj/https://www.tent.org/wp-content/uploads/2021/09/TENT_FPI-Refugees-as-Employees-Report.pdf

Kane, Tim. 2021. *The Immigrant Superpower: How Brains, Brawn, and Bravery Make America Stronger.* Oxford University Press.

Kelleher, John. 2024. "Daniel Aaron." Immigrant Entrepreneurship. https://www.immigrantentrepreneurship.org/entries/daniel-aaron/.

Keohane, Georgia Levenson. 2016. *Capital and the Common Good.* Columbia Business School.

Khan, Yasmin Sabrina. 2010. *Enlightening the World: The Creation of the Statue of Liberty.* Cornell University Press.

Klesse, A., J. Witte, and P. Woldin. 2022. "Without Knowledge of German, It Will Be Difficult to Get Started." *Welt*, April 10. https://www.welt.de/regionales/hamburg/article238069309/Ukrainische-Fluechtlinge-auf-dem-Arbeitsmarkt-Unsere-Mitarbeiter-muessen-Deutsch koennen.html?icid=search.product.onsitesearch.

Kluge, John, Tim Docking, and Joanne Ke Edelman. 2018. *Paradigm Shift: How Investment Can Unlock the Potential of Refugees.* Refugee Investment Network, October. https://refugeeinvestments.org/wp-content/uploads/2019/06/RIN_Paradigm_Shift.pdf.

Korfhage, Matthew. 2022. "After Decades of Decline, Buffalo Boasts a 'Refugee Renaissance.' Can It Last?" *USA Today Network—Democrat & Chronicle*, March 28. https://www.democratandchronicle.com/in-depth/news/2022/01/10/buffalo-ny-refugees-resettlement-gentrification/8766544002/.

Lakuma, C. P., R. Marty, and F. Muhumuza. 2019. "Financial Inclusion and Micro, Small, and Medium Enterprises (MSMEs) Growth in Uganda." *Journal of Innovation and Entrepreneurship* 8:15. https://doi.org/10.1186/s13731-019-0110-2.

Landay, Jonathan, Patricia Zengerle, and Erin Banco. 2025. "Trump Administration to Keep Only 294 USAID Staff Out of Over 10,000 Globally, Sources say." Reuters, February 7. https://www.reuters.com/world/us/trump-administration-keeping-only-294-usaid-staff-out-over-10000-globally-2025-02-06/.

LAVCA. 2022. "2022 LAVCA Industry Data and Analysis." Lavca.org. https://www.lavca.org/research/2022-lavca-industry-data-and-analysis/.

Legas, Habtamu. 2015. "Challenges to Entrepreneurial Success in Sub-Saharan Africa: A Comparative Perspective." *European Journal of Business and Management* 7, no. 11.

Loy, Irwin. 2025. "IRC cutting thousands of staff after US aid freeze." *New Humanitarian*. https://www.thenewhumanitarian.org/news/2025/02/19/irc-cutting-thousands-staff-after-us-aid-freeze

MacArthur Foundation. 2020. https://www.macfound.org/press/article/catalytic-capital-consortium-faqs

Mahe, Stephane. 2022. "Temporary Work: Adecco Launches a Job Posting Website for Ukrainian Refugees." *La Tribune*, March 16. https://www.latribune.fr/economie/france/interim-adecco-lance-un-site-d-offres-d-emplois-pour-les-refugies-ukrainiens-906258.html.

Mahoney, Christine. 2016. *Failure and Hope: Fighting for the Rights of the Forcibly Displaced.* Cambridge University Press.

Mastercard. 1994–2025. "Smart Communities Coalition: Enabling Public-Private Collaboration to Empower the Forcibly Displaced and Their Host Communities." https://www.mastercard.com.ph/en-ph/business/governments/find-solutions/smart-communities.html.

Mawejje, Joseph, and Rachel K. Sebudde. 2019. "Constraints or Complaints? Business Climate and Firm Performance Perceptions in Uganda." *Journal of Development Studies* 55, no. 12: 2513–25. https://doi.org/10.1080/00220388.2018.1502878.

Maxmen, Amy. 2018. "Migrants and Refugees Are Good for Economies." *Nature*, June 20. https://www.nature.com/articles/d41586-018-05507-0.

Mbiyozo, Aimee-Noel. 2023. "Record Numbers of Displaced Africans Face Worsening Prospects." Institute for Security Studies, February 15. https://issafrica.org/iss-today/record-numbers-of-displaced-africans-face-worsening-prospects#:~:text=According%20to%20the%20United%20Nations,Most%20(60%25)%20are%20IDPs.

Mercy Corps. 2025. "Refugee Finance Playbook." February 28. https://www.mercycorps.org/research-resources/uganda-refugee-finance-playbook.

Migration Policy Institute. 2025. "U.S. Annual Refugee Resettlement Ceilings and Number of Refugees Admitted, 1980–Present." https://www.migrationpolicy.org/programs/data-hub/charts/us-refugee-resettlement.

Morgan Stanley. 2020. "Refugee ETF Wins 2020 Kellogg-Morgan Stanley Sustainable Investing Challenge." Morgan Stanley, April 21. https://www.morganstanley.com/press-releases/refugee-etf-wins-2020-kellogg-morgan-stanle.

NAE. 2017. *From Struggle to Resilience: The Economic Impact of Refugees in America*. New American Economy, June. https://www.newamericaneconomy.org/wp-content/uploads/2017/06/NAE_Refugees_V5.pdf.

NGO Refugee Group. August 2025. "Kenya Refugee Response Under Strain: Funding Cuts, Differentiated Assistance, and the Rising Social Cohesion Crisis." https://reliefweb.int/report/kenya/kenya-refugee-response-under-strain-funding-cuts-differentiated-assistance-and-rising-social-cohesion-crisis-august-2025

Nicholls, Alex, Gayle Peterson, and Eric Sukumaran. 2022. *Oxford Faith-Aligned Impact Finance Project Phase 1 Report*. Said Business School, Oxford University.

Noorani, Ali. 2022. *Crossing Borders: The Reconciliation of a Nation of Immigrants*. Bloomsbury.

OCHA. 2024. *Global Humanitarian Overview 2025*. December 4. https://www.unocha.org/events/global-humanitarian-overview-2025 https://www.sbs.ox.ac.uk/sites/default/files/2022-10/oxfaif-phase-1-report.pdf.

OECD. 2015. "Indicators of Immigrant Integration 2015." OECD, July 2. https://doi.org/10.1787/9789264234024-en.

OECD/UNHCR. 2024. *Safe Pathways for Refugees IV: OECD-UNHCR Study on Pathways Used by Refugees Linked to Family Reunification, Study Programmes and Labour Mobility between 2010 and 2022*. OECD, May 23. https://doi.org/10.1787/cdf4c629-en.

Opportunity International. 2020. *The Financial Lives of Refugees Living in Uganda*. Project brief, June. https://opportunity.org/content/News/Publications/Knowledge%20Exchange/The-Financial-Lives-of-Refugees-Living-in-Uganda.pdf.

Özgen, Ayşegül Balta. 2020. "Buffalo, NY: Good Practice in Refugee Resettlement." *Global Dialogue* 10, no. 1 (February). https://globaldialogue.isa-sociology.org/articles/buffalo-ny-good-practice-in-refugee-resettlement.

Kempner, Jessica. 2020. "Youth Unemployment in Uganda Has Been Misdiagnosed." The Palladium Group. January 29, 2020.

Plett Usher, Barbara, and Anna Soy. 2025. "'People Will Starve' Because of US Aid Cut to Sudan." *BBC*, February 24. https://www.bbc.com/news/articles/cy7x87ev5jyo.

Pontifical Academy of Social Sciences. 2022. *"Mensuram Bonam": Faith-Based Measures for Catholic Investors: A Starting Point and Call to Action.* https://www.pass.va/content/dam/casinapioiv/pass/pdf-volumi/other-publications/mb_eng_final_14_11_22.pdf.

Re:BUiLD. 2025. "About Re:BUiLD." https://rebuild.rescue.org/about/overview.

Reed-Hurtado, Michael. 2013. "The Cartagena Declaration on Refugees and the Protection of People Fleeing Armed Conflict and Other Situations of Violence in Latin America." UNHCR, June. https://www.unhcr.org/en-us/protection/globalconsult/51c800fe9/32-cartagena-declaration-refugees-protection-people-fleeing-armed-conflict.html?query=Cartegena%20protocol.

Roots of Impact. 2019. *Empowering Clinicas del Azucar to Attract Investment and Create Impact at Scale.* Social Impact Incentives (SIINC) Case Study, 2017–2018. https://www.roots-of-impact.org/wp-content/uploads/2019/09/SIINC-Case-Studies-CdA-Update-Results-2019.pdf.

Roots of Impact. 2020. SIINC Definitions and Applications. https://www.roots-of-impact.org/siinc/.

Rowan, David. 2018. "The Inside Story of Jan Koum and How Facebook Bought WhatsApp." *Wired*, May 1. https://www.wired.com/story/whats-app-owner-founder-jan-koum-facebook/.

Saad, Lydia. 2022. "Americans Widely Favor Welcoming Ukrainian Refugees." Gallup, April 26. https://news.gallup.com/poll/392069/americans-widely-favor-welcoming-ukrainian-refugees.aspx.

Samit, Laurence Mondon. 2022. "Employment of Ukrainian Refugees: Companies in Vienne Encouraged to Get Involved." *La Nouvelle République*, September 15. https://www.lanouvellerepublique.fr/vienne/emploi-des-refugies-ukrainiens-les-entreprises-de-la-vienne-incitees-a-s-engager.

Sciubba, Jennifer D. 2022. *8 Billion and Counting: How Sex, Death, and Migration Shape Our World.* Norton.

Seibel, K. 2022. "Tech Entrepreneurs Launch Job Exchange for War Refugees." *Die Welt*, March 7. https://www.welt.de/wirtschaft/karriere/article237361333/UA-Talents-Tech-Unternehmer-starten-Jobboerse-fuer-Kriegsfluechtlinge.html?icid=search.product.onsitesearch.

Selee, Andrew. 2018. "How Guadalajara Reinvented Itself as a Technology Hub." *Smithsonian*, June 12. https://www.smithsonianmag.com/innovation/how-guadalajara-reinvented-itself-technology-hub-180969314/#LujseDuqXuw8uD7D.99.

Shahani, Aarti. 2019. "Bill Clinton Owes My Father an Apology." *Atlantic*, November11.https://www.theatlantic.com/ideas/archive/2019/11/time-bill-clinton-apologize-immigrants/601579/.

Sheridan, John H. 1997. "1997 Technology Leader of the Year: Andy Grove—Building an Information Age Legacy." IndustryWeek, December 15. https://www.industryweek.com/leadership/companies-executives/article/21963786/1997-technology-leader-of-the-year-andy-grove-building-an-information-age-legacy.

Simon, Morgan. 2019. "GEO Group Running Out of Banks as 100% of Known Banking Partners Say 'No' to the Private Prison Sector." *Forbes*, September 30. https://www.forbes.com/sites/morgansimon/2019/09/30/geo-group-runs-out-of-banks-as-100-of-banking-partners-say-no-to-the-private-prison-sector/#1990a07c3298.

Solidarité 2023. "Comment la Creuse aide cinq Ukrainiennes à s'intégrer par l'emploi." (2023, May 15). Retrieved July 6, 2023, from www.lamontagne.fr website: https://www.lamontagne.fr/saint-vaury-23320/actualites/comment-la-creuse-aide-cinq-ukrainiennes-a-s-integrer-par-l-emploi_14310004/

Solman, Paul, and Jeffrey Sachs. 2016. "What's the Economic Impact of Refugees in America?" *PBS News*, April 7. https://www.pbs.org/newshour/economy/whats-the-economic-impact-of-refugees-in-america.

Sridharan, Swetha. 2008. "Material Support to Terrorism—Consequences for Refugees and Asylum Seekers in the United States." Migration Policy Institute (MPI), January 30. https://www.migrationpolicy.org/article/material-support-terrorism-consequences-refugees-and-asylum-seekers-united-states.

StartupBlink. 2016. "Guadalajara Startup Ecosystem." *StartupBlink* (blog), October 13. https://www.startupblink.com/blog/guadalajara-startup-ecosystem/.

Statista. 2025. "Estimated Number of Refugees from Ukraine Recorded in Europe and Asia Since February 2022 as of Mary 2025, by Selected Country." https://www.statista.com/statistics/1312584/ukrainian-refugees

-by-country/?srsltid=AfmBOop8eEyTIljjBR9whhd7no_6n7jYnLqkZo DtiwgfsgRw8iak2rTt/.

Strom, Stephanie. 2009. "Billionaire Aids Charity That Aided Him." *New York Times*, October 24. https://www.nytimes.com/2009/10/25/us/25donate.html.

Struwig, F., J. Krüger, and G. Nuwagaba. 2019. "The Influence of the Business Environment on the Growth of Informal Businesses in Uganda." *Sajesbm: Southern African Journal of Entrepreneurship and Small Business Management* 11, no. 1 (February 14). https://doi.org/10.4102/sajesbm.v11i1.200.

SudOuest. 2023. "Amazon, Hilton, Marriott . . . Companies Are Promising Tens of Thousands of Jobs for Refugees in Europe." SudOuest, June 19. https://www.sudouest.fr/international/crise-des-migrants/amazon-hilton-mariott-des-entreprises-promettent-des-dizaines-de-milliers-d-emplois-aux-refugies-en-europe-15628384.php.

Swaminathan, Suma, Aleem Remtula, and Justin Sykes. 2020. "Anticipating the Humanitarian Crisis with Innovative Financial Means." International Trade Centre, June 17. https://www.intracen.org/news-and-events/news/anticipating-the-humanitarian-crisis-with-innovative-financial-means.

Terry, Ted. 2019. "Refugees Made Our City Great. Turning Them Away Is a Moral Disaster." *BuzzFeed News*, September 13. https://www.buzzfeednews.com/article/tedterry/how-refugees-made-our-city-great-clarkston-georgia.

Tran, Van C., and Francisco Lara-García. 2020. "A New Beginning: Early Refugee Integration in the United States" *RSF: The Russel Sage Foundation Journal of the Social Sciences* 6, no. 3 (November): 117–49.

2X Global. 2025. "What Is Gender Lens Investing?" https://www.2xglobal.org/new-to-gender-lens-investing/what-is-gli.

Uhlenbroich, Burkhard. 2022. "German Rail Plans to Hire Ukrainian Refugees." *Bild*, March 28. https://www.bild.de/politik/2022/politik/arbeitsmarkt-bahn-will-ukraine-fluechtlinge-einstellen-79575112.bild.html.

UK Parliament. 2023. "UK Acknowledges Yazidi Genocide by Daesh/Islamic State." House of Commons Library, August 9. https://commonslibrary.parliament.uk/uk-acknowledges-yazidi-genocide-by-daesh-islamic-state/.

UNHCR. 2018a. *Financial Inclusion of Forcibly Displaced Persons and Host Communities: A UNHCR and UNCDF Joint Initiative*. https://reporting.unhcr.org/sites/default/files/UNHCR_UNCDF_FinancialInclusion_ForciblyDisplaced_HostCommunities.pdf.

UNHCR. 2018b. *Submission by the United Nations High Commissioner for Refugees for the Office of the High Commissioner for Human Rights'*

Compilation Report Universal Periodic Review: Mexico. https://uprdoc.ohchr.org/uprweb/downloadfile.aspx?filename=647&file=EnglishTranslation.

UNHCR. 2018c. *The MIRPS: A Regional CRRF Application*. https://www.acnur.org/fileadmin/Documentos/BDL/2017/11416.pdf.

UNHCR. 2019. *Sida, UNHCR and Grameen Crédit Agricole Foundation Join Hands to Promote Access to Financial Services for Refugees and Host Communities in Uganda*. https://www.unhcr.org/afr/5df234214.pdf.

UNHCR. 2025. "Figures at a Glance." UNHCR: The UN Refugee Agency. https://www.unhcr.org/about-unhcr/overview/figures-glance.

UNHCR—Iraq.2024.« Global Focus—Iraq.https://www.unhcr.org/emergencies/iraq-situation

United Nations. 2024. *Global Humanitarian Overview 2025*. Office for the Coordination of Humanitarian Affairs, December 4. https://digitallibrary.un.org/record/4083203?v=pdf.

US Department of State. 2019. "Mexico." Travel.State.Gov. https://travel.state.gov/content/travel/en/traveladvisories/traveladvisories/mexico-travel-advisory.html.

US Department of State. 2020. "2020 Investment Climate Statements: Uganda." https://www.state.gov/reports/2020-investment-climate-statements/uganda/.

US Department of State. 2024. "Milestones in the History of U.S. Foreign Relations." https://history.state.gov/milestones/1921-1936/immigration-act.

US Development Finance Corporation. 2021. *Public Information Summary: Kiva Refugee Investment Fund LLC*. https://www.dfc.gov/sites/default/files/media/documents/9000103696.pdf.

US Embassy of Uganda. 2024. "DFC and USAID Partner with Opportunity Bank to Launch the First-ever U.S. Lending Program to Refugees and Host Communities in Africa. November 18, 2024. https://ug.usembassy.gov/u-s-government-agencies-dfc-and-usaid-partner-with-opportunity-bank-to-launch-the-u-s-lending-program-to-refugees-and-host-communities-in-africa/

USA for UNHCR. 2021. "Refugees Find Safety and a New Life in Mexico." USA for UNHCR, June 16. https://www.unrefugees.org/news/refugees-find-safety-and-a-new-life-in-mexico/.

USA for UNHCR. 2025. "Ukraine Emergency." https://www.unrefugees.org/emergencies/ukraine/.

USAID. 2023. Smart Communities Coalition Innovation Fund | Power Africa. (n.d.). Retrieved July 13. https://www.usaid.gov/powerafrica/sccif. link no longer active; archived program information available via EnDev, 2021

USCIS. 2024. "Immigration and Naturalization Service Refugee Law and Policy Timeline." https://www.uscis.gov/about-us/our-history/stories-from-the-archives/refugee-timeline#:~:text=1948&text=The%20Displaced%20Persons%20Act%20of,and%20Records%20Administration%2C%20College%20Park.

Valiu. 2019. Investor Deck 2019.

VisionFund. 2025. "Delivering Refugee Microfinance in Uganda." https://www.visionfund.org/our-focus/fragile/refugee-lending.

Viwala. 2023. *Impact Report*. April 2023. https://cdn.prod.website-files.com/638775d2ff77f3c2eff83cd5/646f8ef8d918b625d5bba7e7_VIWALA%20Impact%20Report%2023-min.pdf

Vries, Stefan de. 2022. "Ukrainian Refugees Welcome in the Dutch Labor Market." *Les Echos*, April 4. https://www.lesechos.fr/monde/europe/les-refugies-ukrainiens-bienvenus-sur-le-marche-du-travail-neerlandais-1398258.

WBJ. 2023. "Nearly 1 Mln Refugees Already Working in Poland." *Warsaw Business Journal*, February 27. wbj.pl/nearly-1-mln-refugees-already-working-in-poland/post/137221.

WEDI. 2025. "West Side Bazaar." https://www.wedibuffalo.org/westside-bazaar.

Weidmann, D. 2023. "Ukraine: German Company Gives War Victims A New Life." *Berliner Morganpost*, June 10. https://www.morgenpost.de/politik/article238643915/ukraine-krieg-prothesen-ottobock-opfer.html.

White House. 2016. "Fact Sheet: White House Launches a Call to Action for Private Sector Engagement on the Global Refugee Crisis." Press release, June 30. https://obamawhitehouse.archives.gov/the-press-office/2016/06/30/fact-sheet-white-house-launches-call-action-private-sector-engagement-0.

White House. 2025. "Realigning the United States Refugee Admissions Program." January 20. https://www.whitehouse.gov/presidential-actions/2025/01/realigning-the-united-states-refugee-admissions-program/.

Wikipedia. 2026. "Mexico City," last modified January 26, 2026, https://en.wikipedia.org/wiki/Mexico_City

World Bank Group. 2016. "Publication: An Assessment of Uganda's Progressive Approach to Refugee Management." Open Knowledge Repository. https://openknowledge.worldbank.org/handle/10986/24736.

World Bank Group. 2017. "Record High Remittances to Low- and Middle-Income Countries in 2017." Press release, April 23. https://www.worldbank.org/en/news/press-release/2018/04/23/record-high-remittances-to-low-and-middle-income-countries-in-2017.

World Bank Group. 2018. *Concessional Financing for Refugees and Host Communities in Middle-Income Countries*. World Bank Case Study. https://documents1.worldbank.org/curated/en/546681546962326545/Concessional-Financing-for-Refugees-and-Host-Communities-in-Middle-Income-Countries-Overcoming-Challenges-in-Financing-Refugee-Assistance-Case-Study.pdf.

World Bank Group. 2019a. "Informing the Refugee Policy Response in Uganda: Results from the Uganda Refugee and Host Communities 2018 Household Survey." World Bank Group Factsheet, October 1. https://www.worldbank.org/en/news/factsheet/2019/10/01/informing-the-refugee-policy-response-in-uganda-results-from-the-uganda-refugee-and-host-communities-2018-household-survey#:~:text=What%20is%20the%20report%20about,and%20Host%20Communities%20Household%20Survey.

World Bank Group. 2019b. "The World Bank in Mexico: Country Overview." October 10. https://www.worldbank.org/en/country/mexico/overview.

World Bank Group. 2020. "Publication: Uganda: Jobs Strategy for Inclusive Growth." Open Knowledge Repository. https://openknowledge.worldbank.org/handle/10986/33342.

World Bank Group. 2023. *Refugee-Related Investment: Myth or Reality?* Private Sector for Refugees Platform (PS4R) Policy and Research Paper, September 5. https://thedocs.worldbank.org/en/doc/0f3e72aaa017792e24d18959a560d35205700220023/original/FINAL-PS4R-Refugee-Related-Investment-Myth-or-Reality.pdf.

YGC Recoupling Awards 2022. "Global Solutions – Young Global Changers – 2022 Recoupling Awards" https://www.global-solutions-initiative.org/collection/2022-recoupling-awards/

Yucatán Magazine. 2019. "Merida, Home of More and More Foreigners and Out-of-Staters." *Yucatán Magazine*, February 9. https://yucatanmagazine.com/merida-home-of-more-and-more-foreigners-out-of-staters/#:~:text=9%20delicious%20ice%2Dcold%20treats%20to%20keep%20you%20cool%20in%20Yucat%C3%A1n&text=Yucatan's%20population%20of%20non%2DYucatecans,made%20up%20of%20recent%20arrivals.

Yucatan Times. 2019. "Real Estate Boom Would Raise the Population of Merida by 2 Million Before 2030." *Yucatan Times*, May 22. https://www.theyucatantimes.com/2019/05/real-estate-boom-would-raise-the-population-of-merida-to-two-million-before-2030/.

Zhou, Yang-Yang, Guy Grossman, and Shuning Ge. 2023. "Inclusive Refugee-Hosting Can Improve Local Development and Prevent Public Backlash." *World Development* 166 (June): 106203.

ZPP. 2023. "ZPP's Comment: Poland—a Good Place for Ukrainian Entrepreneurship." Union of Entrepreneurs and Employers, June 14. https://zpp.net.pl/en/zpps-comment-poland-a-good-place-for-ukrainian-entrepreneurship/?utm_source=rss&utm_medium=rss&utm_campaign=zpps-comment-poland-a-good-place-for-ukrainian-entrepreneurship.

INDEX

GPSR Authorized Representative: Easy Access System Europe, Mustamäe tee 50, 10621 Tallinn, Estonia, gpsr.requests@easproject.com

www.ingramcontent.com/pod-product-compliance
Lightning Source LLC
LaVergne TN
LVHW091328060826
844950LV00022B/67/J

* 9 7 8 0 2 3 1 2 1 8 1 2 2 *